Thank you for praying with & for us over all these years! In Christ,
Peter & Valerie Limmer

# —— ON THE ——
# POTTER'S
# WHEEL

VALERIE LIMMER

# ON THE POTTER'S WHEEL

TATE PUBLISHING
AND ENTERPRISES, LLC

*On the Potter's Wheel*
Copyright © 2016 by Valerie Limmer. All rights reserved.

No part of this publication may be reproduced, stored in a retrieval system or transmitted in any way by any means, electronic, mechanical, photocopy, recording or otherwise without the prior permission of the author except as provided by USA copyright law.

All Scripture quotations, unless otherwise indicated, are from the Holy Bible, *New American Standard Bible*®, Copyright © 1960, 1962, 1963, 1968, 1971, 1972, 1973, 1975, 1977, 1995 by The Lockman Foundation. Used by permission.

Scripture quotations marked ESV are from the ESV® Bible (*The Holy Bible, English Standard Version*®), copyright 2001 by Crossway, a publishing ministry of Good News Publishers. Used by permission. All rights reserved.

Scripture quotations marked KJV are from the Holy Bible, *King James Version*.

Scripture quotations marked NIV are from the Holy Bible, *New International Version*®, NIV® Copyright © 1973, 1978, 1984, 2011 by Biblica, Inc.® Used by permission. All rights reserved worldwide.

Scripture quotations marked NLT are from the Holy Bible, *New Living Translation*, copyright © 1996, 2004, 2007 by Tyndale House Foundation. Used by permission of Tyndale House Publishers, Inc., Carol Stream, Illinois 60188. All rights reserved.

Scripture quotations marked YLT are from the Holy Bible, *Young's Literal Translation*.

This book is a work of nonfiction. With the exception of those who have explicitly requested that their true names remain,[1] all names have been changed to protect the privacy of the individuals described herein. The events and situations are true.

The opinions expressed by the author are not necessarily those of Tate Publishing, LLC.

Published by Tate Publishing & Enterprises, LLC
127 E. Trade Center Terrace | Mustang, Oklahoma 73064 USA
1.888.361.9473 | www.tatepublishing.com

Tate Publishing is committed to excellence in the publishing industry. The company reflects the philosophy established by the founders, based on Psalm 68:11,
*"The Lord gave the word and great was the company of those who published it."*

Book design copyright © 2016 by Tate Publishing, LLC. All rights reserved.
*Cover design by Albert Ceasar Compay*
*Interior design by Caypeeline Casas*

Published in the United States of America
ISBN: 978-1-68352-652-0
1. Biography & Autobiography / Personal Memoirs
2. Religion / Christian Life / Spiritual Growth
16.07.04

# Dedication

Mr. Milne was my elementary school gym teacher, and the fact that I remember him fondly shows what an amazing person he was because I absolutely abhorred Phys. Ed. class. It gave me ample opportunity to showcase my well-honed klutzdom, and I generally found the sports to be mortifying exercises in futility.

Mr. Milne was a Christian, and when he found out that I was too, he would come to me at the start of each week and ask what I'd learned in Sunday school. I was too young to yet experience embarrassment when I hadn't paid attention or couldn't remember, but as time wore on, the underlying meaning of his weekly challenges sank into my psyche: I was not to simply be a hearer of God's word, but a doer.[1] My faith was not something that should be passively accepted, but actively engaged.

So, thank you, Mr. Milne. I've no idea whether you've now passed on to heaven or whether you're still out there in the world somewhere. One thing I do know is that you left an incredibly precious spiritual legacy in the heart of an awkward little girl who was also your sister in Christ.

# Acknowledgements

I'm so blessed to have many people in my life who helped and encouraged me through both writing my story and living it! First of all, thank you to my husband, Peter. It's such an honour to be your wife and to go through the good and bad times with you. You are such a gift to me. Thank you to my sister, Julia, for your gentleness and strength in my darkest times. Thank you to Manfred, Beth, Emmanuel, and Marion, for helping us to have a godly perspective in the midst of suffering. Thank you to my beta readers and editors, Nozomi, Jenn, Velma, Melvine, Marcia, and Lily. And lastly, thank you to all our other ministry partners. We treasure each of you and are so blessed to be on this adventure together with you.

Does the clay say to him who forms it,
"What are you making?" or
"Your work has no handles"?

—Isaiah 45:9b (ESV)

# Contents

| | | |
|---|---|---|
| 1 | Early Snapshots | 15 |
| 2 | Peter | 21 |
| 3 | Peter's Call | 28 |
| 4 | Married Life and Ministry | 30 |
| 5 | Setbacks and Setups | 36 |
| 6 | Partnership Development | 48 |
| 7 | Speed Bumps | 54 |
| 8 | Living Now | 58 |
| 9 | Rhythmic Interlude | 63 |
| 10 | Working Again | 65 |
| 11 | Okinawa | 68 |
| 12 | Attack | 70 |
| 13 | Running the Race | 72 |
| 14 | Waiting on God | 74 |
| 15 | March 11 | 77 |
| 16 | Attitudes of the Heart | 81 |
| 17 | Preparing to Leave | 84 |
| 18 | Arriving | 94 |
| 19 | Kobe | 101 |
| 20 | Moving In | 104 |
| 21 | Whatever Is Pure | 110 |
| 22 | ESL Training | 114 |
| 23 | Have Thine Own Way | 118 |
| 24 | Prayer Walks | 122 |
| 25 | Following and Feebleness | 125 |
| 26 | Setback | 131 |

| | | |
|---|---|---|
| 27 | Charred | 134 |
| 28 | Chomping at the Bit | 136 |
| 29 | Not Every Question | 143 |
| 30 | Christmas | 146 |
| 31 | Meltdown | 149 |
| 32 | The Parable of the Lost Ring | 154 |
| 33 | Acceptance | 158 |
| 34 | ESL Classes | 163 |
| 35 | What Do You Desire? | 167 |
| 36 | Love My Chains | 171 |
| 37 | Strength for the Moment | 174 |
| 38 | A Hug from God | 181 |
| 39 | Matters of Faith | 183 |
| 40 | Scribbles and Scratchings | 186 |
| 41 | Fellowship of Suffering | 189 |
| 42 | Time Marches On | 191 |
| 43 | 'Potential' | 193 |
| 44 | Friends of Job | 195 |
| 45 | The Spring | 199 |
| 46 | Compassion and Suffering | 202 |
| 47 | Glimmers of Hope | 204 |
| 48 | A Change in Plans | 208 |
| 49 | Releasing | 215 |
| 50 | In the Park | 218 |
| 51 | Surrounded | 221 |
| 52 | Betrayed | 227 |
| 53 | Endings | 230 |
| 54 | A New Family Member | 235 |
| 55 | Followed by Evil | 238 |
| 56 | Connecting | 241 |
| 57 | Offerings of Faith | 246 |
| 58 | Obon | 253 |
| 59 | Surviving or Thriving? | 255 |
| 60 | Changes | 260 |

| | | |
|---|---|---|
| 61 | Typhoons | 263 |
| 62 | Thanksgiving | 267 |
| 63 | Unstuck | 270 |
| 64 | Faith Without Risk | 272 |
| 65 | The Pendulum of Grief | 275 |
| 66 | The Terror of the Telephone | 277 |
| 67 | An Unusual Encounter | 280 |
| 68 | Strong in Me | 284 |
| 69 | According to Plan? | 288 |
| 70 | The Little Giant | 294 |
| 71 | Where You Are | 298 |
| 72 | Appointments | 300 |
| 73 | Compassion | 308 |
| 74 | New Doors | 312 |
| 75 | The News | 316 |

Afterword ............ 323
Glossary ............ 325
Notes ............ 327
Bibliography ............ 335
About the Author ............ 339

# CHAPTER 1

# Early Snapshots

It was a sunny August afternoon in 1983 when I clambered onto her lap and popped the question. "Mummy, how do I let Jesus into my heart?"

My parents had hosted a backyard Bible club for the neighbourhood children that week. I'd heard the Bible stories and pronouncements of Jesus' love, and now there was only one burning question left.

Mother told me later of her internal reactions. *Oh my goodness*, she thought. *This child is only three! There's no way she can possibly understand what she's asking!* So instead, she decided to explain the entire story of God and His relationship with mankind to me: from Genesis to Revelation.

At the end, I sighed. "Yes, but Mummy! How do I let Jesus into my heart?"

*Not distracted! Well, it's almost her nap time. She's sure to get tired soon.* We were sitting in my favourite rocking chair, and she began to slowly sway me back and forth. "You see, Valerie, at the very beginning of the world there was nothing. Only God…"

Twice more, she would go through the entire biblical history of God's relationship with mankind, and each time I responded with dogged impatience, "But how do I let Him *in*?"

Finally, she relented. "You have to pray, Valerie. You have to ask Jesus to forgive you for the wrong things you've done and ask Him to come into your heart to make you clean and be with you always."

"You pray first, and I'll say it after you," I responded. This was, after all, our pattern when we thanked God for our food. Mummy would pray first, and I would repeat after her.

"No, Valerie, this time you need to pray to Jesus yourself. This is between you and Him."

And so, I talked with Jesus for the first time at the age of three, sitting on Mother's lap in my favourite rocking chair, gently swaying back and forth, back and forth.

I've always been very sensitive to visual stimuli, particularly colour. My memories reflect this, alternating between vivid swirls of pigment in the happy times and listless, flat monochromes in times of sadness.

My childhood was both happy and unhappy. To put it simply, I was abused physically, sexually, and emotionally by an adult and an older child.

Yet even in the midst of childhood grief, God had already begun to write the theme of His sustaining power into the pages of my life. I had a cat of partial Siamese descent whose claws and bite were the terror of veterinary assistants everywhere. Her name was Scamper. One of my early memories starts out in an unhappy greyish monochrome, with me arriving home and sitting on my bed, weeping tears of hopelessness. And there is my little black cat, who hops onto my bed, purring and cuddly, to lick my tears away. The memory ends in a gentle yellow—the colour of my old bedroom—with a measure of peace and happiness.

A therapist whom I saw years later would suggest that Scamper was an angel sent from God, perhaps to help my childish heart not shut down in the midst of suffering. I've never been able to shake the idea, and can't help thinking that sentiment holds a substantial degree of truth.

My family was largely responsible for the happy times. A hearty Romanian, Mum passed on her emotional expressiveness to us. In our home, fights were loud and reconciliations even louder. Mum's spirit brimmed with creativity, and she fostered this in us as well. Our house was the place to be for all the neighbourhood kids. We made crafts with my mum and played with the myriad toys provided by my father.

Dad had a knack for the ludicrous. He would sing us lullabies at night, but these were not the ordinary ones. Sometimes they would involve actions; at other times, he would adopt a funny voice. One of his favourites was to sing "Silent Night" in a ridiculously high, cracking falsetto voice. His antics always cheered me up.

And then there was Julia.

Our shoes squeaked on the linoleum floor, an anchor to reality amidst the psychedelic harshness of fumes and flickering lights.

"We're going to see Mummy and your new sister," Daddy lilted.

Mummy I knew. But Sister? It was a term I'd heard often in the preceding months, but a three-year-old brain has difficulty grasping such an abstract.

My chubby legs easily followed Daddy's gentle pace. Soon we were at a door. We entered. There was Mummy, sitting in bed and holding a package.

She smiled, tired. "Here's your sister. Here's Julia."

I gazed into the blanket. A crinkled face stared back at me, black hair sticking out in every possible direction, bright eyes shining like a doll's, and tiny toes wiggling without pause.

Our eyes locked, and the world faded away. Only the two of us remained. My heart filled with love. So this was Sister.

We were rather naughty children. At nap time, our parents would precariously lean laundry hampers against our closed bedroom doors to alert them with a thump if we left our rooms. We would fashion bodies out of stuffed animals, with tufts of doll hair the same colour as our own sticking out from the top edges of the covers; contort ourselves around the laundry hamper alarm systems; and still get out to play. Mum's screams when she found the plastic cockroaches I'd put under her pillow and the rubber snake on her shoulder are ones I'll not soon forget.

Growing up in a Toronto suburb, our sole goal in life—particularly in the summer—was to make money to buy candy from the local convenience store. Parades of our schemes march across my memory in a comical salute to childhood inventiveness.

We would set up lemonade stands with our friend, Beatrix, who would ride up and down the street on her bicycle, directing potential customers our way. Once we conned the local kids into coming with their parents—and paying scaled admission!—to one of our plays in exchange for some poorly executed face painting. On another occasion, we tried selling off some of Mum's art supplies to the neighbours and were very disappointed by their lack of interest in our wares.

The three of us—Beatrix, Julia, and I—spent hours at a creek by our house sloshing around in Mum's big rain boots, catching minnows, and building a fort at the base of an elderly tree. There we stashed our candy and treasures, away from the prying eyes of adults.

In second grade, my teacher gave us an assignment to draw what we wanted to be when we grew up. It's the first time I remember being asked that question, and I still remember the answer: a missionary.

In my late teens, I internally, if not externally, abandoned following Jesus for a season. Tired of emotional and spiritual pain,

I thought perhaps if I weren't following Him quite so closely I could avoid more of it and manage my life better than He had been doing. The results were not as expected. I found myself mired in unhappiness to a much greater degree than ever before.

After a few years, I finally came face-to-face with my failure. I had not made my life better without God, but worse. With this realization, I threw myself at His mercy, pledged my life to Him once more, and asked Him to cleanse and heal me. At the age of twenty, I took a sabbatical from my university studies. God used this time to build and plant me back into His kingdom and to "restore the years that the locust had eaten."[1]

My scars may have been deep, but God's grace flowed deeper still. The tides of His love lapped at my wounds and washed the grit and infection away. I stopped thinking of myself as a victim. From that point on, half the time I would forget about the things that had happened to me. In the other half, I would appreciate that they had happened because they'd helped to shape me into the person I had become. And I liked, and still like, that person. Jesus covered my scars with His own and transformed me from victim to victor.

A few months after my initial repentance, and during my sabbatical from school, I attended a Campus Crusade fall retreat. God spoke to me through one of the people at the conference who led a "Spotlight on Japan" segment about the need for Christian recruits. The hearts of Japanese university students were open and hungry to hear the good news about Jesus, but there weren't enough workers.

Up until that time, I'd felt a strong pull to missions, but not to a specific place. Now it was as if God had turned on a light in my soul and was saying, "Valerie, this is where I want you to go."

From that moment on, I considered my course to be set. Less than a year later, I signed up to go on a short-term mission trip to Japan. Unfortunately it was cancelled for lack of participants. Instead, I served in France for a month with my sister.

This redirection was intensely frustrating at the time. Reflecting on it later, I realized that if my plans for Japan had panned out, I might have considered the call God had placed on my heart to have been discharged.

But that was not God's plan.

## CHAPTER 2

# Peter

*Blessed be Your name*
*In the land that is plentiful,*
*Where Your streams of abundance flow,*
*Blessed be Your name.*
*Blessed be Your name*
*When I'm found in the desert place,*
*Though I walk through the wilderness,*
*Blessed be Your name.*
*Every blessing You pour out*
*I'll turn back to praise.*
*When the darkness closes in, Lord,*
*Still I will say:*
*Blessed be the name of the Lord,*
*Blessed be Your glorious name.*
*You give and take away,*
*You give and take away.*
*My heart will choose to say,*
*Lord, blessed be Your name.*

—lyrics of "Blessed Be Your Name"[1]

On returning to university, I changed my specialty within engineering, moved to Toronto, and roomed with two girls I knew from my previous activities with Campus Crusade. Our apartment was large and sunny, on the second floor of a three-storey duplex, and right on a transit line to campus.

Having transferred a few credits from my former studies, during that first term I was a part-time student. With lots of extra time and not many new friends yet, I spent many hours alone at my apartment. God used that period to continue building me up from a spiritual standpoint. Devotions with Him were very rich. Spurred on by the similar passion of an elderly friend, I began to memorize loads of scripture. For many years after, I would look back on those months of solitude with fondness and thanksgiving.

During that time I wrote a life purpose statement:

> My desire is, at the end of my life, to have nothing that God has given me left which I have not used in His service in some way. To serve Him until I die, and to love Him to the abandonment of all other people and possessions: I can think of no greater joy.

New to the area, I spent weeks scouting around for a local church community where I could belong, be fed, and also contribute. After more than a month of searching for a fit, I was becoming increasingly frustrated.

One evening I finally sat down with one of my roommates. We prayed together about the situation and opened up the Yellow Pages to the section on churches. I closed my eyes and jabbed my finger onto the page. It landed on an entry for Bridgeway Baptist Church. I recognized the address: this was the place where a mission prep meeting for France had been held the year before.

The following Sunday, I went to Bridgeway Baptist and immediately experienced a strong sense of belonging. This was where I was supposed to be.

Peter and I have different memories of how we first met, but I still maintain that I'm right, so mine is the story I shall share here.

On that first Sunday at Bridgeway Baptist, I met the associate pastor, Timothy. He was new to the church and was in the process of setting up high school and college and career groups. He invited me to that week's meeting.

I enthusiastically trekked to church the following Thursday and spent the first while wandering all over the building, exploring and searching for where the group might have stowed themselves. Eventually, I found them in the basement gym playing badminton. We later played a game of Cranium, a guessing game that mixes charades, drawing, and verbal descriptions. Peter was there, and the first memory I have of him includes a painfully gawky charade of a palm tree.

*Oh my goodness, what a geek!* I thought.

Peter says his first thought of me was, *My, what big glasses she has!*

So neither of us made a favourable first impression on the other.

It turned out that we were remarkably similar in personality, our love for God, and even our favourite television shows. Friendship was inevitable. Soon it was apparent to most of our friends that we had a certain chemistry as well. Only a few months in, I remember one person saying that we should get married. I was nonplussed by the statement and shrugged it off as a misinterpretation of the fun in our relationship.

A year and a half later, Peter asked if I would date him. I panicked. I didn't feel ready to date. In any case, I didn't think I wanted to date *him*. Not wanting our friendship to suffer because of my refusal, I didn't know what to do. That weekend, I went home to visit my parents and spent a good hour crying and praying to God over my next course of action.

By the end of it, He had given me a measure of peace in my heart about my response: "No, I won't date you. I'm not ready to date anyone yet. You're welcome to ask me again in a year, but I won't guarantee I'll say yes."

Peter took it rather well. By that time, he had started going to Bible college after his own hiatus from his original degree in music. When he told his friends of my answer, they thought he was crazy to wait for a girl for a year with no guarantee of anything. But wait he did.

Almost a year later, our church started making announcements about Urbana, an upcoming missions conference held every three years by InterVarsity Christian Fellowship. I didn't pay any attention to those announcements. Urbana was too expensive for me, so I didn't even consider whether I was interested in going.

Meanwhile, I began to doubt the call God had placed on my life. Had I understood Him correctly? The short-term mission trip to Japan hadn't panned out, and I questioned whether the spark I'd felt at the mention of Japan was just self-made, perhaps because of my natural interest in missions. I prayed that God would make it clear whether going to Japan was something He really desired of me.

Soon after, Timothy told me that an anonymous donor at Bridgeway Baptist was sponsoring my participation in Urbana. I was astounded. God had confirmed my call to missions swiftly and decisively.

As it turned out, three of us from Bridgeway attended Urbana that year: Timothy, Peter, and me. It was held at a university campus located a few hours outside of Chicago. Thousands of students crammed into the stadium to worship and listen to deep teachings. Never before had I been in a place where so many people were interested in missions to the same degree as me.

I attended one seminar run by a mission agency that focussed primarily on Japan. The stories from people who had gone on both short-term mission trips and longer stints impressed me: the agency seemed ready and willing to use whatever talents and interests its workers had to further the gospel. I liked such flexibility and versatility, and felt in my spirit that this was the organization with which I would eventually go to Japan. I found myself excited again by the call God had placed on my heart.

Urbana takes place between Christmas and New Year's Day. That New Year's Eve turned out to be one of the most painful and joyous of my life.

By then, Peter's year of waiting was almost up, and I recognized my feelings for him went further than I'd formerly realized. Feeling torn, I desired more than friendship from Peter, and yet he seemed not to share my passion for missions. Whenever he talked about ministry, it was always in the context of the North American church. I was by no means willing to give up my own calling, so I prayed that God would make the way clear to me.

"I have something I need to tell you," Peter said during a break in the New Year's Eve programme. "I've been having leftover feelings for my previous girlfriend."

This was an enormous shock to me. I felt as though the world had gone topsy-turvy. My expectations were suddenly very different than reality, and my heart flinched. But I knew God had answered my prayer for guidance. The intermission ended, and the band came out again to lead us in worship and bring in the New Year. When we came to the song "Blessed Be Your Name", I sang with all my heart.

That was one of the most intense times of worship I've ever experienced. It was aching and beautiful. My Father had heard my cry and had answered me. Grateful for His love, all I wanted to do was proclaim His goodness.

Three weeks later, Peter asked to visit my apartment. He and I sat on the couch in the living room. My roommates made themselves scarce. I tucked my feet under me and tried not to think of the piles of homework waiting for me.

"What do you want to talk about?"

"At Urbana, God told me to deal with my feelings for my old girlfriend. He also told me to tell you about what was happening. I was afraid to do this because I knew it would probably be the end of a possible relationship between us. But since then, I've gotten the closure I needed. She's not in the picture anymore. Would you consider dating me?"

I was very resistant to that course of action. "What about our different calls?" I asked.

"I don't actually feel a call to a place, but to ministry in general," he said. "When I was a missionary with Lifespring Singers—travelling all over the world—I became passionate for God's church wherever we went. Based on those experiences, I'm sure that if I end up in Japan, I'll become passionate for the Japanese too."

To me, there was no possibility of anything more than friendship with him. I had already said no in my heart but was a little more ambiguous in my verbal response.

For a week, I didn't give the issue much thought. Then, during a discussion with Timothy's wife, Nadia, I realized that my reluctance to consider dating Peter stemmed in large part from fear of making the wrong choice and of wrecking my friendship with him. By that point, he was one of my best friends, and I couldn't bear the thought of him leaving my life should we break up.

I realized that I couldn't allow myself to make decisions for this reason. I knew that fear has no place in a Christian's life; how could I claim to be filled with the Holy Spirit and filled with fear at the same time?[2]

God used that conversation with Nadia to calm my anxieties. He said to me, "Don't worry about this, Valerie. I know you want to honour Me. I'll take care of the details."

On February 5, 2004, Peter and I made our usual trek to church for college and career group. We chatted for awhile before both falling silent.

"Yes," I said.

"Yes what?"

"Yes, I'll go out with you."

He was driving at the time, making a tricky left-hand turn at one of the busiest intersections in Toronto. In retrospect, my timing could probably have been better. Peter tells me that in his ecstasy, he nearly drove into the median!

During our period of dating, Peter modelled to me God's graciousness as we come to love Him. Peter fell in love with me before I returned his feelings. He was patient as I explored my new, healed personhood in the context of a romantic relationship. When I tentatively tried out the phrase "I love you" and then realized it wasn't quite true, he waited. Just as God tenderly woos us, so Peter was a shining example of that same tenderness in my life.

In the last few months of our dating, I'd known a proposal was coming and made him promise not to go into debt over my engagement ring. Instead, he worked three jobs in addition to his schooling to save up for it.

On December 17, 2004, Peter proposed. To this day, I still feel sorry for him. Nothing went right.

We went out for dinner. Afterward, he intended to take me to the Science Centre for a special exhibit, but the website listed the wrong closing time. We ended up seeing a sad movie instead, followed by a walk in our favourite park. There, he sat me on a bench and read me his version of Elizabeth Barrett Browning's poem: a list of thirty things he loved about me.

When he took out the ring and asked me to marry him, I reacted strangely. I was very happy, but there was also lingering sadness from the movie.

He saw my strange reaction. "Is it too small?"

"It's perfect," I replied.

Eight months later, we were married.

# CHAPTER 3
# Peter's Call

Peter is half-Japanese. His Japanese grandmother was sent to an internment camp in British Columbia, Canada, during the Second World War. When his grandfather visited the camp, a matchmaking friend paired them together. His grandmother was a Christian, but his grandfather was not. They were married for almost sixty years.

Over the course of their marriage, Grandma encountered several health problems. Following a stroke, the doctors said that she would never walk or talk again. But she was a very determined lady and eventually did both. The only residual was a slight slurring in her speech. On another occasion, she fell down the stairs in their house. The prognosis for her ability to walk again was dire, but once more, she recovered fully.

She was always concerned for the spiritual welfare of her husband. He was a practicing Buddhist, and though his wife and children were all Christians, he was never interested in their beliefs. The household rule he instituted was: "I don't try to convert you; don't try to convert me." In typical Japanese fashion, that was the end of the discussion.

Over the years, Grandpa's family continued to pray that God would soften his heart toward Jesus. Pastor Ito, from Grandma's church, eventually started to visit him. Sitting in the kitchen, Grandpa and Pastor Ito would talk for hours, one relating tales of years gone by and the other sharing about the love of God. They soon grew dear to each other, and Pastor Ito began to call Grandpa *'otousan'*, which means 'father'. After many years, Grandpa agreed to attend a weekly Bible study at his wife's church. The group was studying a book called *The Purpose-Driven Life*.

A month before their sixtieth wedding anniversary, Grandma had a heart attack. While she was at the hospital in critical condition, Grandpa turned to Pastor Ito with his questions about Jesus and eternity. He eventually decided to become a Christian himself. The last time Grandma opened her eyes, Grandpa was at her side. He told her that he had asked Jesus to be his Saviour.

To this day, her family believes that for all those years, through all her health problems, Grandma had been holding on to hear her husband say those very words. She couldn't speak, but acted happy. Within twelve hours, she died. She was seventy-nine, and Grandpa was almost ninety.

As Peter tells it, he had always thought Japan was out of reach for him both culturally and linguistically. Though his mother is of Japanese descent, neither she nor he had ever learned the language. When missionaries to Japan came to talk at his church, they always mentioned the difficulty of ministry there. They frequently burned out because of the stress and toil. In his mind, Japan took on the reputation of a missionary graveyard.

When Peter and I met, he was intensely interested in ministry; however, he had previously prayed, "God, I'll go anywhere you want me to go, but please don't send me to Japan."

When Grandma died, everything changed for Peter. God spoke to his heart: if He could bring Grandpa to faith at the age of ninety, then there was hope for 130 million other Japanese people just like him who needed Christ.

# CHAPTER 4
# Married Life and Ministry

My skin hummed with electricity. Everything seemed slightly artificial. I smiled and laughed and tried to act normally. The music started and off went Nadia, Beatrix, and Julia. My little cousin followed them, biting his lower lip in concentration.

The music changed. My turn.

Take Dad's arm. Don't drop the flowers. Take your time. Step. Pause. Step. Pause.

Peter started singing at the piano. So this was the song he'd been working and reworking for months.

"If your eyes are the window to your soul…"

The lace and satin of Mum's old wedding dress rustled with each step as I made my way past the blur of friendly faces. Soon we were at the front.

Senses on overdrive, I felt frozen in time and pleasure as I listened to Peter's musical declaration. It was the best song he'd ever written, and he'd done it for me.

The song ended. Peter approached us, and I kissed my dad on the cheek. The ceremony began.

"She's got a great smile, doesn't she?" someone commented to Peter afterward.

Peter told me many years later that he noticed my smile for the first time on that day.

"Yes, she does," he responded. What a treasure to know that on that special day, his love for me—and mine for him—deepened a little more.

We'd graduated from our respective universities a few months before our wedding. I was twenty-five; Peter was twenty-six. Peter had a degree in pastoral studies, and I was an industrial engineer. We both got good jobs after graduation. Peter was a clerical worker at a telecommunications company. I worked as a consultant at a firm called Imaginia, in my field of specialty. For me, this type of work was intellectually stimulating and right in line with the courses I'd enjoyed most at university.

My new job was located west of Toronto. We decided to settle in Mississauga and did our best to centralize our lives there. To that end, we made the painful decision to leave our beloved Bridgeway Baptist and find a church closer to our new home.

We spent several months searching. Finally, with only a handful of churches left in the directory for our city, we found our way to Haven Community Church. Each week, it met in a school gymnasium where teams of volunteers had set up instruments, audiovisual equipment, and row upon row of green plastic chairs. Our first Sunday there was the last Sunday for the previous worship pastor. We raised our eyebrows over this, particularly since Peter had always been very focussed on worship leadership. It didn't take us long to realize this was the place where God wanted us to settle.

Within a few weeks, Peter was asked to lead worship. Within a few months, he was doing so on a weekly basis. When the church advertised it was looking to hire a new worship pastor, we prayed. After much discussion, we had the mental picture of a nursery. Haven Community Church would be a safe and nurturing place for us to grow in our ministry skills as a couple. God had set this opportunity before us as another phase of training for whatever He had planned in the future.

Peter applied, with the proviso that we intended to leave in a couple of years to serve as missionaries in Japan. The leadership took this under consideration and then offered him the position.

The first few months were emotionally awkward for me. I was not prepared for the adjustment of being a pastor's wife. As it turned out, I had some internal expectations of what a pastor's wife should be. But as time went on, I became more comfortable with the title, realizing I didn't have to meet expectations of my role, whether internal or external. I had the freedom to be the person whom God had uniquely fashioned.

During that time, I also felt emotionally adrift. We had nurtured deep and meaningful relationships with the people at Bridgeway; it was very difficult to not have that same relational depth at our new church. For awhile, I tended to blame others for this lack. I remember on at least one occasion also harbouring some jealousy toward Peter, since he seemed to be developing deeper friendships than me. But eventually, I realized this situation was no one's fault but my own. If I desired deeper relationships, I couldn't passively expect others to come to me. I had to go to them. When I started intentionally spending time with several people in the church, my own friendships began to blossom as well.

A year after Peter started working at Haven, the church board approached him with an offer. They wanted to help further equip us for mission work in Japan and suggested he also take on the role of outreach pastor. Peter told them that were he to accept, outreach would be a joint effort between us as a couple. They agreed, and we gratefully stepped into our new position.

Though the church was small, it had two worship teams. The fellowship and growth—both musical and spiritual—of those teams was refreshing for both them and us. God knit us together in love and blessed those ministries far beyond our own efforts.

We created and led training courses on evangelism; conducted Alpha courses, encouraging people to get to know their neighbours; and also branched out into the community to share

## On the Potter's Wheel

God's love with people, handing out free water bottles in the summer and windshield washer fluid in the winter. Those years of ministry are a shining, bright spot in my memory. We learned so much about how we served best together and came to deeply cherish each person in the church.

In the months preceding our marriage, a pain had developed in my right hip. It was excruciating and rendered me unable to stand or walk for more than a few minutes at once. At the time of our wedding, I was still trying to figure out what was wrong, so Peter and I were married sitting down.

Despite a series of misdiagnoses, I finally found a doctor who could determine what was going on. I've had scoliosis—a curvature of the spine—since childhood. One of the discs in my back had softened somewhat and was no longer properly supporting my vertebrae. One vertebra in particular was rubbing against a nerve, resulting in pain transferred to my hip. Physiotherapy was prescribed, and over time the problem was resolved.

I remember one night before this, when I was utterly tired of being in constant pain, wondering, *Why doesn't God answer my prayers? He's supposed to be my Father, and care for me. A request to not be in pain anymore seems pretty basic. I'm not asking for extravagant riches or power. Why doesn't He take care of me?*

I struggled to understand. I was only twenty-five. Was God punishing me? Did I not have enough faith?

Eventually, I decided to trust Him even if He didn't heal me right away. Little did I know that years later, some of those same questions would resurface, though many times larger.

Time rolled on, and soon it had been seven years since God had placed the call to Japan on my heart. In the interim, I'd done whatever I could to prepare myself for ministry there: studying Japanese religions in university, learning about different techniques for evangelism, and interacting with as many Japanese people as I could find. My eyes were focused on the singular goal of reaching Japan with the good news about Jesus.

Somewhere along the way I began to wrap up my identity in that goal. It wasn't pretty; Peter can attest to that fact. Soon, my identity became so entangled with my call that I panicked at the thought it might not be fulfilled. As we approached our second wedding anniversary, which was when we'd initially planned to leave for Japan, I realized how twisted my outlook had become. Opening up my journal, as I'd done sporadically over the years, I began to write.

June 5, 2007

> I've been absolutely miserable in recent months. I've struggled to have devotions, to pray with passion, and to live a life that loves God. My spiritual highs have not so much been mountains as small hills, and my lows have not been valleys so much as deep chasms. I have been afraid of God, and afraid of the future.
>
> Peter and I had an argument last weekend. I was frustrated once again, and we started talking about being surrendered to God. My old fear came up: that we would never get to Japan, that we would never go on *any* mission, that God would ask us to stay here forever. Everything within me cringes at the thought.
>
> But Peter pointed something out. Every time we're talking about our fears, every time I'm frustrated or scared, this comes up. He said that maybe God is asking me, "If I want you to give up missions, will you do it?"
>
> I've been so afraid of facing that question that I've run off in every other possible direction.
>
> God, I'm tired of running away. I want to follow You, but I don't have the strength to give up my dream—the

dream I've had since I was seven. Please help me to dream Your dreams instead.
    "Will you give up missions for Me?"
    I don't know. But 'missions' was Yours to begin with.

Am I scared of <u>not</u> following You?<br>
OR<br>
Am I scared of <u>following</u> You?

Please help me to seek You with all of my heart, regardless of the outcome.
    "You will seek Me and find Me, when you search for Me with all your heart."[1]

Eventually, I came to accept that God was the owner of my call to missions, and I was not. I was only responsible for my own obedience and submission to His working. Finally, my death grip on those future plans loosened, and I was freed from my own expectations of what getting to Japan would entail.

# CHAPTER 5

# Setbacks and Setups

To us, the idea of including loan repayments in fundraising for missionary work never felt comfortable. So our first order of business was to settle our educational debts so we could be single-minded once on the mission field. Based on our calculations, we would realistically be able to leave for Japan in two years.

Buckling down, we were able to pay off three-quarters of our debt within the first year. We were elated. Then Peter's boss told him that the company was downsizing. Peter had proven himself to be an excellent worker and had earned much favour with his boss. However, his position was unionized and as the most junior member of his team, he was the first to be let go. His boss did manage to secure him two months of additional working time so he could find a new job before being terminated for good.

A man who attended our church soon hired Peter as a car emissions tester. By this time, Peter had also become a part-time worship pastor. His new boss understood Peter's need to accommodate his pastoral duties, and such a benefit helped to offset the stress of lower pay.

At around that time, my sister Julia decided she wanted to move back to Ontario. She'd spent the previous year working temp jobs while living in the Arctic. Without a position already lined up for her in Ontario, she had nowhere to stay. So we offered her our couch for a few months. Though this move would slow down our financial progress toward Japan, we didn't view my sister's situation in a negative light but rather as an opportunity to invest in her life.

Peter was cautious before she moved in. Concerned about the impact that living together in adulthood might have on our sisterly relationship, he said to me, "If she's going to live with us, you'd better be prepared to have her stay for years."

"I don't think that will happen."

"Really? Are you sure?"

"Well, I guess it's possible—"

Peter smiled.

"We'd have a lot of fun. Would it be okay with you if she were to live with us?" I asked.

"I realized long ago that if I want to take care of you, I also need to take care of your sister. You two are really close. I'd be happy for her to move in."

In the end, Peter was right. My sister stayed with us for four years. They were absolutely wonderful. Julia and Peter came to love each other as a dear brother and sister, and I was happy to have the two people whom I loved most under the same roof. We were indeed a close-knit little family.

The next problems we encountered revolved around our car. My dad had graciously given us his used one as a wedding present. It was a godsend, but following its sixth birthday, the repair bills began to pile up. Eventually, we were paying more for repairs than we would have for a new vehicle, so once more we underwent a large cash outlay.

A few days after we purchased the new car, I began to experience doubts over what God was doing. He'd allowed us to pay off the bulk of our debt very quickly, but now we were approaching our original two-year target for departure and were struggling to make any headway whatsoever. What was He telling us? Was He rescinding our call? Surely the enemy couldn't stymie God's plans. It was at this point that I realized my need to release ownership of the call God had placed on my heart and the responsibility of making it happen.

We laid hold of Proverbs 16:9 as our motto: "The mind of man plans his way, but the Lord directs his steps." We were God's servants. If He wanted us to go to Japan, He would make a way. If He wanted us to stay in Canada, He would make it clear. As far as we were concerned, we were still called to Japan and would continue on that assumption until God told us otherwise.

We also made an important decision. While in Canada, we desired to spread the good news of Jesus and realized we couldn't be so focussed on getting to Japan that we ignored present opportunities. God's call to us didn't start in a different time or place. It started right then and eventually would include Japan. God would get us there according to His schedule, but we needed to be good stewards of the time we were given along the way. If we were to die the next day, we wanted to stand before Him unashamed, knowing we hadn't squandered opportunities He had given us in our homeland. This mindset framed the rest of our time in Canada. Perhaps it made us more sensitive to the myriad opportunities God brought across our path—both to disciple and to share the good news of His love with many others.

As I continued in my consulting work for Imaginia, the demands of the job got heavier and heavier. I'd proven myself to be a good worker and problem solver. Eventually, I became the person who was always slated to clean up projects in trouble—in addition to managing new, high-profile ones. This role consumed more and more of my time. I worked enormous amounts of overtime and entered into a continuous cycle of being sick and not-sick, but not quite healthy. I would go on important business trips even when ill and felt as though work were eating up my life.

Peter was very patient as he waited for me to realize the truth he could clearly see: this lifestyle was not good for me or for our little family.

At one point during a flight on a solo business trip to northern Ontario, I experienced severe pain in my ears. I'd had a sinus infection a few weeks before and hadn't realized it wasn't completely resolved. That evening, when talking on the telephone with Peter, I expressed my reluctance to get back on the plane after such pain. Peter, my knight in shining armour, wasn't scheduled to work the following day. He drove eight hours to pick me up after my business meetings and conveyed me home on that same day.

In the summer of 2008, my sister, Peter, and I vacationed together for a week in Nova Scotia. It was a magical trip. We rented a cottage there and spent the majority of our time by the ocean at Peggy's Cove, and in Halifax. Within less than a week of returning to my job, I felt as though I'd never been on vacation and was in desperate need of another one. I finally realized I couldn't continue in this pattern. It was time to change employment. Once more, I dusted off my journal and, through writing, began to understand the workings of my own heart.

September 21, 2008

> I'm reading a book today: *Crazy Love* by Francis Chan. At the moment he's talking about God's magnificence, and how He has exhibited Himself in our world and universe. I am—to be honest, I don't know what I am. Can you be amazed and numb at the same time? What about amazed <u>at</u> your numbness? When reading all sorts of facts about God and His creation, when seeing some pictures of the universe on a website, then I was amazed. But how quickly it faded.
>
> Chan talks about our 'spiritual amnesia': constantly having to be reminded of God's glory. What about what

I've got? A lack of wonder. Amnesia after 5 minutes, like something from a movie. How do you resolve that?

Oh Lord, let me not pride myself in some intellectual understanding of You. Just as a person deeply in love does not merely want to know <u>about</u> the object of his affection, just as he does not wish to engage in a dispassionate discourse on love and its merits, so I do not want to simply observe You as a curiosity and move on. I want to be in You, surrounded by You; engaging, relating, performing the <u>act</u> of loving. I want to have Your picture in the locket of my heart; songs about You flowing from my soul. I want to want You with every fibre of my being.

I am tired. My job at Imaginia is ending. Please let me not sin in my fatigue.

I want to live a life that will make You proud of me. I'm proud of You, and somehow I want to bring You a measure of the happiness You've brought me. What can I do? Who can I be? Holy Spirit, not through my strength can I accomplish this, but only with You.

You <u>are</u> amazing.

I soon found a new job at an engineering company called Methodico. In the interval between my old and new positions, I took almost three weeks off to decompress, so I could give my best work to my new employer. However, it would be many months before I could completely let go of my stress-saturated mentality.

The pastor at Haven Community Church was very fond of finding one-line sayings that imparted important truths. One such saying was: "The set<u>backs</u> we encounter in life are often God's set<u>ups</u> for something better which God has for us." With that mentality, we began to see some of the ways in which God was using our circumstances to set us up for something greater.

In February 2008, we had the opportunity to go on a mission trip to Mexico with a team of six from our church. If we'd been able to leave for Japan according to our original plan, we never would have considered going. However, the relationships developed during that time would be crucial to our preparations and eventual well-being in ministry. The trip was led by Joshua and Sophie Thompson, a missionary couple who had spent almost two decades in Mexico.

We had several preparatory meetings with Joshua, Sophie, and the rest of the mission team during the months leading up to the trip. Tall, passionate, and quick-witted, Joshua was initially a little intimidating. By contrast, Sophie's shy and gentle demeanour masked a different kind of strength. Joshua was full of pithy and insightful statements and would form conclusions quickly; but every once in a while, Sophie would lay her hand on his arm and say, "Joshua…" in a certain tone of voice before going on to offer a different point of view. His eyes would soften as he took her in, and his passion would be tempered by her gentle wisdom. We quickly grew to respect their experience and wholehearted desire for godliness.

When they found out that Peter and I were interested in becoming missionaries, Joshua and Sophie made us an amazing offer: if we could come up with twenty-five questions about missions and missionary life, they would like to meet with us to answer them. We excitedly set to work with our list. Later, Joshua told us that he had made similar offers to other potential missionaries, but many had a hard time coming up with the full complement of questions. However, I had been interested in missions for most of my life, and I'm sure my obsessive list-making personality also helped. We had thought of fifteen questions by the time we finished the drive home from that evening's team meeting! When we e-mailed our list within a few days, they were taken aback at the speed of our response. In the end, we included over thirty queries, many with multiple parts.

Joshua and Sophie faithfully met with us several times to answer our questions. Their answers helped to frame both our mindset and remaining preparations for missionary work. We can't help thanking God for wisely providing the delays we encountered because they meant our lives, relationships, and future ministries would be much more enriched and fruitful.

By this time, I'd developed a new life philosophy that helped me to find things for which I could be thankful. If I encountered something that could help me to empathize with people in their struggles, then I'd decided to be grateful for the experience because it enhanced my understanding of others and also hopefully increased my usefulness to God. Along that vein, I found myself grateful for the stress I'd encountered in my job at Imaginia. It provided some valuable lessons in understanding people who are overworked and stressed. These experiences would help me to later be more compassionate toward people in similar circumstances and to better understand the Japanese themselves, as theirs is a culture of overwork.

In the fall of 2008, we were finally within a few months of paying off our debts, so we began the application process to become missionaries. Our chosen organization later told us that the process typically takes six months to complete. Ours took a year.

Several items got lost in the mail and had to be resent, schedules didn't line up for the various interviews, and each stage of the process seemed to incur unexpected delays.

We asked ourselves what God could possibly be doing. At the time, the only explanation we could find was that the dollar-to-yen exchange rate was particularly horrible at the beginning of the process but improved as we went onward. As a result, when we finally were approved as missionaries, we had less fundraising to complete than if we'd started earlier.

In hindsight there was another benefit. Over the course of our application, we were able to engage in regular monthly fellowship with some friends from Haven Community Church: Kesler, Naveen, and their two girls, Phoebe and Madeline. We'd always intended to develop a deeper relationship with them, but in that year, it actually happened. Naveen was a truly vibrant person. She loved God deeply, was musically gifted, and had a heart to serve children and empower them to serve God. She had a unique habit of greeting people with a perky "Hello, friend!" The first time she addressed an e-mail to me as "Dear Friend," I felt so loved and special.

On the last Monday of each month, we made the trek from work to their house. Sometimes they cooked us dinner; at other times, we brought take-out. We spent time sharing our lives, playing games, and enjoying each other's stories and company.

In August 2009, Peter and I contracted the H1N1 virus, which my sister, a nursing student, had brought home from her job. She experienced a very light case, but we were put out of commission for several weeks. When we'd sufficiently recovered but were still struggling with residual fatigue, Peter and I led a worship service at church. It was our habit to do so alone, without a worship team, on the last Sunday of those months that had five weekends. This was intended to give the worship teams a well-deserved rest from their duties. Still very weak, but no longer infectious, we led the service sitting rather than standing.

At the end, Pastor Alvin thanked us for our efforts despite being so frail. Naveen and Kesler were sitting in the front row. At Alvin's thanks, Naveen spread her arms wide, as if she were hugging us across the distance, and spoke tender words of appreciation. I felt so loved in that moment, and the image of Naveen with her arms open is one I will never forget. There she was, loving us through our weakness and through our recovery from the illness she herself would contract two months later.

In October 2009, we successfully completed the missionary application process. We immediately began a blog to share our new ministry with friends and family. That day, it read:

October 2, 2009

> We're sitting here in our hotel room, in San Francisco, still absorbing the fact that we've finally made it past the interview process and have been accepted as missionaries! This journey has taken almost ten years so far, but as we look back on that time it's amazing to see the care with which God has guided us.
>
> Though our journey hasn't been as lengthy as Moses' forty years, we start to appreciate his season of preparation in light of our own. We can't help thinking that later in life perhaps Moses looked back on that time with great fondness. He'd had so many experiences which would likely have helped him to get through the trials he later faced as leader of Israel. God's wisdom is truly far above our own.

Later that October, I received an e-mail from Naveen. She told me that she'd decided to take a weekly fitness class on Monday nights until Christmas. This would mean she would have to skip out of our monthly visits for about an hour.

I was a little annoyed. We'd made sacrifices to keep our time with her sacred, but she wasn't going to do the same for us. I considered telling her not to worry about our visits, then, until after Christmas. But I realized this was an issue of pride for me; after all, why should one night per month, spent with us, restrict her activities over the rest of the month? I decided not to allow my unsettled feelings to cause our relationship to sour.

That October, we had a lot of fun together with the whole family. When Naveen left for fitness, we continued our visit with the others. When she returned, we lounged around on plump couches and reminisced about the first time we each met our respective spouses.

"I'm so blessed. After fourteen years of marriage, I'm still madly in love with my husband," Naveen said.

That night, we also engaged in the age-old conversation of what we would want our spouses to do if we died.

Less than a week later, Naveen caught H1N1. By that time, the virus had been labelled a pandemic, and the words 'swine flu' were frequent visitors to small talk. Though many millions had been infected worldwide, only a fraction required medical help to recover.

However, Naveen was vulnerable to the virus. Complications with her asthma put her in the ICU.

A few days later, she was dead.

I was at work when the email from Kesler arrived. I couldn't stop shaking. My boss sent me home.

I'd known Naveen was in the hospital and that it was serious. But this? Never in my wildest speculations had I considered she might die.

In shock, I didn't emerge from my numbness and truly start to mourn her until several months later.

Before Naveen's funeral, Kesler shared with us a prayer she'd written in the front of her Bible: asking that she would follow God all the days of her life.

*What an amazing thing*, I thought. *God honoured her prayer.*

She'd loved Him, and she'd loved people.

Peter and I had the privilege of taking part in the funeral. Her family chose a few favourite songs, and Kesler requested that we form a worship team in which he would take part. That funeral was sad and funny and joyful. Kesler was up at the front, heartbroken, playing his guitar, and dancing in praise to God for the gift of his beloved wife. Phoebe and Madeline, Kesler and Naveen's preteen daughters, also danced at the front, doing the actions to "Days of Elijah": the wonder of mourning with hope.

The following Sunday, I learned that many people in the church had taken the day off after Naveen died. In the service, we sat in a circle and shared our feelings and memories. At the end, we sang "Blessed Be Your Name". We started out strong, but at the chorus voices began to drop off. By the end of the song, we'd dissolved into sniffles and a few whispers as some tried to finish the words. Most of us were silent, washed in rivers of tears, and thanking God in our hearts though our mouths and voices had failed.

A few days later, I wrote a poem for her husband and children:

> Colours in my memory dance together to make you.
> You were beautiful.
> Passionate.
> Alive.
> And now you're gone.
> And we, left here below, look around and
> Realize.
> Things are not the same.
> You're not here.
> The place you've gone is real now,
> More than before.
> And one day we'll follow:
> Reunited.
> At last.

There are several things I learned from Naveen, but I will mention two major ones here. The first is a grim reminder that we never know what the future holds. We never know when a person's life might be cut short. I shudder to think of how close I came to cancelling our get-togethers based on a petty grievance that was more in my own mind than in anything she had done. As it was, we had the opportunity to intimately interact with Naveen and her family less than a week before she died. I will ever cherish my memories of that time. How much Peter and I would have lost if I had made a different choice!

The second is the value of a kind word or a unique greeting; the worth of making small kindnesses a habit so they are second nature. We can never know who might be in need of some sort of uplifting contact. We can never tell how a small act might change someone's life.

In elementary school, I believed that I was ugly. Everyone but my mother said so. I assumed she was blinded by love. A few people, like my sister, were silent on the matter. I assumed they remained so out of kindness.

It never occurred to me to ask, "Am I pretty?" Everyone my age, whether classmate, friend, or foe, agreed on this point. I was ugly. And I knew they couldn't be wrong.

One day in Sunday school, the teacher made a comment: "There isn't one girl in this class who is not beautiful."

I shrank down in my chair and thought, *She must have forgotten about me.*

Then one day, everything turned upside down. A sweet, popular girl, whose name still remains precious to me, said six words that indelibly changed my perspective. One of my other classmates had made a snide comment about my looks, and her innocent response rang out clear across the room and to my ears: "What do you mean? Valerie's pretty."

Never did I think of myself in the same way again.

Naveen was a similar type of person. She often took the time and went out of her way to say or do something kind for another person. I didn't realize how habitual this was for her until that church service when we all sat around in a circle, sharing our memories.

CHAPTER 6

# Partnership Development

Now that we were officially missionaries, our next hurdle was to raise the finances that would sustain us in Japan. This process would entail meeting with many people, sharing our story, and inviting them to join us in the work God would do in and through us. Missionaries typically call this phase 'support development'. However, Peter and I use the term 'partnership development'.

In preparation for these meetings, Peter stepped down as associate pastor of Haven Community Church at the end of 2009. This change came with its own upheaval, and I once more turned to my journal as an emotional outlet.

December 15, 2009

> Over the last few weeks I've had an increasing sense of *mono no aware*. That's a Japanese term for an awareness of the transience of things and a bittersweet sadness at their passing. This has become more acute with the death of my friend, Naveen; and Peter wrapping up his pastoral responsibilities. Our time with Haven Community Church has been an amazing period of growth and encouragement. I find myself feeling very sad at the prospect of leaving behind our friends and family, and I miss them already!
>
> That's the one thing I've not been looking forward to in all of this: homesickness. Peter and I know a couple who were missionaries for many years, and they had some fierce struggles with this while away. I'll never

forget them telling us, "Every tear that falls, every ache of homesickness, will be a sacrifice—an offering—going straight to the feet of Jesus." Somehow that makes leaving a little easier, a little more worthwhile—knowing that these pains are precious to Him.

Philippians 4:13: "I can do all things through Him who strengthens me."

In January 2010, we attended a course called Support Bootcamp. It was created to train missionaries in using healthy approaches for finding partners to pray, and financially contribute to their work. Both Peter and I found this course revolutionary to our way of thinking. We were not compelled to approach fundraising as a form of begging for money. Instead, we were empowered with the thought that this phase of ministry could be a joy rather than drudgery. God had blessed us with many friends and family with whom we could share our lives. Our sole responsibility was to describe our vision for ministry and the call God had placed upon our hearts. He would do the rest.

This liberated us to be joyful and trusting. We did not have to see people as potential donors with little dollar signs above their heads; we were freed to think of our preparations in Canada as another form of ministry. From this mindset came our use of the term 'partnership development'. To us, our friends and family weren't simply passive buttresses to our work, but active partners. God's spiritual economy resulted in a worldwide ministry: both to people at home as well as overseas in Japan. It was amazing to see how prayers, like ocean currents, cycled around the world and often ended up bringing nourishment and blessing to many of those in the Body of Christ.

With these realizations, my attachment to our former life loosened a little more. As I journaled about this, I began to realize some of the other costs of leaving.

February 17, 2010

I think that intellectually I'm beginning to accept leaving the church, and Peter resigning as pastor there. We're very busy with missions-related things now, and it's nice to have a break from all the work involved in church life. It's nice to sit through an entire worship service together and not jump up every time there's a problem. However, emotionally it's still very hard to attend and not actually be involved.

So, the question is: what do I really miss? Surely not getting up early on Sunday mornings. Maybe it's more the sense of belonging; perhaps, the knowledge that I may not have that sense again in my life—ever again. We may become people of two countries, and belong to neither; not understanding Japanese fully—but also forgetting our English vocabulary. Not fitting in anywhere. We won't be able to come back to Canada and simply re-acclimatize. Things will change while we're gone. We are essentially giving up all earthly ties, and the only thing that will remain is our citizenship in heaven. Are we willing to do that?

The answer is unequivocally, 'Yes.'

"Forgetting what lies behind and reaching forward to what lies ahead, I press on toward the goal for the prize of the upward call of God in Jesus Christ."[1]

We officially began partnership development in February 2010; that month, we also launched a newsletter—published every other month—to update several hundred friends, family, and church members on our progress in getting to Japan.

Peter still worked at his emission testing job on a half-time basis, using the other half to organize our engagements and take care of the many administrative tasks involved. I still worked full-time for my employer. Since I had switched from Imaginia to Methodico, overtime was reduced, and I could reliably get to our plethora of dinner meetings on time.

In April, our newsletter read:

> I was walking through downtown Toronto a few weeks ago and happened to glance at a sign which helped me determine my route. I was startled to realize, on reflection, that soon I won't be able to 'just glance' at anything anymore. It will be quite an adjustment to be a university-educated person living in a foreign land and be functionally illiterate. That thought has definitely helped to spur us on in our language classes!
>
> There are three distinct writing systems in the Japanese language; all three can be mixed together within the same sentence. *Hiragana* has over 100 phonetic characters and permutations of characters, as does *katakana*. The third, *kanji*, is a set of Chinese characters. Japanese, like many Asian languages, has imported characters from Chinese into its own written language. The meanings and pronunciations are slightly different than Chinese ones, but the basic written forms remain the same. In Japan, school kids are expected to learn about 2,000 *kanji*. In order to be literate, we will need to learn all three of these character sets. No wonder the Harvard scholar Edwin O. Reischauer once said that Japanese is "possibly the world's most difficult writing system!"[2]
>
> I've now learned *hiragana* and *katakana*, but will likely wait to learn most of the *kanji* characters until we're actually immersed in the culture.
>
> A book I've been reading talks about the fact that some people seem to have a special knack for looking at Chinese characters—with next to no guidance—and recognizing their meaning. In this way the American poet, Ezra Pound, was able to accurately translate the writings of Confucius.[3]
>
> My prayer, the day I read that passage, went something like this: "Dear God, Please make either Peter or me a

genius in reading *kanji*!" I'm sure God has quite a good laugh at some of the things we pray for!

By this time, our lives solidly revolved around Japan. We generally had three or four appointments every week to tell people about our future work, plus two nights of language classes. This, coupled with our jobs, meant that by May we needed a break.

We vacationed in Quebec City at the beginning of June. Unfortunately, Peter got sick right at the start. We spent the majority of our days holed up in the condominium we'd rented for the week and got much more rest than if we'd gone sightseeing more extensively.

Whenever I'd previously contemplated learning the two thousand *kanji* characters required for literacy, I had panicked. It takes Japanese people until the end of high school to learn them all; such an undertaking seemed too gargantuan for me. I had laughed at my desperate prayer to become a genius in *kanji* and was sure that God was similarly amused.

However, we had been encouraged by some former missionaries to take the verse "we walk by faith, not by sight"[4] as our mantra while in Japan. When one of Peter's cousins in all seriousness joined me in praying that one of us would become a genius in *kanji*, I realized a few things.

My previous prayer was born of desperation. But God said to me, "I've prepared you in so many other ways for ministry in Japan, ways that you're still learning about. Why do you not seriously ask Me to enable you to learn *kanji*? Is this too big for Me?"

So I started to pray, not out of desperation, but trust—recognizing the ways in which God had already prepared us and asking Him to continue those preparations so we could be more effective while in Japan.

During our holiday in Quebec City, while Peter was sick, my boredom soon became intolerable. Surveying the options for amusement, my eyes fell upon a book of Japanese characters. I decided to give it a try. Over the course of our vacation, I learned 250 *kanji* characters, with an additional 250 polished off over the following month. I was thrilled with such an amazing answer to prayer.

Within the first six months, the ministry partners with whom we met pledged 50 percent of our required funds. God had provided for us quickly and thoroughly, and all seemed to be progressing smoothly. How glad I am that He doesn't tell us what the future holds.

# CHAPTER 7

# Speed Bumps

Peter thinks of the delays we encountered as speed bumps on our road to Japan: intentional points where God placed obstacles in our path to slow us down. A significant speed bump came up in August 2010.

One day I woke up with no energy. It was a Tuesday; by the time I was finished getting ready for work, I was spent. This continued for weeks. I eventually remembered my journal and used it to meditate on my situation.

*August 20, 2010*

> Here I am, sitting on the couch after three weeks of illness: complete and utter fatigue. I could—and, if this had been another time in my life, probably would—have treated this sickness as an enemy: something to be conquered, an obstacle between me and Japan. But I can't help feeling it's a friend God has sent my way to slow me down and teach me something.
>
> I'd been too self-reliant in the days leading up to this. Christian activities had become just that: activities, with no stillness or unscheduled communication with God.
>
> I can't help feeling honoured that He would place such high value on me, saying, "That's enough. I want to spend time with you, and if I have to let you get sick to do it, so be it." He values me more than I valued Him, and that thought makes me want to weep.
>
> Faith is not activity; faith is resting in You. I have not been living a life of faith, yet I plan to be a missionary?

Lord God, help me to see that I am at my most active when sitting here before You. Please help me to prioritize this, to prioritize You.

I don't want to exist outside of You anymore.

The fatigue showed no sign of lessening. We cancelled our partnership appointments. I went to a few different doctors, but no one could find anything wrong with me.

Our August newsletter read:

> I've struggled over the subject for this month's update. I've battled with my desire to always be positive and sharing about our progression toward Japan, showcasing how God's power is apparent in our lives. But would sticking to only positive things, even in the midst of negatives, be truly showcasing how God is working, or would this simply be hypocrisy presented in a wrapping of religious self-sufficiency?
>
> In the Bible God says, "My grace is sufficient for you, for My power is perfected in weakness."[1] If we are therefore to truly show God's presence in our lives, then along with Paul we will choose to say, "Most gladly, therefore, will I rather boast in my infirmities, that the power of Christ may rest on me."[2]
>
> Over the last month I have been virtually incapacitated by extreme fatigue, vertigo, and a few other symptoms. A diagnosis is still elusive (one doctor suggests post-viral fatigue), but during this time I've felt as though God has brought me to an oasis where I can eat and drink my fill of Him. I am improving, slowly, and hope to be back in operation over the next few weeks. But I believe some of the lessons we're learning now will be invaluable in Japan.
>
> I've always been a very task-oriented person. However, during this time most tasks either have been out of my reach, or need to be rationed out a little at a time. I've

been learning to step back from my to-do list, and just be. In my journal last week, I wrote, "Faith isn't about doing; it's about being. Doing flows out of being." I think I'd gotten too caught up in the busyness of getting ready for Japan and hadn't spent enough time just being one of God's children.

In my lack of strength, I have also been learning the meaning of the phrase, "[In Christ,] I can do all things, through Him who strengthens me."[3] Serving Him with busyness is not what our God desires; serving Him with a still Spirit, relying on Him, being connected, drawing strength from Him for each moment—that's what He wants. And that's what we're learning again to give Him.

I love being around people, even if it's just one other person. However, with that illness I found myself largely alone. After more than three weeks of it, the solitude began to take its toll.

For several days I'd been feeling down. Peter and I had been fighting as he struggled with the fatigue of taking care of me and the frustration of my slow recovery. I had felt relationally adrift, and guilty because I thought that God should be enough for me.

*Why should I be affected this way?* I wondered. *I must be doing something wrong.*

Weeping over all of this, I opened the Bible to my psalm for the day. There it was: Psalm 22. It expressed exactly what I was feeling. Forsaken. A worm. Poured out like water.

And then—the verse that was like a thunderclap in my psyche; the loud noise where time stopped, all sounds afterward were muted because I'd absorbed everything I could in that one instant, and the rest passed by like a dream:

> For He has not despised nor abhorred the affliction of
> the afflicted;

Neither has He hidden his face from him;
But when he cried to Him for help, He heard."
(v. 24)

"You hear! You heard me, my Lord and my God!" I prayed. "How merciful You are, how tender in my weakness. A waterfall of thanksgiving could not begin to portray my gratitude. Thank You for providing this Psalm. Thank You for being my Father, ever-present in times of trouble. There is none like You, not even close."

Strangely, though we still couldn't get a diagnosis, after this time with God I felt very little anxiety. I couldn't shake the feeling of His tender care. Poor Peter, though, went through a great deal of worry. For all we knew, I might have cancer.

By this time, it had been almost ten years since God called me to Japan. We'd told our story over and over to many people; and in the telling, the truth of God's guidance and provision had sunk into my heart.

"My life is Yours," I said to Him. "I've already committed it to You. What You want to do with it is Your prerogative. Please help me to trust You, and please use me for Your kingdom, whatever happens."

CHAPTER 8

# Living Now

While sick, I listened to podcasts on the Internet. Sometimes I would meditate on them in my journal.

September 15, 2010

Yesterday I watched a *Meeting House* videocast which featured Eckhart Tolle, a new-age guru. It talked about how we can potentially go from cradle to grave and never truly live in the present moment. Consider, for example, the act of taking a sip of water. There are three parts to this action:

1. Picking up the glass and moving it to your mouth,
2. Sipping, and
3. Putting the glass back down.

Typically, we are already anticipating the sip when we pick up the glass; we are already expecting the water to ease our thirst when we sip; and we've moved on to the next task in our minds while putting down the glass. But how often do we stop to just enjoy the simplicity of the task?[1]

As I write this in my journal, I can't help but wonder: how often do I appreciate the simple act of writing? Writing means I have functional hands and arms, a useable brain, eyes that can see, and education to know the letters. How many things there are to be thankful for, even in this one action! Instead, I complain when I get writer's cramp—the height of ingratitude.

God, please forgive me! Thank You for showing me this slower pace of life and for not allowing me to simply let life pass by as I live in some time other than now.

Now is the time I have been given. Now I will give thanks. Now I will live my life to glorify Him.

In September 2010, a co-worker recommended that I visit a naturopath. I was diagnosed with adrenal exhaustion. Apparently, blood tests don't show anything until the glands have already failed, but a saliva test will highlight problems. According to one doctor, there are fifteen stages of adrenal health: stage one is optimal, and stage fifteen is failure.[2] In August 2010, I was at stage fourteen, dangerously close to the edge.

Under the naturopath's care, my health began to improve. In total, it would be two months before I was able to start working again, albeit part-time and from home.

By mid-October, I was able to leave our apartment for brief excursions, which I thoroughly enjoyed after having been isolated for so long. I could regularly attend church on Sunday mornings and, though small activities could still render me exhausted, I appreciated engaging in a few social connections again.

However, even in the midst of this improvement, my life seemed largely static. I felt as though I were standing, isolated, on a busy street. People were milling about everywhere, living their lives in fast-forward, marching on in different directions, while I stood still, alone, silent. I was most alive in my inner self. My private dialogues with God became the chief expression of my existence, the thing that distinguished me from just being a human paperweight. There was no energy for anything more. But even as I write this, I realize the truth: there was no energy for anything less.

Soon Thanksgiving arrived and brought with it another lesson that I chronicled in my journal.

October 11, 2010

Last night I woke to Peter cuddling up to me, stroking my hair, and saying, "I love you." It sounded desperate, wild, tender, ripped from his soul, deep, pure, passionate. It was an expression of love I have never heard from anyone before; fuller and more profound than anything I had ever experienced.

He told me that he had been having trouble getting to sleep and had gotten up to do several things. At one point he stared out the window of our apartment, looking at the twinkling lights in the other buildings. He suddenly felt heart-wrenchingly alone, even though I was in the other room. For a moment he had a small sense of what it might be like to lose me. He cried.

As I sit here, God brings that conversation back to me, and it hits me: His love is even greater than that intensely beautiful, guttural expression of Peter's last night. I am one of the bride of Christ. How many times have I passed Him by, effectively dead to Him? Oh, the remorse and overwhelming sadness! In grief, I bow before my Maker, the Lover of my soul.

Thank You for loving me so much. Thank You that my love means something to You, and that You desire it.

You blow me away. You're infinitely more than the furthest limits of my imagination, more beautiful and tender and majestic than anything this world—this universe—can begin to reveal. Happy Thanksgiving, God.

One evening, Peter said to me, "That's it! I'm getting you out of our apartment. We're going to have fun!"

# On the Potter's Wheel

We went to the local mall and walked around. Though never much of a shopper or browser, I really appreciated this outing and recorded the experience in my journal.

October 30, 2010

I'm sitting here, savouring the energy humming in my veins. It's funny, but before getting sick, I never noticed it. I never thought of energy as being a blessing. It wasn't really ingratitude—just ignorance of what can go wrong with one's body. They say you never really know what you've got until it's not there.

I found the same thing when I was having problems with the disc in my back. Until feeling pain at every step, I had never really savoured the simple pleasure of walking, of strolling around, carefree, without a plan of what needed to be done before the pain became unbearable. Now that my back is stronger and I don't experience this anymore, I do notice. I savoured strolling around the mall last night: both the walking and the energy slowly returning to my body and enabling me to browse around stores, shop for Christmas cards, and enjoy the fact that I'm alive and returning to health.

Some might say that the past few months have been a desert time of struggle, but I have a hard time thinking this way. They've been more like an oasis. Though physically it has not been pleasant, spiritually I can't imagine a more lush and vibrant place. I pray that God will find me to be faithful when I exit the desert and enter the Promised Land. But for now, I'll just sit here and enjoy the hum of energy in my veins.

The following day in my devotions, I read Luke 10. At the end of that chapter, Jesus visited His friends—Martha, Mary, and Lazarus—at their home in Bethany. Lazarus entertained

Jesus and His disciples; Martha cooked in the kitchen; and Mary—where was Mary? Listening to Jesus, seated at His feet.

Frazzled and frustrated, Martha piped up. "Jesus, please send in Mary to help me."

Jesus gently replied, "Martha, you are worried about many things, but only one thing is really needed. Mary had chosen it, the best thing."

As I finished reading, a light went on in my mind.

"That's what You've been doing, isn't it Lord?" I prayed. "Through the past three months You've been changing me from Martha into Mary."

CHAPTER 9

# Rhythmic Interlude

I've always been rhythmically challenged. In seventh grade, we had to choose instruments for music class. The school owned items in all the different sections, with the exception of strings. I'd already been taking piano lessons for several years; in my timidity, I chose to play the piano rather than try something new.

What I didn't realize was that my music teacher had little use for the piano; volunteering for that instrument meant I would be consigned to the drums. I learned fairly quickly that I had no rhythm, so I played quietly, hoping no one would hear my mistakes.

"Valerie!" Mr. Stanza once said, "I think you're the only drummer I've ever taught whom I had to tell to play louder!"

I enjoyed eighth grade music much more. There was a new boy in the class who also wanted to play the drums. The school had two kits, and his rhythm was even shakier than mine. Somehow that gave me more confidence, because I wasn't the worst. Still, I'm sure those two years of my drumming really tested Mr. Stanza's patience.

While working at Imaginia, a co-worker and I were sent to a conference in Nashville, Tennessee. We ran into a client there who wanted to visit a blues bar one night. He sat us right in the front row for the live music. The singer liked audience participation. To my mortification, he chose to include me. I can't remember the song, but he asked me to repeat a line he sang. I messed up the rhythm the first time…and the second…and the third. By the fourth time, he gave up and settled for 'good enough'. Our client got a kick out of the whole episode and had a lot of fun showing pictures to his co-workers the next day. I was just glad his phone wasn't equipped to take video.

Fall 2010

I have no rhythm. This is a fact that over the years I've grudgingly come to accept. Though I love clapping to worship songs, I invariably start on the wrong beat or lose the spacing between beats quickly.

When my friend, Naveen, was alive she also loved to clap. The difference was she had rhythm. So, I would follow her lead, enjoying the activity without self-consciousness.

When I was on the worship team at church, Peter actually had us practice clapping to "Go Tell It on the Mountain" each Christmas for my benefit. I still need the practice.

Yesterday during the worship service, I really wanted to clap to the first song, but there was a problem: no one else was clapping. There was no one to follow. After a moment's hesitation I started clapping anyway…and a wonderful thing happened. I was on-beat! I wasn't losing the beat! Other people started clapping too—they were following my lead! It was incredible. Here I was worshipping God and clapping without a second thought to getting it right. What elation! Move over gift of tongues—for that song I had the gift of clapping! And boy, did I enjoy it.

## CHAPTER 10

# Working Again

In November, I reached a stage where I was well enough to resume full-time hours at Methodico. I started working from home, taking breaks when I needed to rest and generally maintaining a more relaxed atmosphere than in an office as my body continued to strengthen. As with many recovery processes, improvement wasn't always linear. Several days of good progress might be followed by a bad day, so we knew I still needed to be careful.

Before my adrenal issues, our jobs and partnership development kept us very busy. At this point, we decided to dial back my working life to ensure that we didn't over-stress ourselves with the ongoing preparations. I arranged to work four days per week, rather than five, and soon was ready to start going into the office once in a while.

In preparation for our missionary work in Japan, Peter and I also attended a language acquisition course. This was a two-week program that trained our ears to hear and our mouths to pronounce a variety of sounds not present in English. If our ears were more tuned to hear these sounds, then we would have better accents in Japanese. The course taught us many new methods of learning, and helped to dispel a lot of our fears about communication while in Japan.

November 15, 2010

We are at linguAcademy, in the Colorado mountains, taking a course in linguistics and learning methods. It's been a challenge; our mouths are tired of being contorted to make sounds from languages all over the world. We've just learned about some of the pitches available in tonal languages, and our instructors warned us about the importance of hearing and enunciating these differences. They told us a story.

There were once some missionaries who were ministering to a native tribe in Alaska. The tribe didn't have a written language, so the missionaries created one for them at the same time as translating the Bible into it. As their translation effort progressed, they were puzzled to observe that the natives didn't seem to care at all for Psalm 23. They thought that perhaps there must be some sort of cultural factor preventing the people from identifying with sheep and the practice of shepherding.

These missionaries hadn't been trained linguistically, and couldn't hear the difference between some of the tones in the language. After they finished the translation, they asked an expert to come and check their work. When he examined Psalm 23, he found a few discrepancies because of inaccurate tones. The missionaries' translation read:

> The Lord is my sheep herder.
> I don't want him.
> He knocks me down in the field,
> And drags me to the river....[1]

I'm sure the mistakes we make when we get to Japan will also be quite amusing!

The people we met at linguAcademy were from many different agencies and were at varying stages of preparation for their own ministries. Some would soon be leaving for the mission field while others were just starting partnership development.

However, we all had a similar passion for sharing the good news about Jesus, and the two weeks we spent together refreshed us for the challenges ahead.

CHAPTER 11

# Okinawa

Japan is divided into prefectures, similar to Canada's provinces. When we first applied to become missionaries, we stated a strong preference to be placed in Hokkaido, the northernmost prefecture in Japan. We felt certain that not many missionaries would want to brave its piles of snow and frigid winters. Peter, in particular, really loves the snow. By contrast, his body sometimes has problems dealing with hot temperatures, which are common in the rest of Japan. We felt Hokkaido would be the best fit.

In 2010, the conditions of Peter's job were quite often sweltering in the summer. He worked outside and tested cars to make sure their emissions met the government's environmental standards. That year, his body started to change so that warm temperatures caused him less discomfort.

Our hearts also began to change, and we felt our preference for Hokkaido slipping away. The week before our organization determined where new missionaries would be assigned, I said to Peter, "You know, with all the differences we've been experiencing, I wouldn't be surprised if God sends us south."

Sure enough, the placement committee decided to route us in that direction. We would be serving in Okinawa, which is the most southern prefecture in Japan and home to over a million people. The main island is just over a hundred kilometres long. Given the size of their home soil, the Okinawan sense of distance is very different from our own. In fact, many people won't consider traveling the length of the island without an overnight stay.

In the path of the East Asian Typhoon System, Okinawa experiences monsoon rains in the spring and usually encounters a number of typhoons from July to November. Humidity consistently hovers around 100 percent in addition to the heat.

Japan is a very long country, and Okinawa is quite distant from the rest of the islands. In fact, it's closer to Taiwan, Shanghai, and Manila than to Tokyo.

Grateful for the changes to our physiology and emotions, we couldn't help marvelling that God never throws us into the deep end without first preparing our hearts and bodies to serve Him. Little did we realize how deep that end would be.

CHAPTER 12

# Attack

Spiritual warfare is a reality of every Christian's life. Sometimes it's veiled and almost indistinguishable from normal, flesh-and-blood experiences; at other times, it's much more overt. In Paul's epistle to the Ephesians, he said, "For our struggle is not against flesh and blood, but against the rulers, against the powers, against the world forces of this darkness, against the spiritual forces of wickedness in the heavenly places."[1]

At some points we'd previously come up against overt spiritual opposition to our activities, but none was so forceful as our encounter in December 2010.

One morning, I came under attack. It seemed that every single wrong and sinful thing I'd ever done was thrown up in my face. I felt the overwhelming burden of my guilt. So I ran to my Bible and started reading all God's promises of forgiveness and redemption to those who repent and believe in His name for salvation.

About a week later, Peter, Julia, and I were having our regular Sunday night Bible study when we started talking about spiritual warfare. We came to some startling realizations.

My mother has always struggled with depression, but in recent times, she'd begun to exhibit some troubling symptoms of further health problems. Julia and I became very concerned at the prospect that something might be seriously wrong. We started working with the doctor to try and get her help. I realized that I was feeling panicky over the thought of leaving Julia to trudge through the medical diagnostic process alone. It was difficult to consider leaving her and my mother at such a time of need.

Meanwhile, we also recognized struggles within our home church. Shortly after Peter resigned from his role as associate pastor, several people in key positions left; and by this time, several more were in the process of leaving. Those in our church loved us dearly, and Peter was distressed to be leaving for Japan at such an unfortunate time.

Lastly, we'd noticed a disturbing trend with those who had signed on to be our partners. Within months, weeks, or sometimes even days of them expressing their commitment to financially join us in our ministry, several lost jobs, loved ones, or their own health. We both struggled with the idea that the devil was attacking us and those around us, and the lie that it was somehow our fault.

Through the previous six months, a battle had been intensifying around us. Peter and I were personally confronted with temptations of every kind to stay in Canada rather than go to Japan—temptations that struck at areas nearest and dearest to our hearts.

As Julia, Peter, and I sat in our living room coming to these realizations, we couldn't help but be grateful that though we're frail beings, we serve an immense God. Before Him, our enemy can do nothing but tremble and flee.

That day, God asked me to turn these areas of attack over to Him. He didn't give any guarantees of protection for the ones I love, so obedience was a struggle—almost physically so. In an intensive time of prayer and worship, God enabled us to hand over the lives and well-being of my mother, our partners, and the church to His care.

Finally, I came to the point where I looked each of these temptations in the face and declared, "You have no power over me. Jesus has power over you!"

CHAPTER 13

# Running the Race

January 10, 2011

Yesterday in church, the pastor spoke on 1 Corinthians 9:24-27, which talks about the need to "run in such a way as to get the prize" (NIV), and to make our bodies our slaves so we won't be disqualified. I couldn't help thinking that though we often focus on discipline and training when looking at this passage, there's another element we often miss: mindset.

A friend of mine used to babysit and play tennis with a now-famed European tennis star. Something she once said remains imprinted on my mind: "Really, when you're looking at the top five people in a sport, any of them could win the match. It often comes down to athletes' arrogance and how much they believe they will win. Eduardo Ricardo is a really arrogant guy. He always has been. That's why he's so good."

How does that arrogance translate into our own experience, when we as Christians are told to be humble? Perhaps the solution lies in the mentality with which we approach our lives. Perhaps the key is to daily claim the victory Jesus has already won on our behalf. How many times have we allowed ourselves to get sucked into defeatist attitudes? How many times do we use 'perseverance' and 'faithfulness' as terms to insulate ourselves from the reality that we are not living in victory or joy—that we are not living the abundant life Jesus has graciously given us as an inheritance?

The more I think about it, the more I am convinced that living in victory is itself a spiritual discipline.

When disheartened, we might be tempted to read these things and respond, "That's all well and good, but what if in my life there are no apparent victories? What if everything around me is crumbling?"

That, I think, is when true discipline and faith come in. Some of the most joyful, triumphant Japanese missionaries I have ever met shared this verse with us last year:

"We walk by faith, not by sight."[1]

What if that's the key?

In those times when sweet triumph is lost in the dissonance of defeat, when our hearts are pummelled and broken, when we grope blindly for hope—that is when, through Jesus' strength, we can choose to claim victory by faith. The sweet incense of our offering of faith curls its perfume up to the throne of grace; He inhales deeply, and smiles.

## CHAPTER 14

# Waiting on God

Again juggling full-time work and partnership development, I found myself struggling with those former 'Martha' tendencies. As much as I liked to be organized and fill my time with things that made me feel productive, I realized that I needed to let go of busyness and simply abide in Jesus. Many of my thoughts on this matter finally came together early in the new year. I recorded them in my journal.

*January 2011*

> A friend recently told me that he spent his Christmas reading, writing, and gazing at little delights from his window. It's sad how busy people are these days—they often miss doing those very things.
>
> I've come to the conclusion that busyness is really a disease gnawing at our society. We look to our level of activity to define our own importance and self-worth, rather than rooting our identities in less-transient things. I must admit that at times I, too, have fallen into the trap of thinking of my full calendar with a sense of pride; as if the more things I have pulling at me, the more important I am. How far from the truth this is! I've concluded that busyness, like leprosy, numbs us to the things that truly matter.
>
> Today, I'm challenged to sit down and consider what makes me valuable as a person. Because if it's my level of activity, I will ultimately become an emotional leper: numb to my surroundings, consumed by my busyness, robbing myself of the abundant life.

"I came that they may have life and have it abundantly."[1]

By February, my adrenal functions had climbed to stage 10 from 14, and the speed of recovery was increasing.

"Please guide us with our finances," I said to God when all of this started. "You know when I'll be healthy enough to leave for Japan. We don't want to live in fear, so we're trusting that when we get to 100 percent of our financial requirement, You will have prepared us physically as well."

From that prayer onward, my energy levels began mimicking our fundraising status, and we were deeply thankful for God's reassurance in this.

Our supervisor's family planned to come back to Canada for a few months that summer. With our organization we discussed the logistics of their departure from, and our arrival in, Japan.

"We don't want to leave you in the lurch during the first months of your time in Japan. You should be settled in your new home before your supervisor leaves for Canada."

We nodded, pausing to work through the timeline. "So the options are either to arrive in Japan a few months before they leave for Canada or to arrive a few weeks after they return to Japan."

"That's right," the human resources lady said. "If you've completed 75 percent of your target fundraising by the end of February, then you can leave for Japan by May."

We did some quick math. "Based on how things have been going so far, it should be easy to reach that level soon. We should be able to leave before May."

"Great!"

We were all gung ho to continue meeting with potential partners and prepared for my job resignation. But God had other plans. Historically, we'd seen a cancellation rate of 10 to

15 percent for partnership appointments. However, in February, this number soared to 90 percent. At every turn that month, there were delays, and even people saying "Wait", in our path. At Methodico, the walls of my office cubicle felt as though they were closing in on me, but the messages God sent us remained constant: "Wait on Me."

One day, when I was listening to a Christian song during devotions, the truth hit me. I'd been feeling a measure of failure to meet expectations: to get to Japan in others' timing and, more dominantly, in my own.

The truth is that only God's plans matter, I wrote in my journal. I am a success because I am following Him. We are not serving others or ourselves. We are serving Him.

Once more He freed me from my own expectations.

"Grow in me, Lord God," I prayed. "You must increase; I must decrease."[2]

As the end of February approached, we realized that we would not be leaving for Japan until our supervisors returned there in September.

We sometimes questioned why God would let matters proceed so rapidly at the beginning of the partnership development process, only to slow us down in the following months. I think maybe He wanted us to see what could be accomplished when the timing was right. We needed to know there wouldn't always be struggle. When everything was ready for our departure, He would move swiftly and powerfully.

CHAPTER 15

# March 11

*God is our refuge and strength, an ever-present help in trouble. Therefore we will not fear, though the earth give way and the mountains fall into the heart of the sea.*

—Psalm 46:1–2 (NIV)

On March 11, 2011, the country of Japan was radically changed. A powerful earthquake set off a tsunami that tore through the Sendai region. Though designed to withstand earthquakes and tsunamis larger than any on historical record,[1] the nuclear plants of Fukushima were overwhelmed by the deluge that swept over their fortifications, and a nuclear failure also ensued. This triple disaster took thousands of lives and left many more thousands suffering and broken.

I remember staring blankly at the news, trying to absorb the enormity of the events that had transpired and feeling physically sick at the pain and suffering of so many people. The devastation was horrific and the need immense, but we knew our God was bigger than any disaster. Jesus could tenderly transform the situation for love, hope, and life.

Okinawa, though a small island, is sufficiently distant from the rest of Japan that it was lightly affected by the various disasters. For instance, it didn't even feel the earthquake, and the tsunami it experienced was minimal. The main effect was that there would eventually be many displaced people who came to Okinawa. On Honshuu (mainland Japan), more than half a million people lost their homes. The government opened up free public housing across the country as the homeless tried to get their feet back under themselves over the coming year.

Our organization had developed connections with a number of church congregations across the country, so there was a great opportunity to work together in the name of Jesus and show His love in a myriad of ways. Japanese Christians were remarkably self-effacing through that time. They helped others, not in the name of their churches or organizations, but only in the name of Christ. In fact, those who were suffering started to address Christians as "Jesus" or "Mr. Christ."

"Grandma, Jesus brought us food!" children would call out.

"Mr. Christ is having a barbeque!"

As time progressed, the needs of the people in the affected regions shifted from food to shelter and other forms of relief. Because churches were in constant contact with the people, they were able to identify deficiencies and act as first responders to the requirements of the moment. The job of missionaries was to serve and empower local people who, in turn, could then help the community with grace and meaning.

This was a special period for the church of Japan. It was not looking to exploit or capitalize on this tragedy as a gimmick. This was one of those moments when people were most obviously in desperate need of hope: a need that had been there all along but at times was easier to ignore than others. There had been problems with societal hopelessness for some time in the form of suicides and people voluntarily shutting themselves in their bedrooms for years on end (termed *hikikomori*). But we trusted that the love of Christ, and the hope found only in Him, would transform hearts and lives to heal and restore. We felt privileged to be a part of this amazing work.

In the wake of the crisis in Japan, several people came to Peter and me, exclaiming, "Thank goodness you're still in Canada. Thank goodness you're safe!"

Peter and I had the exact opposite reaction. We felt the urgency of getting to Japan and frustration that we weren't there to help in the immediate aftermath.

During the previous year, when our congregation collectively read through the book of Acts, I noticed that though the early church went through intense persecution, whenever they gathered to pray there seemed to be something missing. They didn't pray for physical safety. In fact, they arguably asked for the opposite: boldness in the face of persecution.

With the disasters in Japan, I was reminded of this observation. I started to wonder if perhaps I was missing a deeper lesson. What if our North American obsession with safety was unfounded? What if we'd somehow been tricked into pouring massive amounts of time, energy, and money into creating something that didn't—and never would—exist? What if security was just an illusion and, for all our hype and hyperventilation, we would never achieve our goal?

I did a personal Bible study and found that neither Jesus nor His disciples mentioned physical safety once. Our physical safety was not a given; but His love for us, and our spiritual safety, were promised with full assurance.[2] Where did that leave us? What if we'd lulled ourselves into a sense of false security and complacency and had contentedly rendered ourselves ineffective?

Tacitus, a senator and historian of the Roman empire, said that "the desire for safety stands against every great and noble enterprise."[3]

I realized that I, too, had bought into this obsession. "Lord, help me to shed my preoccupation with safety and embrace Your risk," I prayed.

"Security is mostly a superstition," Helen Keller once said. "It does not exist in nature nor do the children of men as a whole experience it. Avoiding danger is no safer in the long run than outright exposure. Life is either a daring adventure or nothing."[4]

CHAPTER 16

# Attitudes of the Heart

Missionaries have to be very careful of their heart attitudes toward their ministry partners. This was one of the most valuable lessons that Joshua and Sophie imparted to us in our question-and-answer sessions several years earlier. As time went on, the contours of this lesson came into sharper focus. The heart attitudes of a missionary will colour his or her relationship with partners and will profoundly impact ministry in the target country. An attitude of entitlement during the partnership development process can be exhibited as arrogance on the field. Conversely, an attitude of timidity, fear, or embarrassment does not build a foundation of boldness and victory for future ministry. We realized that God was far less interested in our service than He was in the state of our hearts. Service could be duplicated by others, but the purity of our hearts was ours alone.

As our remaining time in Canada dwindled, I started to think more and more about the people and things we were leaving behind. The gravity of our possessions and jobs didn't pull at me much, but people were a different matter. I comforted myself with those words of Jesus: "And everyone who has left houses or brothers or sisters or father or mother or children or farms for My name's sake, shall receive many times as much, and shall inherit eternal life."[1]

One day, I sat down with my journal. Well aware of the people we would be giving up, I needed to remind myself of the One we were giving them up for.

May 1, 2011

What are You worth? You are worth all the treasures this world has to offer, whether jewels, or soil, or money. You are worth ambition, extravagance, and diligence. You are worth the most extreme effort and worth risking devastating defeat. My strivings, struggles, and trials do not attain You, for no one is deemed fit to climb Your Holy Mountain. But Your Son has made a way when no one else could; through Him I experience joy and peace in abundant measure.

How wide, how deep, how magnificent You are. There is none like You. No one else is worth so much, worth all I have or could ever hope to have, all I am or could ever hope to be.

It's not because of me that I come. It's because of You. You draw me. You are perfection personified. Love embodied. Grace poured out, plentiful and free.

You are greater, You are higher, You are purer, You are lovelier. You are more in every way. You are overwhelming. You surround me like a cocoon, and I am secure.

Synchronize my heartbeat with Yours. What can I give You today, Lord? Love? Obedience? Surrender? Take me, take all of me, and mould me into Your image more and more today.

Later that month, God asked me something new during my devotions. "Would you give up your Canadian citizenship? If I requested it of you, would you become a Japanese citizen?"

I love my country, am proud to be a Canadian, and feel I've won the genetic lottery. But God was the one who gave me this gift in the first place, so the question remained: would I give it up if He asked?

"But…my country!" I protested.

"You are a citizen of no earthly country, but of heaven, of My kingdom," He responded.

I opened my Bible: "More than that, I count all things to be loss in view of the surpassing value of knowing Christ…count them but rubbish in order that I might gain Christ…I press on toward the goal for the prize of the upward call of God in Christ Jesus."[2]

"Please help me to honour You in all of my choices," I prayed.

For two days, I wrestled with this question.

"You are my Father, and You are my Lord," I finally prayed. "If You want me to give up my citizenship at some point, I'll do it."

That day, I shared with Peter what God had asked of me.

He looked stunned. "In my devotions over the last two days, God has been asking me the exact same question."

## CHAPTER 17

# Preparing to Leave

At the beginning of June, we decided to visit a Japanese garden near our apartment. Peter took a picture while there. He thought it simply showed me looking at the garden; we didn't realize its profundity until we got home. In it, my back was to the camera as I gazed at a wooden pagoda that stood over a shimmering pool and was framed with tufts of cherry blossoms, a monument to the sensitive artistry of the Japanese. A hazy, distinctive Canadian skyline was painted in muted blues in the background. The picture was so perfectly absurd that it looked fake. However, it spoke volumes about our mentality as we approached our last few months in Canada. Things of our native country had started to fade into the background, and Japan was becoming much more imminent and real. I meditated on this in my journal.

June 4, 2011

> We walk around the mall, and everything seems kind of foreign. The merchandise which used to tempt us before now barely leaves an imprint on our consciousness. We find ourselves ferociously craving those last few precious moments with family and friends, and there's a general detachment towards anything other than people.
>
> I wonder if this is the same feeling people get as they're dying: the reality of things that are truly important comes sharply into focus, and distractions start to fade away. In a sense, I feel like we're living out the concept of dying to the old self. We're dying to our education, occupations,

former ministries, and even a little to our relationships here. They'll not be the same as they were before; the ability to interact—to smell, see, and touch—will be so diminished.

I suppose we're setting out on the mourning process that we were warned would happen as we approach our departure date.

"But whatever things were gain to me, those things I have counted as loss for the sake of Christ. More than that, I count all things to be loss in view of the surpassing value of knowing Christ Jesus my Lord...."[1]

I decided to finish my employment with Methodico on June 16, my birthday. For the following three weeks, I would tackle the many tasks to be completed before our vacation in July.

Leaving a job is stressful at the best of times, and the added knowledge that we would soon also be leaving our country only added to the difficulty of my last week at Methodico.

I'd initially thought finishing on my birthday would be a wonderful present: "Happy birthday, Valerie, now you no longer have to go to work at a job that's not your passion. Now you're free to do the things for which God made you."

However, I discovered my feelings were far from congratulatory. Instead, they were the inevitable sadness of transition, and the mourning of relationships that would ever be changed from their previous state because their comfortable, familiar routines were altered.

It was quite depressing, really, and I found myself in a rather deep funk. Peter and Julia came to the rescue though. They gathered around me in love, and we had a wonderful time together that evening. Quitting a job on my birthday is one thing I will never do again.

One of the first things I did in my new role was to sit down and plan the tasks that needed to be completed each day until we left. To my mildly obsessive self, this was the best way to keep us organized. After three hours and six pages of minuscule handwriting, our master schedule was finally ready. It would seem that no matter how minimalistic we'd tried to be, there were still many things to do before our departure.

Peter completed his employment at the end of June. In early July, we left with Julia for vacation. It had been more than a year since our last one, and because Peter had been sick for most of that earlier holiday, we were sorely in need of rest.

Though I'd been unable to work for several months over the previous year, the helplessness and inactivity of illness weren't restful. In fact, they were the polar opposite. As author Amy Carmichael once wrote, the truest rest is found in healthy vigour and ability: in the freedom to run, or swim, or play.[2]

By this point, I was well again, and we had hit 100 percent of our required funding, which we saw as a gift from God. It meant we didn't have to worry about doing any more fundraising when we returned from holiday.

We loaded our car with stacks of camping gear and trekked off for a week in Fundy National Park, New Brunswick, home to the highest tides in the world. We played zany car games, took a side trip to Prince Edward Island, flew kites (Julia and I for the first time), ate ice cream, and explored several of the charming cities in New Brunswick. Then we rented a condo in Mont Tremblant, Quebec, and enjoyed the luxury of real beds for a few nights.

On the way back to Ontario, we dropped Julia off in the small town of Huntsville so she could catch a bus home to Mississauga. Her vacation was over, but we wanted one more week in our favourite camping spot: Algonquin Park.

It seemed as though God caused everything that depended on chance to turn out in our favour. We were able to secure our favourite nonreservable campsite. Though there was some rain, most of the time it was at night: just enough to keep the risk of forest fire down and ensure we were allowed campfires.

I love animals, so I prayed that we would get a chance to see some creatures I'd not encountered in the wild before. God granted that request too. We saw a moose cow and her two calves less than fifteen feet away, and a family of wild turkeys (two hens and two poults).

I was very impressed with the turkeys' care in parenting. They were really protective of their babies, who were too small to fly. The first time we saw them, we got out of our car to take some pictures. When they decided to cross the road, the babies were a little sluggish in following the adults. This put them at risk of getting hit by an approaching car. One of the mothers was about to attack the car, at risk to her own life, when we stepped in to slow down traffic and aid in their crossing. Over that week, I grew quite attached to the little family.

On the morning of our departure, we saw a turkey acting strangely by the side of the road. She didn't have a poult by her side, so at first I thought it must have been a different bird until Peter said, "Oh."

I turned and saw the dead baby in the middle of the road. It had been run over by a car. The mother was craning her neck toward it, trying to see her offspring, acting listless and not caring to get out of the way of oncoming traffic.

I cried my heart out.

God had orchestrated a perfect vacation for us—only to cruelly show us this sad, sad tableau at the end. At that moment, I hated the world and all its suffering, pain, and death.

"I would have been happy to give up our favourite campsite if it meant the little turkey baby could have lived," I said to Peter and to God. "Why bless us with so many things only to allow such suffering at the end?"

I woke up the next morning with the answer. This world, with all its suffering and loss, heartache and death, is the best many people will ever know. This will be the bright spot in their existence. They will never know a place where death is conquered, where love reigns, and where there is no suffering and sadness.

That was our mission. That was what drove us. That was what I would remember when thinking of the baby turkey. We were compelled by the love of God to reach out to the lost and perishing, so we might snatch some from the diseased clutches of hell.

I was ready.

Julia struggled with clinical depression for several years during her late adolescence and early twenties. At university, she once attempted suicide. I was also in university and knew in the days beforehand that she was more down than usual. I took to calling her every night in an attempt to encourage and ground her. On finding out what had happened, I was grief-stricken at the depth of her pain and horrified at how close I'd come to losing her. As a result, I felt very protective of her. At some point, I'd fooled myself into thinking that if I held on to my sister tightly enough, I could take care of her. But this was a lie.

When we were growing up, if our parents wanted to share really personal thoughts or feelings, sometimes they would write us letters. This practice became part of our family dynamic; into our adult lives, Julia and I still followed it on occasion.

As Peter and I prepared to leave for Japan, Julia realized my mentality, and wrote me an email.

> "I know you're a 'natural worrier', but stop! It's not going to get you anywhere; it's going to distract you from what you should be focused on; it gives the devil a foothold;

and it takes away from believing in the power God has over my life, and over yours.

"The opposite of worry is faith and trust. Do you have faith in God, that He's in control of everything? (I know you do.) Do you trust Jesus with my life, my sanity? If I told you right now that I was going to kill myself tomorrow, or the week after you left for Japan, would you still go? What if you knew that by not going to Japan, you could prevent me from being institutionalized for the rest of my life?

"You need to give me over to Jesus. I'm crying right now as I write this, because I know how hard this is for you. I know how much you want to protect me, and that you would give up your life for me. But what if I am the sacrifice God asks of you? Would you be willing to give up my life for Jesus? Or my sanity?

"You can't hold on to me and go away to serve God. You need to let go of everything and everyone and leave them in God's hands. Who better to entrust with the people you love most?! By not letting go, you are saying to Jesus that He can't take care of me as well as you can. Is this true?"[3]

Reading her words, I heard the voice of my Father in them and realized the need to surrender my sister to Him. I'd never done that before. But just like Mum and Dad, she was His already. He was her Father, just as He was mine. I didn't naturally want to give her up. God might do something with her I didn't like. But since when did I have a say over His decisions?

Giving Julia up was the hardest thing I'd ever done.

"Please help me to open the hands I've got so tightly clenched around her," I prayed. "Lord, this too I surrender."

Departure loomed. Our emotions were raw as we savoured each gathering with family and friends. These were now our final moments together for the next several years.

There were a few people with whom we particularly cherished the remaining time. We deeply loved our young nephews, aged two and three, and shuddered at the thought that when we returned, they'd be much older and might not remember us. Peter's grandfather was elderly, and we weren't sure whether he would still be alive when we returned. Lastly our friend, Angela, was terminally ill with cancer and had been given only a few months to live. We knew we'd probably not see her again in this life.

One Sunday, when we were at Haven Community Church, I had a chance to spend a little time with Angela after the service. By then, she was deteriorating very quickly and was wheeling around an oxygen tank and tubes. Many people came up to her to chat. I pulled up a chair and sat nearby, listening to her responses and drinking in the sight of her.

After most of the others left, we had a chance to talk privately. She expressed the sadness of a woman who should be in her prime, and the wistful desire to live a little longer. There were still all sorts of passions and dreams flowing through her heart.

I leaned forward and took her hand. "Over the last months, it's been such an honour to send you little encouragement notes. I really appreciate your spirit of service to those around you even when you're going through such a hard time yourself."

She smiled. "I'm so glad you're going to be sharing Jesus with people in Japan." Tears filled her eyes. "Find a little Japanese child and give her a hug from me."

"I will," I promised. We cried and embraced. Though I would see her once more, this was the time when we said goodbye.

Time marched on. Soon we were embroiled in packing, redesigning our ministry website, and planning a worship and thanksgiving service that would give us and our partners a chance to thank God for all He had done in our lives and the lives of the people around us. Finally the date of the worship service arrived: August 20.

That morning, I was nervous. We were going to be saying goodbye to many of our friends and family later. People would be coming just to see us, and I didn't want to disappoint them. When I realized the source of my nerves and focused instead on serving God, those other distractions dropped away.

That night was a beautiful time of thanksgiving and love. Ten of our friends participated on a worship team we specially assembled for the evening. We didn't plan it that way, but on the team there was at least one person from each of the five churches that had chosen to partner with us.

Even though the event was in August, a traditional month for vacations, many people were able to attend. Julia, an avid scrapbooker, made an encouragement book. Everyone brought along pictures of themselves and wrote little notes to us, which Julia pasted onto her pre-made pages. We would later refer to those encouragements while we were on the mission field, allowing God to minister to us through our partners back home.

At the end of the evening, our love meters were off the charts. The people around us had poured themselves and their affection so much into our hearts that we were overflowing with gratitude to God for His goodness toward us.

By September, we'd worked our way through the bulk of our to-do list. The swirling mix of emotions was something we'd never experienced before. It could sometimes be quite draining. As we experienced periods of mourning, stress, and anxiety, we found ourselves snapping at one another. Thankfully, these weren't the only emotions we felt; the sense of excitement and anticipation was potent as well. Praying for grace with each other, and for unity, we practiced "taking every thought captive"[4] in earnest, and kept coming back to some of our favourite verses about God's power and presence with us through each moment.

We will not fear, for the Lord is on our side, I wrote in my journal one day. He is on our side not because of anything that we are or have or can contribute, but because we are on <u>His</u> side. Because He has seen fit to call us for His good purpose.

The difficulty of giving everything up continued to build. Leaving our jobs and possessions was relatively easy. Leaving people was hard. One day I sat down with my journal to record a haunting thought.

September 7, 2011

> Do I love God more than I love anyone?
> Yes!
> Do I love God more than I love <u>everyone combined</u>?
> That's the hard part.

On September 10, our hearts were heavy as we gathered for our final goodbye with Peter's family, including Grandpa and our two toddler nephews. We savoured every word, cuddle, and kiss.

The following day, we attended Haven Community Church for the last time. Angela had passed away the day before. She was an integral part of the church, the sister-in-law of the pastor, and the second Haven member to die in the past two years; her loss affected us all profoundly.

Peter and I were asked to speak briefly in the service.

I cried. "Our spirits feel like they are beaten to a pulp, and we're heartbroken to be leaving at this time of loss. But when I said this to Peter, he made an interesting comment: when we're reduced to pulp, that's when God can form us, like papier-mâché, into the shape He truly desires. I have a vision for this church: God is refining and transforming you into something pure and beautiful."

"Tomorrow we're leaving for Japan," Peter ended. "The culture will be different. The food will be different. The language will be different. The weather will be different. But we will serve the same God."

That evening we finished up the few odds and ends of moving, and stayed at Peter's parents' house. Peter spent most of the night packing and repacking our suitcases, cleverly distributing our belongings to minimize potential overweight charges at the airport.

We left Canada on September 12—eleven years to the month after God first called me to Japan. All but one of the tasks on our to-do list was complete. Though I'd prayed to be at adrenal stage seven by the time we left, in actuality I was at stage five—even better than I'd hoped—and within normal range. Our flight, scheduled to leave at around noon, was delayed for over an hour. We savoured the extra time with the people we loved and eventually said goodbye to our parents, my sister, and some friends who'd come to see us off.

# CHAPTER 18

# Arriving

Our plane touched down at Narita International Airport in Tokyo on September 13. We rushed to get our bags but were unable to clear customs in time for the connecting flight to Okinawa. Apart from language, the airport looked like those in North America, though cleaner. I found my head swivelling every which way as I tried to take in whatever Japanese writing I could.

The airline officials helped us change our flight to one leaving from Haneda Airport, also in Tokyo, a one-hour bus ride away. When we stepped onto the bus, we were greeted by homey curtains in the windows and doilies on the headrests.

By the time we got to Haneda Airport, it was too late to check our luggage, and we were held up going through airport security. That plane left without us too, and the airline put us up in a hotel for the night. By Tokyo standards, our room was luxuriously large, and we enjoyed our complimentary steak dinner immensely.

The following day, we boarded another plane for the last leg of our journey. When we disembarked, parades of colourful orchids lined our way.

*How can the Japanese make even an airport so beautiful?* I thought.

We collected our luggage and followed the other travellers to the exit.

When they saw us, a small-statured couple with grey hair and kindly wrinkles stepped forward tentatively. "Valerie? Peter?"

"Yes, that's us."

"I am Higa Motofusa. This is my wife, Higa Tsuneko."

He said his last name first, just as we'd been taught in Japanese class. So this was the pastor of Seaside Chapel, where we would be working for the next several years. Along with the rest of the church, we would call them Higa sensei and Tsuneko sensei. The word *sensei* means 'honoured teacher'.

They both smiled and bowed.

Remembering our training, we reciprocated, carefully considering the depth of our bow so as not to cause offense.

They gave us each lei necklaces in welcome and escorted us to their waiting car.

After some lunch, we started the weeks-long process of establishing our paperwork: going to the town hall to sign up for our alien registration cards and National Health Insurance (NHI), to the bank to set up a new account, and to the local electronics store to acquire cell phones.

At the town hall, we chose the spelling of our names, using the Japanese character set. Peter's choice was pronounced "Pee-tah." Mine was more of a challenge. There is a *V* sound in the Japanese character set, which some people recommended I apply, but this is a little-used variation. Aware of its uncommonness, I asked the town hall clerk to pronounce my Japanese-equivalent name ("Vah-rah-ree"). Watching him valiantly struggle several times with the awkward sound, I realized that I had to give up my name. I could not allow its very pronunciation to become a barrier between me and the people whom I'd come to serve. In the end, I chose an easier variation: "Bah-rah-ree".

September 15, 2011

We're here. And it doesn't seem as weird as I thought it would. That's probably coming later. But for now, I'll enjoy it: looking around at the Japanese writing, understanding the occasional word in people's conversations, learning about the culture, seeing little differences between what I'm used to and the way the Japanese think and do things, and appreciating the care they take to make the most mundane things beautiful.

Lord God, today I pray that You would take away the nervousness that just exerted itself in my mind and tummy.

Thank You for Your promise to never leave or forsake us. I'm all too aware of how much I need You. I can't do this, but You can. And You are more than enough.

Though Okinawa is part of Japan, its people and culture are very different from those in other areas of the country. Okinawa used to be its own kingdom, called the *Ryuukyuuan* kingdom, a separate entity from the country of Japan. As a result, even now there are many differences between Okinawa and Japan. For instance, there's a distinct Okinawan language. Only the elderly speak it in earnest these days, but select words from that language appear regularly in store signs and conversation.

Having been exposed to Eastern music only in passing, at first I couldn't tell the difference between Okinawan and traditional Japanese music. But when Peter later started to learn the *sanshin*, a three-stringed instrument native to our prefecture, my ears began to make the differentiation.

As someone who greatly appreciates dietary variety, I grew to love Okinawan food. In the rest of Japan, fish and tofu are main sources of protein. However, in Okinawa pork, beef, chicken, fish, and tofu are alternated regularly. *Okinawan soba*, a noodle and pork soup; *goya champuru*, a stir-fry made from the bitter melon that many scientists credit for Okinawan longevity; and *chirashi zushi*, a rice and fish mixture, soon became our favourites.

There are also theistic differences from the rest of Japan. Whereas Buddhism and Shinto are dominant elsewhere, in Okinawa the main religion is matriarchal shamanism. Its adherents worship their ancestors and nature; they navigate a complex web of relationships between the living and dead, the gods, and the spirits of the universe.[1]

For a long time, we had no overt contact with the Okinawan religion, so we gleaned much of our knowledge from our supervisor, research, and a few church leaders. The Okinawan version of shamanism includes priestesses, shamans, various talismans, spirit channelling, and ceremonies to appease the spirits and honour the dead. A young woman who is called by the spirits as a *Yuta* (shaman) but who refuses to obey will go through a time of affliction that eventually leads to her surrender and servitude to the spirits.[2] We didn't know what this affliction involved, and it seemed that much of this process was secretive. However, we were told that *Yutas* have very high divorce and suicide rates.

There are no visible temples in this religion, and if we hadn't known about it beforehand, we never would have guessed at its existence. Shrines are housed in peoples' homes, and food is offered to idols during family celebrations. One core belief is that certain places have spirits associated with them. For instance, hauntings are thought to be quite common. Certain configurations of rocks can denote sacred places outside of the home; but many times, these are generally known within the community after having been declared by a shaman to be sacred. People also regularly worship their ancestors at grave sites.

Many Okinawans live in fear of angering the spirits and will pay high fees to the shamans for protection from the anger and retribution of evil forces around them. Often people will hire a shaman to comb through their religious practices and ensure they've not done anything to offend the spirits. They believe that this in turn will serve to stave off bad things from happening to them and encourage good fortune instead.

The confidence of the Christian church stands out in stark contrast to the uncertainties of shamanistic religion. Japanese churches have on average about twenty members; they make up less than 0.5 percent of the general population. However, perhaps because of the spiritual sensitivity of the people there, the Christian population in Okinawa is double the national average.

Our church, Seaside Chapel—originally planted by Canadian missionaries—had about sixty members at the time we joined. It was located in Itoman, the southernmost city on the island. Higa sensei had been the pastor of Seaside Chapel for more than forty years when we arrived, and it turned out that there were only two degrees of separation between him and us. One of our friends from Canada had known him years ago.

Seaside Chapel had recently changed names and moved locations; it had previously been in an area that was increasingly industrial, and thus less and less ideal as a meeting location. So, the church decided to transplant itself into a new area and continue in effective ministry to people's needs. With the more central location, people from the community started dropping in during the week and for Sunday services, out of curiosity. This had never happened before.

Seaside Chapel had already been instrumental in planting two other churches; we would be involved in helping it with a third. We soon discovered that more than five couples there had been earmarked to engage in church planting endeavours through the coming years.

During our first week in Japan, we stayed at Seaside Chapel while waiting for our apartment to be ready. On the third day, still tired because of the time change, we took a rather lengthy nap. Afterward we'd planned to go grocery shopping but dawdled a bit because waking up was difficult. Just as we were getting ready to leave, there was a knock at our door.

Standing there was a man, a little younger than us. He didn't speak any English. We tried to communicate, but to no avail. Finally Peter had the idea of asking him to write what he wanted to say in *hiragana* (phonetic Japanese). We looked up the words in our dictionary.

His name was Alan. "My life is tired," he said. "I want to talk with someone."

We kicked into gear. The suicide rate is high in Japan. For all we knew, this man might harm himself. We called some of our emergency numbers and finally reached Tsuneko sensei, the pastor's wife. She talked with Alan on the phone for awhile, and he agreed to meet with her. She arrived in about an hour.

After a long conversation, she told us what had happened. It turned out that Alan was a Christian. He lived in the area and felt compelled to come into the church that night. Like so many Japanese, he had fallen away from Christ after his initial decision to follow Him. Alan was feeling increasingly isolated and lonely, and had been taking lots of sleeping pills.

"I feel more hopeful about the future," he said after talking and praying with Tsuneko sensei. "I want to come to church this Sunday and be a student in the ESL classes."

Around that time, we met the six pastors whose churches were involved in an Okinawan network coordinated by our organization, and the five Japanese couples who had been designated by Seaside Chapel to start new churches. Two were in the initial phases of church planting using different methods.

One couple was discipling a professional ballerina who had come to Christ. As a ballet teacher, this woman had a wide array of contacts; the church planters hoped she would develop a passion for reaching those in her sphere of influence with the good news about Jesus.

The other couple, the Andos, were starting their house church as a Bible study, meeting every other week on Saturdays. They had three regular attendees, in addition to themselves, and planned an eventual transition to traditional church meetings on Sunday mornings.

The Japanese place immense value on heritage. Higa sensei, his wife Tsuneko sensei, and the church members seemed to have a special affinity with us because we were Canadian, like the missionary founders of Seaside Chapel.

In one of our first meetings with Higa sensei, he unfolded a pamphlet we'd sent him before our arrival. It contained some introductory biographical information. He placed it in the centre of the table and pointed to our life purpose statement at the bottom. "When I read this, I was so happy you were coming to my church."

"We're so happy to be here," we said. "We've been looking forward to meeting you for a long time."

"God has a plan for you here in Okinawa. He has a special story He will write while you are here. I am looking forward to seeing what He will do."

"We are too!"

So ended one of our first exchanges with Higa sensei and Tsuneko sensei. Carried out in halting English and Japanese, our conversations were more 'stop' than 'go', but even from the first, God instilled a great love for each other within our four hearts.

## CHAPTER 19

# Kobe

At the end of our first week, we flew from Okinawa to our organization's annual fall conference for short-term missionaries on Honshuu, the main island of Japan. Though we planned to eventually transfer to career missionary status, at that point we'd committed to a term of three years and thus fell into the short-term category. Several career missionaries were also in attendance.

The gathering was held at a retreat centre in Kobe. Its stark decor contrasted with the lush beauty of surrounding forest, cobbled steps, and fresh, cool air. Peter and I were asked to lead the morning worship sessions; we thoroughly enjoyed the chance to contribute.

The fall gathering afforded us a first look at some further cultural differences between Canada and our new country. For instance, the retreat centre used peculiar pillows. Rather than the fluffy stuffing to which we were accustomed, these were filled with buckwheat casings, which are much cooler in the summertime. In the temperatures of fall they weren't such an advantage, and the stiffness of the casings made my ears hurt. I would, however, later come to greatly appreciate this Japanese innovation in pillow-dom.

We were also introduced to Japanese breakfasts. Foods that a North American would have considered for lunch or dinner were served, but this wasn't as off-putting as I'd feared. Beforehand, I'd wondered how my stomach might handle eating fishy ingredients early in the morning, but it seemed to balk at nothing. One of my friends happened to be pregnant at the time and was not so fortunate.

During that conference, we first experienced public bathing in the nude. This was in a place called the *ofuro*, where women and men bathed in separate locations. We removed our shoes at the entryway (*genkan*) to the *ofuro*, before passing through a curtain and into the tatami-covered changing area. Clothes and other possessions were deposited in small plastic baskets and stored in the compartments of a wooden shelving unit on the wall opposite the entrance of an inner room. We went into that room with only our small *ofuro* towels (35 × 75cm). It was tiled, with washing stations lining two sides of the perimeter. Each station was equipped with a ledge for shampoo and soap, and an attachment similar to a shower head. We retrieved plastic stools from a pile near the entrance, sat, and washed ourselves down at the stations before easing into the hot communal waters. After getting past the initial awkwardness, our times at the *ofuro* were wonderful chances for fellowship with the other missionaries, and a very relaxing experience.

Almost as soon as we arrived in Japan, we felt a different spiritual dynamic than the one to which we were accustomed. Part of it, we believed, was simply our own emotional state and our reaction to a different time zone. However, during our time in Kobe, I also found myself assailed by avalanches of temptations. The sheer barrage was exhausting at times. I continuously had to be vigilant in taking every thought captive and submitting it to the lordship of Christ. Eventually, the barrage became a less-draining trickle.

In our organization's training sessions, we compared our personality strengths with those of the rest of our team, and discussed forms of communication in our new country, strategies for church multiplication, and techniques for evangelism. These sessions were enlightening; they not only helped us to better understand the Japanese people and culture, but also to understand the mindset our fellow missionaries brought to ministry in Japan.

By the end of our training in Kobe, I was once more surprised at the ways in which God had prepared us, and recorded those thoughts in my journal.

September 29, 2011

> Over the past year or so, my communication style has evolved to become much more ambiguous. With this change, several family members and a couple of co-workers have understandably expressed frustration at the amount of time it now takes me to get to the point.
>
> However, it would appear that this move to ambiguity is very close to the way the Japanese express themselves. It's quite interesting to see how this plays out. Sometimes we have the luxury of a translator with us in meetings. Conversation will go on in Japanese for a minute or two, yet the translator is often able to summarize everything in just a sentence. This is because the Japanese communicate not only to relay information or make decisions, but to maintain and strengthen relationships as well. By contrast, the direct approach of North Americans often appears very rude to them.
>
> There are many complexities in the choreography of communication in Japan. We know it will likely take us years (if not decades) to grasp even some of the most basic inflections, but I'm so encouraged to see that God has already been preparing us in this as well.

Even with these realizations, we were only beginning to scratch the surface of the groundwork God had laid in our hearts and bodies.

# CHAPTER 20

# Moving In

During our first weeks in Japan, when not in Kobe we stayed in one of the auxiliary Sunday school rooms at Seaside Chapel. The church owned several futons, but these weren't the ones we were accustomed to. Instead of a thick mat on top of a wooden frame shaped like a couch or bed, in Japan a futon is a two-inch thick mat unfolded directly onto the floor, which can be hidden away in a closet during the daytime. So in those weeks we camped out on the hard wooden floors and took care of turning on and off the church's lights at night and in the mornings.

While there, we met a nemesis. The building had formerly been a food factory. When the church had purchased it a year earlier, it was a mess. The former owners had left behind flour and sugar and all manner of food items. In cleaning everything up, church members literally had to fight off loads of fierce rats trying to protect their food supply. Deprived of their larder, the rats left in search of a new home. However, a few other creatures stayed. The nemesis we encountered was a cockroach—four inches long. He had a habit of crawling into our wet laundry for a nap and scaring us when we later went to fold it.

We also met a few friends: nocturnal geckos who would eat wayward cockroaches and other pests. Their chirping was comforting, and whenever I found one, I would try to bring it to the room where we slept.

By the time we returned from Kobe, the church had found an apartment for us, and we began transferring our belongings into our new home. We planned to move in on a Sunday,

October 1, after the church service. That morning I was antsy and wrote a prayer in my journal.

> October 1, 2011
>
> Lord God, today I feel a little off-kilter. Peter and I have seen a couple of really large cockroaches in the church over the last two days, and it's disconcerting. Would You please stop any from hitchhiking in our luggage from the church to our new home?
>
> It seems silly that I'm concentrating so much on this, particularly when I have no control over it. Lord, help me to give this over to You. These roaches are under Your authority. Thank You that I can trust You.
>
> Please help me not to obsess. You are in control. You are in control. You are in control!

Incidentally, at our new apartment we did see a baby cockroach, which one of our new friends immediately squashed. In a paranoid frenzy, we set up traps all over our apartment but didn't see another inside for almost a year. God was indeed merciful to us!

Our home was located in the Nishizaki district of Itoman city. It was ideally situated: a fifteen-minute walk from the church; across the street from a wonderful neighbourhood park; and close by a grocery store, restaurants, a gas station, and many other convenient shops. We had several adventures in getting accustomed to the niceties of our new culture, which I shared on our blog.

> October 3, 2011
>
> We've just moved into our new apartment, so to celebrate Peter thought he'd make me a breakfast this morning like he did once a week back in Canada. Last night we went

to the supermarket and picked up some eggs, bacon, juice, and milk.

As he cooked the strips of bacon, they started to emit odd smells. Peter called me over to consult, and we couldn't decide what it was. Lamb? Something else? It definitely wasn't bacon.

We gave up on the meat and started the eggs. It hadn't occurred to us in the store that the Japanese don't sell eggs by the dozen; they sell them in metric, by tens.

After he'd started cooking the eggs (sunny side up, my favourite) Peter realized we'd not bought a spatula… and when the eggs were done, he realized we didn't yet have plates!

Oh yeah, we didn't have forks or knives yet either. So, for our first breakfast in our new home, we ate eggs, sunny-side-up, in bowls using chopsticks. Talk about mixing cultures! Our breakfast wasn't the most successful endeavour, but we did have a good laugh. Peter has decided to try this again next week.

The meat? It turned out to be beef—dinner for tonight!

Our home was made out of concrete. Whereas buildings in the rest of Japan are constructed to flex easily with frequent earthquakes, those in Okinawa are built to withstand typhoons, which sweep through the prefecture every year. Though large earthquakes in Okinawa are uncommon, buildings are still replaced every fifty years. The climate is so humid that after five decades, the inner steel rebar begins to rust through. Much of the infrastructure, whether buildings or bridges, requires regular replacement.

In Okinawa, *shisa* dogs abound. These are typically small stone lion-dog statues that are attached to buildings as guardians to ward off evil spirits. Our building had the typical pair, and whenever I looked at them, I was overtaken by a sense of unease.

I later read that in Japanese Buddhist tradition, whenever a picture or sculpture is finished, an eye-opening ceremony is performed. Though the eyes of the picture or statue have already been completed, this ceremony is intended to instil a soul into the object. It essentially becomes inhabited by a god, which afterward is considered worthy of veneration and worship.[1] Reading this information, I was reminded of the Bible's statement that idols are really demons in disguise.[2] I often wondered if *shisa* dogs were similarly endowed with their own inhabitants.

In our building, parking was on the first floor, the owner lived on the second, and tenants occupied the remaining ones. As usual in Okinawa, there was no basement. Our apartment was on the top, the fourth floor. According to Japanese law, buildings of up to four stories don't require elevators, so ours had none.

Our unit was bigger than we'd expected: about 450 square feet. We were fortunate that Okinawan apartments tend to be larger than those in more congested areas, such as Tokyo. Peter loves wood; to his delight, the interior was all wooden panelling. Our apartment boasted at least one window in each direction. Since it was one of the taller buildings in the vicinity, we were able to take advantage of a marvellous cross breeze in the warmer months.

Higa sensei and several of the church elders came to our apartment and prayed with us on the day we moved in. We asked God to cleanse the place and to remove any evil forces that might have made it their playground. We prayed for God to place His protection over us and our new home and for His Spirit to fill it so nothing counter to His purposes could exist there. If idols had been worshipped or witchcraft practiced, we renounced those things and asked for Jesus' blood to wash our home and make it pure and holy.

The church provided us with many basic furnishings, including our couch, kitchen table, refrigerator, and air conditioner. One of our pastor's daughters donated her old queen-size bed for our use—an enormous blessing—and we started saving money to purchase housewares and furnishings in addition to the ones that the church had provided. Within a few months we'd settled in, and Japan had become home.

The day after we moved into our apartment, I developed a painful external haemorrhoid, probably resulting from the long plane flight a few weeks earlier, coupled with extended times of sitting at the fall conference.

Despite having to miss prayer meeting, that night I gritted my teeth through the pain and went around to our neighbours with Peter and the Higas, handing out the expected 'apology gifts'. In Japan, when families move into new neighbourhoods, they present each of the new neighbours with a gift to atone for the inconvenience they've caused, whether because of additional noise, a moving truck, or something else. Our neighbours all seemed to like the idea of trying out Canadian maple tea. On realizing that we'd brought along the exact right number of containers for each apartment in our building, we remarked that God seemed to coordinate even the smallest of details.

I tried applying an over-the-counter cream to the haemorrhoid, but nothing seemed to help. Eventually I went with a friend to the doctor for a checkup. In Japan, doctors are located primarily in hospitals, so whether a person has an earache or a heart attack, the hospital is the place to go for treatment.

When the doctor examined me, he found a blood clot that had formed in tandem with the haemorrhoid; the clot needed to be removed. The procedure, particularly the introduction of the anaesthetic needle, was very painful; but I came away impressed with the Japanese medical system. We could go straight to the specialist for diagnosis and treatment; the entire process—from arrival, to seeing the doctor and having the procedure, to paying our bill—took under an hour; and the bill, including an oral pain prescription and topical ointment, was a reasonable sixty dollars.

    I've always taken a long time to stop bleeding from wounds larger than a paper cut, so I spent the next two and a half weeks in bed, waiting for the bleeding to stop.

## CHAPTER 21

# Whatever Is Pure

During that time, God had some important lessons in store for me. They started when we heard that two of our friends in Canada had passed away. One was a dear lady from the church where Peter had grown up, and the other was a new friend who'd been a pastor at one of our partnering churches. In one month, he had gone from a herniated disc in his back, to cancer, to pneumonia, to deceased. How fragile life is.

"I need You, Lord," I prayed upon hearing the news, "with every fibre of my being, with every atom, with every breath. I need You because You're not fragile, but strong and constant. There is no one else in heaven or on earth in whom my trust lies. You are mine, yet You cannot be possessed. You are not for sale and are never on the discount table. You *just are*, and I need You today."

I continued to pray, using my journal.

Lord, tell me to do anything, and I'll do it, I wrote.

Even as I prayed, God brought something to mind.

"What about *Being Erica*?"

This was a sitcom I'd enjoyed in Canada. However, as I'd watched it, I'd felt a growing uneasiness—as though my conscience were saying, "Valerie, does this honour God?"

Not wanting to give up the show, I'd resisted, pretending I hadn't heard.

"What about *Being Erica*?"

"Well I didn't mean that, God!" I responded now.

But there were my words across the page of my journal: tell me to do anything...

Was it a cop-out to say, "Let me think about it, Lord. I'll get back to You?" (Probably after watching a few more episodes...)

Of course it was.

What's so wrong with *Being Erica*? I reasoned. Maybe this is just my subconscious and not God...

So why had it come up during the last two times I'd had *devotions*?

God kept drawing me back to His Word: "Whatever is true, whatever is honourable, whatever is right, whatever is pure, whatever is lovely, whatever is of good repute, if there is any excellence and if anything worthy of praise, let your mind dwell on these things."[1]

"Ok, I get the message," I said to Him. "I've not been focussing on pure things. I don't want to give this show up. I was tempted to say, 'But it's a good show!'"

*Maybe that's the point*, I thought. *It promotes a morality I don't subscribe to, a way of living He doesn't approve of. It's a compelling show. That's different than good. And the thing I'm most looking forward to: seeing whether Erica sleeps with Kai. How is that good?*

"Okay, God, here I am in Japan," I prayed. "This is a spiritual battlefield. I will not survive if I maintain pet sins or deny Your right to complete control over my life. I can't afford to give the enemy a foothold."

A furtive whisper came to my ear. "You can always watch it back in Canada when you're out of here."

*But doesn't that negate surrender?* I thought. *Putting sin in my back pocket for later is still sin. Spiritual warfare isn't any less in Canada; it just takes different forms.*

"God, it's in my head! Please help me!" I prayed. "I *cannot* indulge in this, but I'm weak. I feel double-minded. Please help me to completely surrender to You."

He brought a verse to mind. "If we confess our sins, He is faithful and righteous to forgive us our sins and to cleanse us from all unrighteousness."[2]

I opened my journal and picked up my pen once more.

October 16, 2011

Ok, God, I confess before You that I have sinned. I've ignored Your prompting to turn off the TV and have wilfully indulged my own desires above Yours. Lord, I give over this area of my life to You. I'm too weak to break these chains. They kind of feel like an addiction. But, Father, when I am weak You are strong. Please help me to cast off "what lies behind and…press on toward the goal for the prize of the upward call of God in Christ Jesus"[3].

Lord—that very title means You are my master—please align my will with Yours. Give me peace in my spirit and help me—help me!—I pray, to live a life that's pure and holy in Your sight. Only You can do this. I can't.

"I have been crucified with Christ; and it is no longer I who live, but Christ lives in me; and the life which I now live in the flesh I live by faith in the Son of God, who loved me, and delivered Himself up for me."[4]

Okay, God. I won't be fearful about the future and whether I'll be able to resist temptation. I'm to live by faith in You. I can't resist, but I can submit myself to You and allow Your Spirit to work through me and resist on my behalf.

I immediately felt a great sense of freedom.

"Thank You for forgiving me," I prayed. "Thank You for convicting me, though I'd said no to You before."

After this, temptations to dodge around obedience continued to flow fiercely. I paced around our apartment, quoting scripture to myself for several hours to keep them at bay. Eventually they abated.

As a child and teenager, I often struggled with overpowering rage. Sometimes the violence of my emotions scared me and those around me. When I rededicated my life to Jesus at twenty, God not only healed me from the hurt and trauma I'd suffered earlier, but also from my problem with rage. It was immediate. Over the ensuing eleven years sometimes I would still get angry, but never to the point of being scary, and never to the point where I felt out of control.

Eventually, Peter and I noticed that we were fighting much more than usual over inconsequential issues. The scary rage was back and entrenched in my spirit. Then we started to notice some disturbing correlations. If we were in the middle of a fight and paused to pray, the feelings of driven fury would completely dissipate. The fight would immediately be over; it would be revealed for what it was: a contrivance.

We realized that the bulk of our clashes seemed to be sparked by some sort of spiritual attack. We began to pray together at the beginning of each day for God's protection over our spirits and emotions, and for marital unity. With this, the frequency and intensity of marital conflict was reduced to its normal level, and my struggles with rage subsided.

## CHAPTER 22

# ESL Training

I visited the doctor twice more in October: once because I'd not yet stopped bleeding from the procedure, and later because I was still experiencing pain in the surgical area.

To offset my boredom with the time it took to heal, and to distract myself from the pain, I began working full-time hours from bed: using my smartphone and tablet to handle correspondence with our partners back in Canada, write newsletters, and provide administrative support to Peter in his activities. I also read books on the Japanese culture and customs, wrote book reports so Peter could quickly assimilate the same information, and engaged in intensive Japanese language study.

We'd planned to have a drop-in open house for the members of our church on October 23 after the Sunday service, but our supervisor advised us not to invite people to our apartment while I was injured. He said that the Japanese tend to be uncomfortable entering a household where someone is bedridden. I was very lonely by this point, and eager to be back on my feet and able to participate in ministry.

Thankfully, within a few weeks, I was once more able to take part in activities outside of our home. Peter and I had never been English as a Second Language (ESL) teachers before, so during our first month and a half in Japan, we learned a number of conversation-teaching techniques. Running ESL classes would be one of our primary forms of ministry with Seaside Chapel over the next three years. In the past, many missionaries had successfully used this type of program to establish new connections with people in their communities.

One day, Higa sensei, the pastor of Seaside Chapel, showed us an article from a local newspaper. Okinawa had just announced that it planned to be the number 1 prefecture for English in Japan within the next five years.

Later, when Peter and I were undergoing ESL training, we asked our supervisor, "Who are our major competitors for students?"

"The two main companies that used to teach English conversation have declared bankruptcy in the last eighteen months," he said. "This wasn't for lack of students, but because the companies extended themselves too quickly. Now there are no competitors."

There is a Japanese term, *nemawashi*, which literally means 'to go around the root'. The word picture is of soil getting cleared away from the roots of a tree in order to more easily uproot and transplant it. In English, the closest equivalent would be 'to clear the way'.

Through these circumstances, we had a strong sense that this was what God had been doing for the time of our arrival in Japan, and we couldn't help wondering what was in store.

As we honed our new skills, we were assigned to observe and eventually practice-teach at an existing English conversation class. According to our organization's model, ESL classes were broken into three segments: a one-hour main session; followed by fifteen minutes of Bible study led by a pastor or leader in the church; and a tea time, complete with drinks and snacks, where there would be an English discussion of something from either the class or Bible study, depending on the inclinations of the students. Tea time would range from fifteen to forty-five minutes, based on the momentum of the conversation.

On the appointed evening, we enthusiastically trooped off to the church where we would be trained. It was a compact building, with two parking spots available for church members. We parked down the block to allow room for the students' cars as they arrived. The meeting area itself was a small multipurpose room, with flickering fluorescent lights providing a sense of habitation to an otherwise dark and empty night. At the door, we shed our shoes and sandals for socks and slippers. Clumsily navigating our way around the linoleum floor in our flopping footwear, we set up folding chairs in a semicircle with a whiteboard and podium as the focal point.

During the first week, our job was simply to observe. However, during tea time, the students had many questions about our hobbies and home country. We enjoyed getting to know them. One of the ladies there, Bianca—about my age—was a Christian. However, her husband, Bob, was not. Bob and Bianca had been attending the class for the past year, and she'd been hoping that he would eventually embrace Jesus as his Saviour.

The next time we attended, we practice-taught. We had to postpone that session by a week because of the pain from my surgery. Ironically, the lesson revolved around the subject of health. In that session's tea time, Bob and Peter discovered they were the same age and thus would have been in the same classes at school. The difference in school grades is an important social distinction in the Japanese mindset.

"We would have been friends," Bob said.

Our training complete, we didn't attend the following week's session. In that tea time, there was an intense discussion of the Bible segment, all in Japanese. Bob sat back and didn't say much. Bianca, when she glanced at him, thought he'd zoned out.

## On the Potter's Wheel

When they got home that night, Bob pulled Bianca aside. "I want to officially become a Christian," he said.

What rejoicing there was then; it continued the next Sunday when the church could also join in the celebrations.

We later wondered if, in a society where age and social ranking are so important, the fact that Peter was a Christian had made an impact on Bob. As far as we knew, up until that point Bob had only ever met Christians who were women, or were men older than him. Perhaps meeting a Christian of his age and gender helped him to realize the things discussed in Bible study could also be applicable to him.

Thrilled to have been links in the chain to Bob's new life, we were happy to hear he'd started praying to God and reading his Bible regularly.

"I want to get baptized sometime in the future," he later announced.

The Japanese place a high value on fitting in with those around them; and the Japanese proverb "the nail that sticks up gets hammered down" is a common motto in Japanese society. By contrast, Christians, who make up less than 0.5 percent of the country's population, can't help but stand out in their monotheistic stance and are often disowned by family members because they refuse to worship their ancestors. We prayed for Bob's continued growth and endurance in a culture that emphasizes homogeneity.

## CHAPTER 23

# Have Thine Own Way

I was able to move about and sit within a few days after the bleeding from my procedure stopped. However, one evening during a relatively short social situation, the pain in the surgical area began to increase. I waited until the earliest appropriate time to excuse myself and went home to rest.

It seemed that there was no progress whatsoever for a day or two; I was incredibly frustrated with the limitations in my abilities. How tantalizing to finally be in Japan after so many years of waiting and yet be unable to do anything! I felt that God was really cruel to allow this.

The day after some of my feelings overflowed, God gave me a few verses during devotions: "You who seek God, let your heart revive. For the Lord hears the needy, and does not despise His who are prisoners."[1]

How exactly that hit the spot! I'd been feeling a prisoner without thinking of it in those precise terms, but God told me that He'd heard my cries and that He would eventually allow me to serve Him.

A few nights after arriving in Japan, I had an unusual dream. On waking, I realized that I'd been angry with someone for quite a while without knowing it. After about a month, I'd accepted my feelings of hurt and anger and processed them enough to approach forgiveness from a place of authenticity.

As a technique for forgiveness, I'll sometimes write a letter to a person who's caused me hurt, and never send it. This can be particularly effective when the person is unable or unwilling to admit any wrongdoing. It allows me to recognize my feelings as legitimate and express them without fear of reprisal or rejection. It also helps me to understand many of the things I'm feeling because the words that flow from my pen often are from some deeper, unknown part of me. After expressing myself, I can recognize the other person's brokenness as well as my own, and come to a place where I turn this over to the Gentle Healer, who enables me to forgive others as He's forgiven me.

One day, during my devotions, God told me to start writing a letter like this. It took some time to bolster my resolve, but I finally obeyed. On the following morning, I cracked open my journal and began to write out a prayer.

November 1, 2011

> Okay God, I wrote the letter. I'm forgiving the person who's hurt me.
> Lord, what else?
> Dangerous question.

I quickly closed my journal and tucked it away.

That evening, I got very downhearted. I was eager to be up and about again, and felt a failure for being injured. Lying in bed was not what I'd traveled around the world to do. I'd allowed these feelings of inadequacy and failure to isolate me and only told our immediate family about my struggles.

However, that night, Peter challenged me. He pointed out that my feelings were not an accurate reflection of reality. The truth was that God had His own purposes and that we should not allow ourselves to hide our problems from our partners. Peter asked me to send out an SOS e-mail to a few people, requesting prayer. I did, and their response was nothing short of marvellous. We both felt uplifted by the love and encouragement of God's family.

"Please show me how I can be useful for Your kingdom even in the midst of this," I prayed the next day. "Help me to bring glory and honour to You."

"*Big Bang Theory.*"

The day before, I'd asked how else I could obey Him.

He'd mentioned *Big Bang Theory*: another of the television shows I enjoyed.

I'd closed Him down, saying, "Dangerous question." I'd felt He was out to get me, to take all enjoyment from my life. I was unwilling.

I sighed. There was no way to win against God. "Okay. Do You want me to give up *Big Bang Theory*? I'll give it up."

"No."

"Are You sure? Did I hear You right?"

"No, it's alright."

"Why did You mention it, God, if you didn't want me to give it up?"

"Because I wanted you to surrender something to Me and know that I don't always take it away. I'm not punishing you, Valerie. Everything will happen in My time. I want you here in Japan, but there are people whom you're not supposed to meet yet. Pray for these people. Pray for this city, this prefecture, and this country. I will heal you in My time."

"Okay, God, in Your time. Thank You for telling me. Is it okay if I share this with Peter?"

"Yes."

"God? I need You. I like talking with You. I love our conversations. Would You please keep talking to me today and on all these other days when I'm in isolation?"

"My grace is sufficient for you, for My power is perfected in weakness."[2]

## On the Potter's Wheel

Pondering this conversation later, I found myself excited. God was using all this pain and effort to orchestrate a meeting. What would follow when it finally happened?

# CHAPTER 24

# Prayer Walks

Around this time, I finished reading through the book of Jeremiah in my devotions and recognized the sinful gravity of people claiming to speak for God when they are imparting only man-made messages. God punished false prophets very severely. I'd been hearing more and more from Him over the previous weeks and realized I needed to be really sure before attributing something to Him. I shuddered to think that I, too, had the potential to become a false prophet if I wasn't careful.

Earlier that same day, I asked God whether I should go out to pray in the park across from our apartment.

"Not now," He replied.

A few hours passed.

"Go."

"Now, God? Is that really You?"

"Go."

"Okay."

I walked around the park, praying for everyone in sight. When I came to two trees, they felt different: evil. Feeling a little awkward, in Jesus' name I bound whatever spirits were associated with them and with the park. During this, the surgical area in my rear started hurting really sharply; but as soon as I mentioned Jesus' name, the pain went away. I finished my walk and came back to the apartment.

"I have a sense that You want me to do this again tomorrow and every day for the next week," I prayed. "Is that right?"

"Yes."

There seemed to be something more, something special about the seventh day. A strong impression came to the forefront of my mind.

"What about the seventh day? Are You telling me I should bring Peter and sing 'Lord We Pray For This City' on that day? Is that right?"

"Yes."

*Jericho*, I thought.

As the walls of Jericho fell after the Israelites marched around them for seven days, so I realized that God planned to break down some of the spiritual barriers built by ancestor worship and witchcraft in our area.

When Peter heard the story about the tree, he joked that my rear seemed to be a spiritual barometer. We had a good laugh, but also wondered if there was a degree of truth in his comment.

The following day, I was skeptical. Maybe God's earlier instructions to walk and pray in the park were a product of my imagination. Perhaps I was just being melodramatic. Not wanting to put words in His mouth, I did want to do His will even if it made me look silly.

"I'd rather be Your fool than anyone else's wise person," I prayed. "Please confirm or deny this course of action. Should I do this?"

"Yes," He said.

"Your voice is so soft today, God," I said. "Okay, maybe it's soft because I'm nervous about singing in the park. What will people think?"

"Be not afraid of their faces."[1]

"Okay, God. I will not fear. Thank You for the opportunity to worship You with my obedience."

On my walk around the park the following day, I stopped at the trees again. I felt mildly uncomfortable, as though there were a shadow of the previous evil still lurking there.

"You are good trees," I said. "You were made by the Father of lights. I proclaim you to be good and ask Jesus' blood to cleanse you from whatever evil forces have been in charge here."

The day after, when walking by that section, I could no longer tell the difference between the individual trees. The area felt cleansed.

I continued my daily walks and asked Jesus and His Holy Spirit to weave themselves into the very fabric of the park—that it would become known as a place of peace because no evil could enter, and that people would flock to it and have encounters with Jesus. I planned to eventually reach out in His name to those who took refuge there.

A week later, when I told our supervisor about the prayer walks, he didn't seem fazed by these experiences at all. "It's quite common for evil spirits to inhabit certain areas. This is a reality commonly accepted by Christians and non-Christians here on the island. I'm glad you took Peter with you on that seventh day. Pastors will typically only go for prayer walks in pairs."

CHAPTER 25

# Following and Feebleness

Over the next few weeks, we experienced a few false starts in my recovery, which helped us to learn the limits of my abilities. Pushing through the pain would result in intolerably more of it; and a certain itchy feeling, as if a bug were crawling on my skin, was a precursor to out-and-out pain.

As I'd experienced with my fatigued adrenal glands, life became more active internally than externally, and my journals became recordings of conversations with God.

November 10, 2011

> Lord, I miss my family today. Peter's parents just sent us pictures of everyone, taken before and after we left Canada. Joshua and Sophie said that every ounce of homesickness, every tear that falls, is an offering that goes straight to Your throne. So, here is my offering. May it be pleasing in Your sight. "I will not give offerings to the Lord my God that cost me nothing."[1]

In mid-November, I learned another painful lesson. We were still setting up our household and hadn't yet purchased all our furniture, so I'd developed the habit of keeping my nighttime water glass on the floor by my side of the bed. When I bent down to retrieve it one night, I felt something in my rear snap. This plummeted me into a state of constant pain so severe that it would wake me up in the middle of the night, and I spent many hours tossing and turning, desperately trying to find some position that would lessen my distress. Through that incident, I learned that further bending was out-of-bounds if I wanted to avoid aggravating my injury.

The false starts probably cost me about three weeks in healing time, but then we stopped making mistakes that caused setbacks. We knew which activities seemed to help and which would cause further injury; we started to see small improvements in my pain level and abilities but were ever aware of the danger of regression. One day, overcome by fear for the future, I opened my journal and prayed.

November 15, 2011

> Please help me to be wise in knowing what I can and cannot do. God, I need Your help. I'm scared of messing this up, of never healing, of telling our partners that for the moment I'm incapacitated, and of having them withdraw from our ministry. I'm scared of being left high and dry and of not even being able to go home to Canada because I can't sit through the plane flight.
>
> Lord, these are my fears. I lay them at Your feet and ask You to take them. I can't bear them anymore. I give them to You. They are Yours.
>
> You have called us here for a reason. You knew this would happen. Help me to relax in the knowledge that You are with me.

Soon my body began to steadily improve. I was constantly on alert to ensure I didn't miss pre-pain signals to return to bed, or inadvertently do something that would cause further injury. Such a level of vigilance was exhausting to maintain, but Peter and I both knew it was necessary.

While bedridden, I grew concerned that I might develop another blood clot. However, in devotions one day, God pointed me to a story in Ezekiel 4. God told Ezekiel to lie down on his side and stay lying in that position for more than a year as an object lesson to the nation of Israel of their own sinfulness.

"I protected Ezekiel," He said. "I will protect you."

Eventually, the pain was reduced to almost nothing, as long as I heeded my body's signals. However, I did start to notice a sensitivity to vibration; in some cases, depending on its strength and duration, I would experience pain.

I also became impatient with the amount of time my recovery was taking. I wanted to be free of bed, of suffering, and of all the restrictions on my activities. I was getting better, but not quickly enough for my own liking.

We'd planned with Seaside Chapel to start a Christmas ESL class at the end of November. As this would be our first ministry with the church, it was at the forefront of my mind. I didn't want to be left out, and prayed zealously for a quick recovery. I wanted to be a 'real' missionary: free to connect with and minister to the Japanese people for whom God had given me such a heart.

ESL class began on November 25. Though my goal had been to physically assist in leading the class, by then my body wasn't sufficiently recovered. Instead, I contented myself with helping in preparatory work: creating flash cards to be used in the teaching times and brainstorming creative approaches for explaining the material.

The class, entitled *Announcing Christmas*, was based on the biblical story. Peter also taught the students a few Christmas traditions, such as singing carols.

Two of his students were a married couple, Charles and Chelsea. Chelsea was a Christian, but Charles was not. Charles proudly came up to Peter on his own initiative every week and recited the memory verse from the week before. He was the only member of the class to do this, and we prayed that God would use the words implanted in his heart to draw him to Jesus.

In Japan, Kumon after-school programs offer tutoring in a range of subjects, including the English, French, and Japanese languages. This concept was new to us: in Canada, Kumon usually offered tutoring only in mathematics. For a few weeks in November, the franchise provided free Japanese classes to potential new students. Peter and I hoped to attend. We set up an appointment with the prospective teacher.

Unfortunately, when the date arrived, I had to stay behind. I wasn't well enough to travel, so Peter went to meet the teacher without me. After the trial period, we decided to learn Japanese reading and writing using the Kumon method. Peter attended class in person and brought my homework sheets to and from our teacher.

Peter had always struggled with reading and writing new languages, but he was very talented when it came to listening and pronunciation. He had an amazing ear; he could hear things in the Japanese accent that I couldn't. I eventually came to trust him beyond my own abilities and tried to follow his corrections, even if I couldn't hear the difference between my own pronunciation and that of Japanese people; he was always right. With a little more practice, I knew he would sound very Japanese.

At this point, my physical limitations were very restrictive, and Peter was feeling increasingly worn as he continued to care for me. He was juggling not only my care but also all the household cleaning, purchasing groceries, preparing meals, and the various duties of ministry with the Japanese church. In his fatigue, he would sometimes get impatient with me in my physical state.

At those times, I would try to help him past the point that it was wise for me to do so. I was concerned he might snap from the stress of our situation.

One evening we had some free time and began to discuss our mutual impatience with my injury.

"What are the opposites of the fruit of the Spirit?" I asked. We made a list.

| Fruit | Opposite |
|---|---|
| Love | Hate/Indifference |
| Joy | Despondency |
| Peace | War/Anxiety |
| Patience | Impatience |
| Kindness | Cruelty |
| Goodness | Evil |
| Gentleness | Harshness |
| Faithfulness | Unfaithfulness |
| Self-control | Being out-of-control |

"Look at this list. Which of these opposites is the least destructive?"

Peter shook his head. "I don't know."

"In our fast-food, instant-gratification culture, we'd tend to say that impatience is minor, but I think this is a lie. Just think about the Israelites wandering in the desert. Look at our own experiences over the past several weeks. If we're impatient, we rob God of the chance to teach and transform us, and we can tear down those closest to us.

"What could have been a time of sweetness for Israel was instead a time of complaint, followed by God answering their complaints."

I made another list:

| Israelites' Complaint | God's Answer |
|---|---|
| Red Sea: "You brought us here to die!"[2] | Parted the sea[3] |
| Water: #1: "What shall we drink?"[4] #2: "Give us water that we may drink."[5] #3: There was no water; "Why have you brought us to die here?"[6] | #1: Changed the water from bitter to sweet[7] #2: Gave water from the rock[8] #3: Gave water from another rock[9] |
| Food: #1: "You have brought us out into this wilderness to kill this whole assembly with hunger."[10] #2: "Who will give us meat to eat?"[11] | #1: Provided manna and meat[12] #2: Provided quail[13] |
| Golden Calf: "Come, make a god for us..."[14] | Smote the people[15] |
| Land of Canaan: "Why is the Lord bringing us into this land, to fall by the sword?"[16] | Allowed the people to wander the desert for 40 years[17] |

"Instead of allowing God to transform them into a people who honoured Him," I continued, "the Israelites allowed themselves to be led by fear. So, they were thrown out at Canaan's door and didn't experience the sweetness of trusting God."

We realized that we needed to be really careful not to allow a spirit of impatience and complaint to dominate our own mentality. If we were to learn the lessons God wanted to teach us, we had to cultivate a spirit of thanksgiving, patience, and trust. We didn't want to be consigned to forty years of wandering in a metaphorical desert because we refused to learn in the time He had set apart for us.

## CHAPTER 26

# Setback

*Some people believe that the personality trait of optimism yields resilience in the face of hardship. Author John Collins once tested this theory in an interview with Admiral Jim Stockdale, who was held captive and tortured by the Viet Cong for eight years.*

*Collins inquired of Stockdale, "Was there any one group of people who didn't have the resilience to weather the conditions of the camps?"*

*"Without a doubt: the optimists," Stockdale replied. "They were some of the first to die. They were confident we would be released by Christmas. When that didn't happen, they anticipated being out by Easter. Time wore on, and their hopes and spirits were dashed. I believe they died from broken hearts."*

—Harvard Business Review article[1]

A positive outlook will only get you so far. Mine broke on November 29, 2011: the day after I encountered my biggest health setback, the day I realized the damage of the previous day's car ride would not be fixed overnight, the day my faith started to unravel.

I'd been injured in my back for several months, largely bedridden, and had finally been making good progress in healing. It was decided by our organization's leadership that another visit to the doctor would be a good next step. For some reason, my body had become sensitive to vibration; and Peter and I were cautious of the consequences a car ride might bring about.

However, after praying, we felt the most godly thing to do was to comply with our leaders' request. Though we firmly stated our objections and reservations, in prayerful submission we finally went.

The doctor was able to determine that my injury was not due to the procedure which I'd had two months before; he suggested the problem might be in my back. This made sense to us: many of the actions I'd discovered were dangerous to recovery (including bending, sitting, and twisting) were related to movements of the back. In addition, there was a plethora of back-related risk factors, many of which we hadn't previously recognized as such, leading up to my injury. A back injury became our working hypothesis, and the doctor told us to return in a week or two for medical imaging if there was no improvement.

Unfortunately, the price we paid for that consultation was very high. The car ride to and from the doctor undid weeks of recovery. I went from being able to engage in a variety of physical tasks to being back in bed in extreme, unrelenting pain; from hope to despair; from stability to spiral.

Following the car ride, my body became hypersensitive to vibration. Peter could no longer sleep in the same bed as me, as his nocturnal movements caused me too much pain; vibrations transmitted from the floor through the bed also caused pain, whether they resulted from Peter simply walking around our bedroom or closing the front door two rooms away. I couldn't even breathe too quickly or deeply, as one does in singing, without the vibration from my breathing causing pain.

My physical activities became very limited. I could only lie in bed. I couldn't stand, sit, use a pillow under my head, turn onto either side in bed, bend, or twist in any form. The pain was intense and constant. I couldn't help comparing my former progress with my current misery; despair seemed the only option.

I applied mathematical and engineering skills to my situation, keeping meticulously detailed records of my pain levels and responses to physical stimuli, and graphing out the data to illuminate trends in my condition. Soon I had enough information to accurately predict how my body would respond to the introduction of various activities, such as bending, sitting, and exposure to vibration. As I examined the data, I couldn't avoid the disheartening conclusion any longer: I could not engage in another car ride to the doctor without courting the possibility of lifelong injury.

As the weeks rolled by and the data piled up, we came to another horrifying realization: the physical trauma of the car vibrations had not added to my body's recovery time but multiplied it.

In my suffering, I blamed our organization for not allowing us to wait a little longer before seeing the doctor. I felt frozen in torment, like a bug caught in amber, but cruelly still alive.

After a few days, we telephoned our friends Joshua and Sophie. We knew their previous decades in missions would enable them to understand some of our struggle.

In our discussion, Joshua said something that shone a beam of light into our darkness: "I know it's pretty elementary, but you're going to have to come to grips with the fact that your organization made a bad decision. You're going to need to forgive them."

With that, the darkness loosened its grip on our throats somewhat, and we began to pray that God would enable us to forgive. When our supervisor's wife visited the following day and we were able to explain the severity of the setback, she cried. Seeing her tears, the gates of my heart opened; love and forgiveness flowed around her. I was free—and thankful for restored relationship.

## CHAPTER 27

# Charred

Following the setback from the car ride, it took awhile for my body to stabilize. Indeed, there were a few days when my condition seemed to worsen before it levelled off. Faced with unrelenting misery, my spirit shrivelled into an agonized lump, incapable of hope. When my tongue failed, my pen took its place.

> December 1, 2011
>
> God, I'm so down. Today I'm not better but worse. Where is the healing You promised? You can't lie. Did I imagine Your promise? Have I nullified it somehow?
>
> Where are You? Why aren't You healing me? Am I still supposed to wait and pray?
>
> I'm about two steps away from breaking. I need You, God! Is that what You want to hear? I NEED YOU.
>
> I can't take being strung along with hope anymore. I'm finished. I have nothing left.
>
> My flesh is wasting away as I lie here, atrophying. My spirit is a charred piece of…something. Unrecognizable as to what it once was.
>
> Here I am: unstable, useless, and unable to go on.
>
> > And the ransomed of the Lord will return,
> > And come with joyful shouting to Zion,
> > With everlasting joy upon their heads.
> > They will find gladness and joy,
> > And sorrow and sighing will flee away.
> > (Isaiah 35:10)

> I have a choice. I can look at these words You've just pointed out to me with bitterness, close my Bible, and walk away.
>
> Or, I can choose to let them sink into my soul and nourish me.
>
> I choose You. I choose to trust You.
> I WILL PRAISE YOU IN THE STORM, GOD!
> This is for Your glory.
> YOU ARE WORTH IT.

In that year's Christmas newsletter, I meditated on what God might be doing in our situation.

> We know God is using this time to refine us. It's not pleasant or easy, but we have a choice: we can walk away from Him, or we can walk with Him. We've seen God already working to guide us, through our limitations, for the good of His kingdom; and we choose to trust in His wisdom, goodness, and love for us. This is not the easy path, but it is the best one. "We emerge from a season of profound disappointment, unnerving chaos, or debilitating pain with a faith worth having. We discover that the place we most want to escape has produced the fertility that we most desperately crave."[1]

# CHAPTER 28

# Chomping at the Bit

*And He will sit as a smelter and purifier of silver, and He will purify the sons of Levi and refine them like gold and silver, so that they may present to the Lord offerings in righteousness.*

—Malachi 3:3

In a sermon a few years before, our pastor had told us a story that I'd always remembered. I decided to meditate on it again.

As the story goes, a woman read Malachi 3:3, which talks about God sitting over His people as a refiner of silver. Without mentioning what had stimulated her interest, she made an appointment with a silversmith to learn more about the refining process.

Sitting in the smithy, she watched him at his craft. He first positioned the piece in the flames. As it heated, he explained that silver must be inserted into the very hottest part of the fire, the middle, in order to properly burn away its impurities.

*If God is refining us as silver is refined, that would explain some of the hot spots I sometimes find myself in,* she reasoned. A memory sparked to life. "Is it true that you have to sit in front of the fire for the entire time the silver is being purified?"

The man nodded. "I always sit right here and watch it. I don't look away for a second. If it's left in the fire for even an instant too long, it will be ruined."

Surprised, the woman queried, "How do you know when the silver is finished? How do you know when it's pure?"

The man smiled. "Simple. It's pure when I can see my own reflection in it."

I prayed that this time of pain and suffering would not be wasted, but that through it God would shape me more into His image.

In the midst of affliction, I found myself constantly fighting obsession. It was easy to become unhealthily focussed on healing and a time where I would no longer be subject to the pain and physical limitations of the moment. This period was incredibly trying for our faith, and at times, we felt close to breaking.

I once read a few books by a man named Geoffrey T. Bull. He was a missionary in Tibet when the Chinese took over, and was imprisoned and tortured for several years. During that time, he composed books in his head. When he got out, he wrote them down. One of his comments stuck with me long after I finished reading: "It's not the strength of my grip on God that holds me, but His unbreakable grip on me."[1]

That's been true for us, I wrote to a friend. Every time we get to the end of ourselves, we encounter God where He begins and have found the strength to go on. Someone recently told me, "It's at those moments when we're in pain and despair, but choose to praise God anyway, that He is most glorified."

It wasn't easy, but I clung to God's promises of healing. He seemed to give me additional ones every time I was at my lowest.

God's patience with us is pretty amazing, I wrote to that same friend. How can we not praise Him when we see our own wretchedness and His desire to use us anyway?

During the nights when Peter was out, I would sometimes watch sermons over the Internet to while away the hours. One day, a message from *The Meeting House* provided a particularly valuable challenge, which I pondered in my journal.

December 10, 2011

Today when I was watching a sermon, the speaker asked, "What would you look like if you were the most awake, most fully alive person you could be?" He pointed out that we often content ourselves with taking small, manageable sips of Your Living Water, rather than allowing You to drench us.[2]

I think that's the key word: manageable. We try to manage You, to shrink You to a size we can handle. Because then we're still in control.

But it's only when we're willing to abandon all control and offer up ourselves—our lives, our resources, our futures—to the uncontrollable God that we're at our most alive.

The question is: am I willing to take the risk? Or, will I satisfy myself with a dehydrated life: rationing out a teaspoon of Living Water for daily consumption? Will I drink just enough to keep me alive, to sustain me, but not enough to really thrive?

The thing is: severe dehydration leads to coma.

> Awake, sleeper,
> And arise from the dead,
> And Christ will shine on you.
> (Ephesians 5:14)

How do I do this, God? I get overwhelmed with You, and can't sustain interaction with Your intensity for long. How do other people do it?

I think the answer lies in the degree of need for You. If I'm desperate for You, I have a higher threshold. But my need for You doesn't change. Only my <u>recognition</u> of it does.

So how do I recognize my need? How do I develop dependence? How do I strip away my own capability to the base knowledge that there's no remedy for my condition except through You?

Here I am, bedridden. My situation cannot be more dependent, yet I still sometimes don't feel the need.

Lord, please teach me to gulp of Your Living Water today.

There were periods when I was able to abandon myself to God's timing and trust Him in all things. But in the uncertainty of how our organization might react to my slow recovery from injury, there were also times when my fixation on healing was stronger than ever, when all I wanted was to be healthy and whole and able to minister as I'd imagined. During December, I was often alone and lonely as Peter engaged in a variety of church Christmas activities. My heart's desire was to be there with him, and there were days where I would have done anything to get my way. Once more, I turned to my journal.

December 15, 2011

God, I want to praise You in this storm, but I don't know how anymore. I'm battered. I'm broken. I don't know which side is up, and I don't have any confidence left.

You gave me the opportunity to pursue You…and I did, at some times better than others. But now I'm winded. I can't run any farther. I'm out of breath, and I'm spent. I'm finished. There's nothing left. Nothing left to pursue You with.

WHAT DO YOU WANT FROM ME?

I've given You everything, and all I've got is a promise left behind to taunt me.

"Is that all?" a little voice asked after I put down my pen. "What about My Son?"

"Yes, and Him," I said. "I have eternal life, whatever that means. What I'm in right now, this is technically life. This pain, this struggle. But I don't want it anymore. It's more than I can bear."

"Is it? I promised not to give you more than you can bear."

"Maybe You overestimated me, God. What I need is rest. What I need is recovery."

"Your heavenly Father knows that you need all these things. But seek first His kingdom and His righteousness; and all these things shall be added to you."[3]

"What do You think I've been doing? I've been seeking You, but I'm done. I can't pursue You any longer. I need You. I need You to come to me."

"I gave My best for you, Valerie. Is My Son not good enough?"

"Of course He is. Please teach me how to rest. I need Your rest."

With this, I realized that I'd been contending with God: working myself into near-hysteria, trying to bait Him into encouraging or healing me. I'd been trying to manipulate Him. I confessed this and asked Him to forgive and cleanse me.

"Please show me that I'm not helpless," I said. "I still have *choice*—the choice to listen to Your voice of truth, the choice to trust. 'I do believe; help my unbelief.'"[4]

One night, Peter and I began to talk about our feelings of increasing depletion.

"You're always trying to help me with chores around the house," he said, exasperated.

"I know. I'm really aware of everything you've got to take care of now that I'm injured, and I want to lighten your load."

"You want to pitch in, and normally this would be a good character quality. It means that you're not lazy, you're motivated. But I think in this situation it's not helping. You still need to rest."

"I want to get better so badly. I just want to help."

"I know." He paused. "Do you think your desire to get better might be bad for you?"

"What do you mean?"

"Well, when you're so obsessed with getting better, you sometimes push yourself to do too much."

"I can't help it. I keep thinking that maybe if I just try harder, I can recover more quickly."

"You're not used to not being in control. I think you need to let go of this obsession."

I nodded. "I can see that. Sometimes I fixate on reaching some sort of physical milestone—like being able to bend down—and endanger the healing I've already got. Why am I like that?" A memory rose to the surface. "One time, when I'd forgotten to pray for healing, God said to me, 'You have not because you ask not.' This obsession started after that. From then on, I took my recovery to be my responsibility, as if I could control it."

Peter looked thoughtful. "You assumed God was talking about healing. But what if He was telling you to pray for something else? Did you ever ask Him what He meant?"

"No."

Later, after recording this interchange in my journal, I came to God in prayer.

"Here I am," I said. "My question to You is simple: *what do You want me to ask for?*"

The next day during devotions, I started praying for the salvation of some of the people in our vicinity.

God said, "Your prayers are too small."

So I prayed for the people of our city.

"Too small."

My prayers kept getting bigger and bigger.

Still He kept saying, "Too small."

Eventually, I prayed for the salvation of our entire city, for the light from that place to spread to the whole prefecture, for Okinawa to become a light to Japan, and for Japan to be a beacon to the nations.

"Now you're getting the idea," He said. "This is the prayer I will answer."

Wow.

"I ask You for signs and wonders, dreams, visions, and miracles," I said. "Please display Your power so people come to You—not as a sideshow, but as the God who is more powerful than their superstitions, more powerful than the forces that would seek to bind and enslave them.

"It seems as though You and I hatched that prayer together. I'm hesitant to put Your name on it because after reading the book of Jeremiah, I'm wary of putting words in Your mouth. But at the same time, I don't think I would have had the courage or imagination to pray this without You."

Later, when Peter and I were reading the Bible together, God gave me Jeremiah 33:9 as a promise for Itoman:

> And this city shall be to Me a name of joy, praise, and glory before all the nations of the earth, which shall hear of all the good that I do for them, and they shall fear and tremble because of all the good and all the peace that I make for it.

I'd thought my dreams for our ministry in Japan were already pretty big, but God had given me a glimpse of His instead. We found ourselves thrilled at the enormity of His plans—and His power.

# CHAPTER 29

# Not Every Question

Around this time, a bird began to visit my window. I called him an Okinawan Robin. His Prussian blue jacket and vermillion waistcoat were pristine, and I thought that he must be quite young. He had a beautiful, melodic song, like none I'd heard before. His visits brought me precious scraps of encouragement. Peter left him pieces of bread on our balcony. The following year, I kept my eyes and ears peeled for him, but he never returned. It was then that I realized God must have sent him especially to me the previous year, to lift my spirits during those darkest days.

A most haunting question had been imprinted on my mind in the extremity of pain a few weeks earlier. "Why have You put this wild and extravagant dream in my heart," I'd cried to God, "and then given me a body that breaks as it has?" I felt He was very cruel.

At one point, I wrote a song. It only had one verse and a chorus, but as Amy Carmichael so succinctly said of her own songs, "They are short, for when one is in pain, one does not want much of anything."[1]

I set the words to a cheesy country music tune and still sing it to myself for cheer on days when God's ways seem inscrutable to me.

>   *Chorus*
>   Not every question needs an answer,
>   Not every song needs a tune,
>   But every heart needs a Lover,
>   And Jesus, I need You.

*Verse*
You may lead me through thickets full of pain and disappointments,
You may lead me through wide meadows full of joy and bliss.
On this endless journey You're my steadfast companion.
If there's one thing I'm sure of, Jesus, this is it:

*Chorus*
Not every question needs an answer,
Not every song needs a tune,
But every heart needs a Lover,
And Jesus, I need You.

As I continued to ponder my earlier question, a new thought gave me a measure of comfort, and I recorded it in my journal.

December 2011

What if pain is not an obstacle to be overcome, but an instrument God is using to prepare me for ministry?

What if, rather than trying to get healed—and this injury being in the way of that healing—this is exactly where I'm supposed to be; exactly where I <u>want</u> to be, because it means I'm drawing near to God and He to me?

What if this injury is the means to a ministry for people with *hikikomori*, that mental illness where they lock themselves in for months and years on end? As a result of this experience, even though I've never had *hikikomori*, I know what pain and isolation are like…

What if…?

In this instance, God saw fit to one day answer my question fully. About a month later, I woke up from sleep in the middle of the night, and He was there.

"Valerie," He said, "your body is the tool I am using to teach and refine your spirit. My grace is sufficient for you, for my strength is made perfect in weakness.[2]"

CHAPTER 30

# Christmas

That December, our Christmas gift from my parents came early: money to purchase a television. In my intense loneliness, I would turn it on while Peter was out; the voices of fictitious people would keep me company as I carried out the tasks of my evening.

Since Christmas is a popular Western holiday, some Asian people try to achieve an authentic experience. In Japan and several other Asian countries, Kentucky Fried Chicken (KFC) has done a masterful job of marketing itself as the Christmas meal of choice for North Americans. We'd decided that we wanted to engage in the custom of eating KFC for Christmas, so Peter signed up for a meal a few weeks ahead of time, according to Japanese tradition. He was able to select our meal and desired pickup time, as well as prepay for everything.

Christmas was on a Sunday that year, so Peter and I planned to hold our personal celebrations on December 23. We'd shipped a small artificial tree and decorations with us from Canada. That day, we opened the presents my sister had sent us, along with the ones we'd purchased for each other.

In the evening, Peter promptly went to KFC at the prearranged time and brought home our celebration meal. It was quite a treat to open up the package. There was a commemorative plate on top, followed by eight pieces of chicken, a salad, and chocolate cake. The whole meal was more delicious than any of our Canadian KFC experiences, and we proudly displayed our commemorative plate for several months following.

As expected, I spent the majority of Christmas Day on my own while Peter participated in activities at church. We both were a little heartsick: I, at home, wishing I could be part of the activities; Peter, the introvert, wishing I could be at his side through all the hustle and bustle.

I'd been dreading Christmas Day and its isolation, but in the end, I had a good talk with God in my journal and gained some new insights into Jesus' experience of His own time on earth.

December 25, 2011

> Lord, today is Your birthday, and it feels strangely fitting to spend it mostly with You.
>
> You and me, alone together.
>
> This Christmas is so vastly different than anything I'd anticipated—and I'd thought it would be very different from before! But I didn't expect to be in bed, not at church, and not with Peter.
>
> Despite these differences, I can't help but feel blessed, because You're here; because this Christmas my focus is more singular, without the distraction of people; because I get to be with You.
>
> I love and trust You, Jesus. Thank You for this time, because I know it will not be wasted.
>
> There's so much to be thankful for. Thank You for coming to earth. Were You ever homesick? I bet You were. You'd exchanged the riches and purity of heaven for the moral and physical filth of everything we've done to pollute Your world.
>
> Were You lonely? Maybe, like me, it was partial loneliness. You could still talk with Your Father, just in a different form. For me, the vehicle is the Internet; for You, it was prayer. It's not the same, though, is it?
>
> Did it help to know that Your Father was proud of You? After all, He sent the angels to herald Your birth, and the dove to affirm the start of Your ministry.

Based on my experience, I would say it helps, but it's no substitute for physical contact.

So, this Christmas I come to You understanding a little more than before. Thank You for Your sacrifice—not just on the cross, but for the thirty years before that, as You lived in a foreign land.

That day, I kept feeling my own belovedness in my Father's eyes and was grateful for His companionship. As night fell, I was relieved: I'd survived Christmas Day and its loneliness without having a meltdown.

# CHAPTER 31

# Meltdown

On December 27, matters finally came to a head. A few days earlier I'd tried to sit on a chair for the first time in a month, but my body had reacted badly. Before sitting, I'd been able to get up from bed for half an hour at a time, but afterward I was only able to do so for five or ten minutes. Unhappy in the days following this, I'd tried to ignore my emotions. When I finally looked at them squarely, my reality grew dark and horrifying.

As Amy Carmichael writes:

> The hardest days of the trouble that follows accident or illness are not the first days. They are the days later on, when a new assault of that strangely dreadful power finds us, as it were, at his feet defenseless...[the destroyer] appears to straddle quite over the whole breadth of the way, and swears we shall go no further: "Here will I spill thy soul."[1]

Over the preceding days, I'd entered into a circuit of accusation, trying desperately to find a reason for my misery. I internally blamed our organization for not listening to our warnings; Peter for allowing me to go on the dangerous car ride; and God for not protecting me as I'd believed He would. I spiralled into an endless cycle of casting blame on everyone in sight, including myself. That day it was God's turn. I ranted at Him for more than an hour.

Back in November, I'd been so sure that despite the danger of the car ride, God would protect me. My faith had been big, but now an insidious voice hissed in my ear. Perhaps God was not as powerful as I'd thought He was. I bitterly questioned if my faith had been bigger than my God.

Confident of nothing apart from my salvation, I knew that at some point God had loved me because Jesus had died for me. But I wondered when He'd stopped loving me, and was convinced that He now hated me. In my mind, He was infinitely cruel, like a powerful cat playing with its powerless prey: me.

I felt great affinity for Job. I, too, had lost everything. I had no children, but unlike Job, I'd <u>voluntarily</u> given up everything—family, money, and position—to serve God. In return, He had stripped me of my health and dreams. Powerless to stand up under the heaviness of His hand, all I wanted to do was escape from Him.

Eventually, my tirades ran out of steam, and God planted a thought in my mind.

December 27, 2011

> My purpose is not to share God's love with the nations. Rather, it is to revel in being beloved, and to love Him in return. All sharing flows out of this.
>
> My focus is to be on Jesus, and on Him alone. I will not make missions an idol any more than I will make the Bible an idol.
>
> Jesus, all this is for Your glory. And You are glorified even when—especially when—no one is watching.

My feelings were by no means resolved. I'd spent the past few days ranting at God—discontent, spent, empty of everything but bitterness and despair. However, in the following days He continued to speak to me. Under Jesus' tender ministrations, my heart stopped its painful spasms, and I began to learn about my own faith.

At one of my weakest moments, Peter made a suggestion.

"I think you need to call someone," he said. "You need to get this off your chest."

"What do you mean? I can talk with you."

"It's not the same. You need to vent to someone other than me. You're struggling, and right now I'm part of that struggle. You feel jealous because I'm out doing ministry and you're not. God called you to Japan first, but I'm the one who's doing everything you've dreamed of. It's really unfair."

I'd never expressed this to him—nor had even consciously thought it—but when he said it, I recognized the truth.

I called Julia.

"Hmm, I just learned something in my devotions the other day that might help you," she said. "As you know, I've been reading through the book of Genesis. The other day, I noticed that though God made extravagant promises to Isaac and Jacob, He chose to bless their brothers (Ishmael and Esau) before them. But the promises made to Isaac and Jacob lasted much longer.[2] I think God will do the same thing with your healing and ministry. They may be delayed, but they'll endure."

After our call ended, I continued to reflect on these things in my journal.

December 29, 2011

> I just read something, and it makes me want to weep.
>
>> For if we died with Him, we shall also live with Him;
>> If we endure, we shall also reign with Him;
>> If we deny Him, He also will deny us;
>> If we are faithless, He remains faithful;
>> For He cannot deny Himself.
>> (2 Timothy 2:11-13)
>
> These verses have always confused me: the part about denying seemed to contradict the part about faithlessness. Until now.

I have been faithless—completely lacking in faith—but He has remained faithful.

I have thought that He hated me. I have desired to escape from His heavy hand. I have been void of faith. And yet He still loves and forgives me. He is faithful.

Perhaps, in this context, faithlessness is not a lack of faithfulness but a lack of faith itself.

What if my faith is like one of those faulty computer programs at my old job? We were trying to solve an operational problem using software for analysis, but the original programmer had made some mistakes along the way, in fundamental structure. I would be called in to fix the programming. Sometimes the most expedient thing to do was to rebuild the coding from scratch, using the lessons learned along the way. The end result was a better program—more robust. The original structure, though discarded, was still useful because it provided valuable lessons for the future.

What if God is rebuilding my faith? What if it had gotten me as far as it could, but now it needed to be changed into something better? The lessons learned are valuable still, but some of the foundations—for instance, basing my faith on myself to some extent—were shaky.

What if God is not content to simply patch things over, but wants to build something better and more robust—for me? For His kingdom?

What if…?

That day, God redefined some of my basic views. My faith was not something I owned. Its beginning and end was external to me and rooted only in Him. I had no power to start or sustain it. Only He could grow it in any way. With this realization came great release. I could throw myself at the throne of grace with abandon and trust my Father to catch me.

The next day, I shared with Peter a letter I'd written to help me forgive someone. Along the way, I'd realized that because of that person's self-protectionism, he couldn't experience the fullness of love as I knew it, and I'd pitied him.

I finished reading aloud.

Peter was silent for a moment.

"Aren't we all kind of like that?" he asked.

This stopped me in my tracks. He was right. What made me think I had love all figured out? My version of it was pale indeed, compared to God's.

*I wonder if that's why we sometimes condemn God as unloving: because our own understanding is too shallow,* I thought.

I could conceivably mistake God's rich and boundless love for something different. In my limited dimensionality, I couldn't begin to comprehend God in all His grandeur, I realized. I could even misread His love as hate. I needed to trust in His character and remember all the times He'd proven Himself before.

CHAPTER 32

# The Parable of the Lost Ring

Mondays were typically our day off, and we would use those days to rest, spend time with God, and mentally prepare for the week to come. On the first Monday of the new year, that didn't happen—at least, not in the way we expected. It was a special day, particularly for Peter, and this is the story he told afterward.

Late in the afternoon, I decided to go for a walk. My hobby is photography, and Val had been encouraging me for weeks to take a field trip and enjoy myself. I'd been reluctant to do this. I always like going out and doing things with her more than by myself.

"I'm still in bed, injured," she said. "Who knows when this will be over? You shouldn't avoid fun in your life just because I can't go with you."

So I went.

Near our apartment was a river with lots of birds and plants. *That would be a good place to enjoy nature and pray*, I thought.

Walking along, I absentmindedly fiddled with my wedding ring. It had been loose for a couple of years. In 2008, I jammed my finger in a door, resulting in what we thought was permanent swelling. My ring would no longer fit, so we got it resized. In 2009, after our bout with H1N1, my finger shrank back to its normal size. But we were accepted as missionaries soon after, life got busy, and reducing the size of my ring fell off

Val's radar. She's the planner. I don't have any radar to speak of, for planning.

When I arrived at the river, there were some white cranes along its banks. The wall by the cranes was quite tall; on my side there was a ten-foot drop to the river. A long way down.

Just as I rested my camera on the wall, the ring slipped off my finger.

Time slowed. I heard the *tink* as it bounced off the wall and turned to watch it fall.

*Splash.*

Looking into the river, I saw it, half-visible. It looked very much like the scene from *The Lord of the Rings* when Gollum reached into the water and pulled his ring out. While it wasn't the 'one ring', it was my wedding ring, and I immediately called Val. I'll admit it: I was crying.

"That's okay, we'll buy you another one," she said on hearing my story. She said a few other comforting things, which I didn't really absorb.

So many things had been going wrong lately. Sometimes it felt like we were clinging for dear life to the promises God had given us: of healing for Val's body, and of His working in our ministry both now and in the future. How much more could I possibly take?

"Wait a minute," she said.

I tuned back in.

"I think God's telling us that we should ask Him to get the ring back for us."

I let her pray. I was too discouraged.

"God, please return that ring to us," she said.

We hung up, but she called back two minutes later.

"Peter, after we finished talking, I kept praying. If God's going to be doing all these amazing things here, then I know this matter of the ring isn't too difficult for Him. He told me to call you back. You're supposed to ask the next person you see on the street for help. I looked up the Japanese word for wedding ring in my dictionary. It's *kekkon no yubiwa*."

We disconnected again. I repeated my line over and over to myself, in Japanese.

"My wedding ring. My wedding ring."

Soon a man and his mother approached, walking their dog.

"Excuse me," I said. "My wedding ring." I pointed down to the water.

They quickly understood and were sympathetic to my plight. After discussing something with his mother in Japanese, the man turned to me again.

"Please wait," he said. Then he left with his mother.

I waited. I took more pictures of birds, and of my ring, and waited some more.

The man returned after about ten minutes, carrying a net and some rope. He said something incomprehensible in Japanese. I guessed it was an explanation of his plan. After tying the rope around a tree and around himself, he pulled it tight and rappelled down the side of the wall. About two feet from the bottom, his hand slipped. He scraped it and got some rope burn. He reached into the water, got the ring, put it into the net, and passed it to me. He tried to get a grip on the wall with his feet but couldn't. Just then, two more passersby saw this problem, and the three of us pulled the man back over the wall.

When all was finished, I asked, "Is there anything I can do to thank you?"

"No," he said, "helping you to please your wife is enough."

I thanked him over and over. Finally we parted ways.

When I got home, Val looked at me expectantly. "Well?" she asked.

I told her the story. When I was finished, she smiled widely. "That's amazing!" she said.

"Yeah, God really answered our prayer."

"No, you don't understand how amazing this is. When you called, I was reading a book. After we were done talking, I went back to reading. It was a Christian book, and at one point, it mentioned a Bible verse. Before I even looked it up, I felt God prompting me to look two verses past it to 1 Corinthians 7:33. It said, 'But one who is married is concerned about the things of the world, how he may please his wife.' I didn't know what to do with this, so I went back to reading.

"Now, you tell me that the man who helped you said almost the same thing at the end!"

If we'd been in any doubt about God working in this situation, He'd gone one step further and autographed the whole story in big bold letters: our benefactor's statement closely echoed the scripture verse God had guided Val to.

In a training session, we'd been told that the Japanese typically won't go to much effort to help someone outside of their own social groups. It's the responsibility of each person's groups to take care of him or her, so strangers won't feel much obligation toward other strangers. However, God used this event to confirm we'd been correctly hearing the things He was telling us.

# CHAPTER 33

# Acceptance

Continuing to meditate on the events of December, I found myself coming to a deeper understanding of what had taken place.

When all I'd wanted to do was escape from God's apparent cruelty, He kept showing me verses from the book of Job that echoed some of the very rants I'd expressed in the days before I read them, sometimes even using the same words. It was as if He were reassuring me that these words and feelings weren't sinful.

I now had a strong sense that God was rebuilding my faith. He was using foundations built solely on Him this time, and a new recognition of the depth of His grace.

This was all in answer to my own prayer, I realized. When God told me about the largeness of His plans for Okinawa, I'd recoiled and been scared that somehow I would puff myself up and take credit for His work.

I'd written in previous journal entries that I needed healing, but upon later reflection, I realized my error. God was the one I needed. Healing would come eventually because He had promised it. My truest need was for Him, and I finally was able to say that He was enough.

Through this time, I began reading the books of Amy Carmichael, a missionary who also went through months—indeed years!—of physical suffering and helplessness. She wrote that those who are ill or injured can find a great deal of freedom in accepting their infirmity. This doesn't mean they surrender to it, but that through acceptance they can find a measure of contentment in the midst of a situation where answers are hidden.[1] At this point, some of her thoughts on acceptance became true of me.

When we'd left Canada, we'd left with a big God. But we realized now that *we* had been too big in our own estimation. If someone had asked me about our purpose in going to Japan, my reply would probably have included the phrase "to give God glory". But the glory was already God's. Who were we to give it to Him? We now understood the only things we could give Him were thanksgiving, love, obedience, and surrender—and we still served a big God!

At the end of December, God in His mercy showed us a little of what He had been doing in our lives. He'd brought us through several distinct phases: October was a time of our own ignorance and arrogance, the introduction to this ordeal; November, a time of softening; and December, a time of breaking and intense transformational growth, of recasting our vision for God's work in Okinawa to be much bigger than we'd ever imagined, and of redefining our views on faith and love.

One day, I spent a portion of my devotional time looking back through my journal at the things God had taught us in December, and listing them in point form. The list filled two pages! I had the clear impression that the next phase for us would include a time of cementing the things we'd learned, and that this step was necessary before complete healing took place.

As I thought back to the start of all this, when God promised, "I will heal you in My time, Valerie, but there are people here I don't want you to meet yet", I couldn't help but chuckle. Then, I'd interpreted this as meaning that God was still preparing their hearts for the gospel, but now I realized it was equally probable that He'd been preparing mine.

And so, for the moment I was content to wait on God and his plans. If I was to be His missionary, then I would have to rely on His schedule and not my own.

One night, Peter and I rewatched the first *Lord of the Rings* movie. I was struck by a scene at the end when Sam practically drowns himself trying to follow Frodo as his comrade leaves the rest of the fellowship behind. It is the truest expression of love and friendship, and brings me to tears every time.

Watching it, I thought of a verse from Job: "Though He slay me, yet will I trust in Him."[2]

"God, I want to be like Sam," I prayed. "Please give life to my faith and trust. Though I may die in the effort, I will follow You. I love You."

Though it was difficult to be away from our families and support systems, I also began to see a little of the sense in our situation. Sometimes we need to go through certain trials alone in order for God to instruct us. Peter and I now recognized that we would never have been able to learn the things God was teaching if we were still in Canada. Only when all the familiar networks were stripped away were we ready for this intensive education.

I finally realized that my healing was delayed so my relationship with God could grow and my faith could be challenged and changed. If I had been distracted by the encouragement of major progress, I doubted that I would have learned these lessons quite so well. For the time, healing continued slowly, so there was ample opportunity for application.

One of the hardest elements of the previous months was the feeling of uselessness. I felt that life was passing me by, and that I wasn't contributing anything to the people whom I'd come to serve. Amy Carmichael's writings greatly encouraged me in this regard:

> A soldier on service in the spiritual army is never off his battlefield....No soldier on service is ever 'laid aside'; he is only given another commission, sometimes just to suffer (we are not told yet the use of that), sometimes, when pain and weakness lessen a little, to fight among the unseen forces of the field....A wise master never wastes his servant's time, nor a commander his soldier's—there is great comfort in remembering that....We may be called to serve on the visible field, going continually into the invisible both to renew our strength and to fight the kind of battle that can be fought only there. Or we may be called off the visible altogether for awhile, and drawn deep into the invisible. That dreary word 'laid aside' is never for us; we are soldiers of the King of kings. Soldiers are not shelved.[3]

Along with my language and cultural studies, God also began giving me a unique new ministry. In our training, we'd learned that each year almost the same number of people leave the church as the number who are baptized. This results from a variety of complex factors, but is one of the reasons the Japanese church has remained small for so long. On hearing this, we were reminded of Jesus' parable of the sower and the seed, recorded in Mark 4.

Up until the beginning of the year I'd not had many visitors, though we'd maintained an open-door policy. In early December Tsuneko sensei, our pastor's wife, asked if the church could do anything for us while I was recovering. Peter knew how lonely I was, so he suggested that people could provide the occasional meal. In the back of his mind, he thought perhaps those who dropped off food could be invited in for a visit.

Sure enough, church members started to respond to this request. Whenever they arrived with food, we would invite them in. They became more and more comfortable with my situation and eventually began to visit even without the excuse of food.

To balance my limited vocabulary, I used scripture verses from a bilingual Bible to communicate or to share some of the different lessons God had been teaching me.

Eleanor, the first lady with whom I tried this, seemed to appreciate my approach. I felt that we connected. However, I didn't realize the extent of the bond until she showed up again at our door a few days later.

"I will come at this time on Mondays, Wednesdays, and Fridays," she said. "I will teach you Japanese, and you will teach me English."

We immensely enjoyed each other's company, and I learned many things about the Japanese language and culture. She wrote me a letter in Japanese, which we studied during one of our lessons.

"I hope you will come to think of Okinawa as a second home," she wrote, "and I will think of you as my second daughter."

The visits with people from the church continued. More than one family remarked, "We came to encourage you, but we are the ones who are encouraged!"

We were told that this was a powerful testimony to the Japanese of God's sustaining power through pain and adversity, and we hoped that perhaps this circumstance would eventually encourage a disheartened person not to give in to defeat when the reality is that we have been granted glorious victory in Christ Jesus our Lord, for "we walk by faith, not by sight."[4]

# CHAPTER 34

# ESL Classes

*We found out the other day there's no such thing as a 'mild flu' in Japan. At one point, when we told the Japanese that we had the flu, they were all very concerned. It turns out that regardless of other symptoms, if you have a fever below 39°C then you've got a 'cold'. Up until now we'd always wondered why people stayed away from English class if they had colds, because in Canada one won't put you out of commission....*

—Journal entry, winter 2012

The ESL class at Christmas was really well-received. In fact, the church wanted to run another one right away after it ended. This was wonderful because in Okinawa new things usually take awhile to get started. However, my internal reaction was mixed. I'd just come through the hardest month of my life, due in no small part to loneliness and isolation from people.

I approached the coming month with apprehension. Peter would be leading two Bible classes. This, coupled with Japanese conversation class, violin lessons, prayer meeting, and working with the church plant, meant I would spend most nights alone. I was not looking forward to this and prayed that God would be my companion through those times.

Our two new English Bible classes started at different churches in late January and early February. They used the same textbook, entitled *People Who Met Jesus*, and introduced the students to Jesus' ministry, death, and resurrection through the eyes of Zacchaeus, the Samaritan woman, Pilate, and others.

As was our pattern, Peter was the teacher; and from bed, I helped to brainstorm lesson plans and prepare materials beforehand. On Friday nights when Peter went off to teach, I would spend the time praying that the Holy Spirit would enable him to communicate well, and that God would enlighten the minds and hearts of the students to embrace Jesus and the life of freedom and victory He has to offer. Fridays soon became my favourite night of the week. I knew exciting things were happening and eagerly awaited Peter's return when he would share the details of each session.

Before we started the new class at Seaside Chapel, we prayed for two things: that there would be a half-and-half split between people who did and didn't know Jesus, and that Charles, who'd memorized Bible verses at Christmas even though he wasn't a Christian, would return. On its first day, the class was already at its maximum capacity of twelve people; five or six of the students attending didn't know Jesus. Two of the attendees were Charles and his wife Chelsea.

During that class, two of our other non-Christian students seemed particularly responsive to the gospel. Felix and Grant started coming regularly to Seaside Chapel's Sunday services in addition to ESL. Felix even started bringing his wife and daughter along.

Over the previous months, everyone in the church and ESL classes had become familiar with my story. Experiencing a building sense of anticipation, we were eager for the day of my healing. We looked forward to the time when we would remind our students of the story they'd learned on the second week: of the paralyzed man who was let down through the roof, and of Jesus' words, "But that you may know that the Son of Man has authority on earth to forgive sins...rise, pick up your bed, and go home."[1]

I said to a friend, "I would love to be able to walk into that class before it's over as a physical demonstration of Jesus' power to not only heal bodies but souls!"

During one of our last sessions in the *People Who Met Jesus* series, we examined the story of the rich young ruler who came to Jesus asking how to inherit eternal life.[2]

"How do you get to heaven?" Peter asked.

"By following the commandments," someone answered.

"By being good," said another.

"How good is 'good'?" Peter drew a graph on the whiteboard. "The ruler was good. He followed all the commandments, but Jesus wanted good plus one."

The class counted up the list of commandments the ruler had followed. "Six out of seven is good," Peter continued, "but only seven out of seven would be acceptable. How do we get into heaven? Do we have to sell our belongings?"

They talked about this for awhile, but eventually Chelsea read a partial verse from the story: "If you want to be perfect…"

Peter smiled. "So to get to heaven you need to be perfect. Can we be seven-out-of-seven people every moment of every day?"

The students looked at their shoes.

"No."

"That's difficult."

"So how do we get to heaven?" Peter persisted.

Daniel looked at the memory verse on the whiteboard and brightened. "All things are possible with God," he read.

"Why is it possible to be seven out of seven with God?"

"Don't know," the students said.

They looked at Peter, expecting him to give the answer.

"Maybe we'll find out in another class," he said.

And so the discussion ended. In the Japanese school system, most learning takes place by means of strict memorization. We were excited to help our students discover Jesus' offer of salvation for themselves. We hoped that as they embarked on this journey of discovery, they would take ownership of these ideas and embrace them personally.

## CHAPTER 35

# What Do You Desire?

At times, when I wrote in my journal, the words that flowed from my pen were prayers to God; and as He answered, I recorded our dialogues. Such was the case one day in January.

January 30, 2012

You have not given me a life that other people lead. You have given me an uncommon one. Yes, I'm experiencing health problems. But You have also bestowed on me uncommon grace. Your bounteous, beautiful, beyond-comprehension grace lifts me up to the foot of Your throne.

You have a purpose, I know it. Am I ready to embrace it? To embrace You? Am I ready to declare that You're enough for every circumstance?

Like Job, I've sometimes waited with longing to hear Your voice. I've ranted at the ceiling, demanded a response—but none came. You do not answer our demands. Instead, You counter with a question of Your own: "Will you wait for Me, beloved? Will you still choose to trust Me when you don't understand?"

And, like Job, when You speak—even if the words are not the things I was looking for, even if Your answer is really no answer at all—I'm content. Because You have spoken. You're here after all. You care for and love me. And that's enough. More than enough.

So, here I am today. Waiting for You, hungry. Only You will satisfy me. All other desires are sickening by comparison.

"Even your desire to be well?" a small voice asked as I finished writing.

"Is that what this is? Is this a test?" I prayed. "Are You going to remove Your promise to heal me? I feel a little panicked, God. A little queasy. What are You asking of me? I don't know if I can give this up."

"You're not answering the question," came the gentle reminder.

"I know, God. I'm avoiding it. Have I made being well into an idol? Is this an idol You will smash or is this just a case where You want me to surrender something to You and then You'll give it back? If I knew, this would be so much easier…but then 'surrender' would lose all meaning, wouldn't it?…if I knew."

I considered the question. My desire to be well was strong. So was my desire to be close to God. If I had to choose between Him and being well…

I paused, and understanding flowed in.

My thinking was flawed.

'Well' denoted wholeness—of body, soul, and mind. I'd long felt that my mental and emotional soundness were intrinsically linked to my relationship with Him. Without *Him*, I wasn't well. I might be physically fit for a time, but not mentally, emotionally, or spiritually. Before long, this would impact my physical health.

I couldn't think of a fuller answer. His question was like asking whether a zebra was black or white. It might be fine in theory, but in practicality the zebra is both black *and* white. Take one away and the animal is no longer recognizable as a zebra.

Take God out of the equation and all possibility of physical wholeness would evaporate. The question could not be 'God or wellness?' The reality was:

GOD  WELLNESS

God causes wellness.

Whether this resulted in physical health was beside the point, I realized. Physical wholeness was subordinate to my need for Him. Without God, the possibility for well-being simply did not exist. Rather than my desire for healing warring with my love for Him, it should only add fuel to my need for Him.

I thought of a scenario:

> Suppose I were once more physically well, but back in my emotionally-ill state of the year 2000. I would drive Peter away and would be alone in my degenerative cycle of manipulation and self-loathing.

And then, an alternate scenario:

> Suppose I were housebound or bedridden for the rest of my life, but close with God and Peter. God would give me a new ministry, perhaps to others like me.

Going back to the original question, I was indeed sickened by the first scenario, especially when contrasted with the second. How much did I want to be well? Very much. But I was unwilling to trade my relationship with God for it.

I opened my journal again and recorded my answer.

January 30, 2012

> I trust You, God. If You want to rescind Your promise, I'm okay with that. I will not make physical well-being an idol. I love to walk, and run, and jump. But I love You more.
>
> Anything less than You is sickening.

## Valerie Limmer

I will wait on You, Father, and trust in Your promises. I don't know what the future holds for my body, but my spirit is Yours.

## CHAPTER 36

# Love My Chains

Through this time, there were moments when I absolutely detested my bed. My skin crawled at the thought of being in it even a moment longer. After the brief times when I could stand and walk around our apartment, it was achingly difficult to lay my body back down on that familiar mattress and yield once more to needed rest.

Yet there were other times where I found a "secret sweetness in…[the] briar"[1] of my infirmity. "But it is not of us," Amy Carmichael once wrote. "It is Love that lifts us up. It is Love that is the sweetness."[2]

In C. S. Lewis' book, *The Last Battle*, there's a scene at the end when everyone is imprisoned in a hut. It's very dreary in there. Then some of the prisoners begin to realize there's a different world that exists in parallel with the hut: they're actually in a heaven-like garden, if only they have the eyes to see it.

I couldn't think of a better illustration of my situation. My flesh recoiled at being in that place for so long, at the helplessness to speed up my recovery, at the complete uncertainty of how much longer I would be there. At times I was very much in the hut. But then God in His mercy gave me the grace to once more see that the chains binding me were actually fine jewellery; that my bed of isolation had been changed into a banquet table, and I was feasting on the goodness of His provision.

It seems that this strange dichotomy exists for many people who are in conditions they would rather not endure; and so, through this experience the words of Madame Guyon came to have special meaning for me.

> I have no desire that my imprisonment should end before the right time; I love my chains. My senses, indeed, have not any relish for such things, but my heart is separated from them and borne over them.[3]

In high school English class, as part of governmental testing, we were required to select one of two poems for analysis. The one I chose impacted me greatly. I've tried many times since to find a copy, unsuccessfully. However, perhaps it shines more brightly in my memory than it would were I to read the poet's actual turns of phrase.

The story is about a child who accompanies his mother to the grocery store each week. While she shops he waits in the vestibule, staring at a children's ride: a horse. Busy people hurry to and fro, and all he can do is imagine what it would be like to ride such a majestic beast, with its proud stance and flowing mane. What lands they would explore together! What adventures they would encounter! The child begs his mother for a quarter so he can ride his horse to far-off places, but she always refuses. Then one day, someone drops a coin. The boy can hardly believe his good luck; his chubby fingers grab eagerly for the piece. He climbs onto his steed in joy and feeds in the quarter. But things are not as he'd imagined. The horse never comes to life. It bucks about mechanically, and worst of all, he never leaves the grocery store. When he disembarks at the end of a terrifying two minutes of shattered dreams, the child is in tears. He cannot stand to look at the beast. It grins tauntingly at him—paint chipped and ugly. The poem finishes with the line, "My true heart's desire was not what I'd wanted after all."[4]

January 23, 2012

> This morning I woke up in the dark, sad. The end of the grocery store horse poem echoed in my mind. "My true heart's desire was not what I'd wanted after all."[5]

That poem has always haunted me, but at the moment its effect is amplified. Is it true in my life, right now? My true heart's desire has been to serve You, to come to Japan and share the good news of Jesus. But now I'm here, and nothing is as I thought it would be. I didn't think that I came laden with a lot of expectations, but I did expect to serve. Am I serving? I don't know. Perhaps I am, and am blinded by my own emotions. I feel more like I'm waiting. Yet again.

I was editing our website yesterday and was struck by our testimonies of all the roadblocks You put in our way before we finally arrived here. It would appear they are not over. Does that mean they're not useful? Does that mean it's Your will to block us perpetually from doing what we believe You've called us to? My heart cries out, "NO!" And a corner of it murmurs, "…at least, I hope not."

But You are the God who is able to do exceedingly, abundantly more than I could ever ask or imagine[6]; the God who will never leave or forsake me[7]; the God who is truth itself[8].

My life is Yours! I will do whatever You ask of me. You are my desire, more than anything else. You are not what I expected; You are MORE.

You are more than my anaemic desires, more than the pale shadows of colour that make up my imagination, more than the stomach of my soul can contain. Let me be a glutton for You—let my soul burst as I feast upon Your bounty—only, let me desire You all of my days. You are different than I expected. Am I disappointed? The truth is: sometimes. I wish I weren't still lying here in bed. But then You come along with Your MORE and I realize again that I'm right where I want to be: with my true heart's desire.

## CHAPTER 37

# Strength for the Moment

*And it will come about that every living creature which swarms in every place where the river goes, will live. And there will be very many fish, for these waters go there, and the others become fresh; so that everything will live where the river goes...And by the river on its bank, on one side and on the other, will grow all kinds of trees for food. Their leaves will not wither, and their fruit will not fail. They will bear every month because their water flows from the sanctuary, and their fruit will be for food and their leaves for healing.*

—Ezekiel 47:9, 12

A bed of infirmity is a place of extremes. It can either be one of wallowing and spiritual degeneration or one of refining and deepening. I asked God for grace and strength each day so I could take every thought captive, enter into the work of prayer, and be patient and open to the lessons He had for me. Some days, as Amy Carmichael describes, the act of persisting was very trying:

> But I have not found myself that illness makes prayer easier, nor do any of our family who have been ill tell me that they have found it so. Prayerfulness does not seem to be a flower of the spirit that grows of itself. When we are well perhaps we rather take it that it does, as though what is sometimes called a 'sickbed' offered natural soil for that precious flower. I do not think that it does. A bed can be a place of dullness of spirit as well as of body, and prayer is,

after all, work—the most strenuous work in all the world. And yet it is our only way of joining the fighting force.[1]

In those times when trudging on was more difficult, I sometimes used scripture to help express myself; at other times, I felt too endlessly weary to pray much at all.

One day, while reading my daily chapter from Amy Carmichael's *Rose from Brier*, I was hit by an amazing truth. All along I'd treated prayer as my mandate. Some days were more successful than others. On 'off' days, when the fatigue was so great that I couldn't even begin to pray, I'd felt guilty for not holding up my part of the bargain. But now I saw that this was false guilt. God knew my frailty and my limitations. He knew, and did not expect more than I could give. A short prayer, like Amy Carmichael's "Do Thou for me...for him...for her"[2] would suffice in those times. This was not an excuse for laziness, but it *was* the outpouring of His grace and mercy.

And so I would struggle on, praying as much as I could and entrusting my Father with the rest. I was much encouraged by the similar trials of others before me, and found great comfort in the knowledge that some good might be extracted from the intense effort of prayerful exertion.

> True valor lies, not in what the world calls success, but in the dogged going on when everything in the man says Stop...Let us face it now: which is harder, to be well and doing things, or to be ill and bearing things? It was a long time before I saw the comfort in that question. Here we may find our opportunity to crucify that cowardly thing, the softness that would sink to things below—self-pity, dullness, selfishness, ungrateful gloom.[3]

It was sometimes difficult to be content, so I prayed that God would teach me how to be satisfied in every circumstance, as He'd taught Paul. During physical affliction, it's natural to become covetous of other people's health, but I knew comparisons were pointless. God continually affirmed that though my experiences were very different from those of most people my age, this did not make my gift of life any less valuable.

As healing progressed, at certain points I would test the extent of my capabilities to see if a new action could be added to my daily routine. However, sometimes my body wasn't ready for new activities. If I was careful to experiment in infinitesimal increments, it would only take a day or two to recover. My spirit would often need recuperation time too.

I wasn't in constant pain anymore. Instead, pain was like my jailer—giving me prods now and then, and kicking me back into line if I tried to do too much. There was always the threat that it would come back with a vengeance if I didn't listen to my body's signals. Grateful for this progress, I prayed that it would continue.

There is an excellent poem in one of Amy Carmichael's books:

> The toad beneath the harrow knows
> Exactly where each tooth print goes
> The butterfly upon the road
> Preaches contentment to that toad.[4]

She likens the toad to a suffering Christian, and the butterfly to one who isn't suffering nor has ever suffered. I sometimes felt the sting of a comment from someone who was well and had never experienced the road that I now travelled. Rather than hoarding the hurt, I decided to examine each statement as it came and learn as much as I could. Perhaps in this way I wouldn't be someone who compounded the hardship of others in the future.

One day, I received a note from a friend. She talked about wanting a pain machine so she could enter into other people's difficulty and commiserate with them. Her remark, though desiring to be empathetic, really struck me as being from someone who has never suffered. It was really my first exposure to the sorts of things people say when they don't understand.

Someone who has gone through affliction does not *desire* to enter into more of it. That may be his lot in life, and God gives him the strength and grace to bear it and grow. But the flesh recoils. A pain machine would be deceptive: friends might be able to feel the physical pain and walk away thinking they understood. Yet they wouldn't, because they could turn the machine off and not feel the emotional pain of helplessness and uncertainty about the future. This pain is at least equivalent to the physical. In my experience, it is more.

If there were a pain machine, friends also wouldn't feel the distress of isolation—of few people (if any) understanding. By its very nature there would be a sense of fellowship, of entering into pain together.

It wasn't my friend's fault that she didn't understand. She'd simply never gone through it.

"Lord, please cleanse my heart," I prayed. "Help me not to feel haughty because I understand these things. Help me not to be embittered against the well. Supply me with wisdom and graciousness to give gentle answers.

"Sometimes I feel so lonely. Not even Peter fully gets it. But I do have someone who understands. You do. Thank You for being with me."

At times, life seemed to drone on continually with no prospect of rest; but every so often God would provide a new promise, and its refreshment would flow over and into my soul.

In reading Ezekiel 47 one day, I came upon a few verses that talk about a river flowing from the sanctuary of God, bringing life to everything in its path, and making sweet the waters of the sea.

"This is My Spirit," God said to me, "in whom everything lives, and moves, and has its being."[5]

The Bible talks about trees planted on either side of the river, perpetually bearing fruit, with leaves that never wither.

"This is you," He whispered. "If you plant yourself along My river you will be abundant and fruitful."

The next morning, in my devotions, I came to Psalm 1. Verse 3 says, "And [the righteous man]…will be like a tree firmly planted by streams of living water, which yields its fruit in its season, and its leaf does not wither; and in whatever he does, he prospers."

Through this time, I began to connect with a few missionary women in our organization and started a weekly Bible study with a lady named Hanna. Together we explored what it means to be on a pilgrimage toward our heavenly home.

We discovered that a pilgrim is someone who foremost has vision, of a better life, for which he or she will leave home, hearth, and family. He or she is willing to endure hardship for the sake of the *better*.

Psalm 84 says, "Blessed is the man in whose heart are the highways to Zion."[6] This speaks of a deep longing for God. The writer even cherished the journey to Zion because the end was meeting with God. Are we as Christians willing to cherish the journey? I wondered. Do we desire God so much that the journey itself becomes a joy?

With another lady, I began monthly encouragement calls. Surveying my circumstances, I realized my ministry could expand even further. I initiated Internet encouragement calls to missionaries outside of our organization, and invited more people from the Japanese church and ESL classes to our apartment for meals.

Though I was ministering to others, my faith was still shaky. Once, while reading *The Necessity of Prayer*, I was assailed by doubt again. The author talked about the need to cast away doubt, to persevere in order to pray effectively. I questioned if perhaps I wasn't healed yet because of my own shortcomings—the weakness of my faith; the fact that I was so often tired, lacking in perseverance; and so on.

But my shortcomings didn't govern God. Along with those times of doubt, there were also times when He'd called my faith into flame—into a raging bonfire.

The next day, as I read *The Necessity of Prayer* again, I was encouraged. Though I'd been discouraged the day before, in the present moment I was filled with trust. Such was the ebb and flow of life. So, rather than feel guilty at my own feebleness, I opted to enjoy that moment of faith and hope and trust, that moment of the Father's provision and sustenance.

I sometimes felt like a child just learning to walk, and kept coming back to an assurance in the Psalms.

> The steps of a man are established by the Lord;
> And He delights in his way.
> When he falls, he shall not be hurled headlong;
> Because the Lord is the One who holds his hand.
> (Ps. 37:23–24)

In reading these verses, I've always had the image of a toddler and her father in my mind's eye. She's wobbling along with halting steps, and the father is patiently walking alongside, holding her hand to steady and protect her from harm.

When first learning this verse in university, I mis-memorized a word. For a long time, I thought the Bible said, "If he falls." What great release and freedom were mine when I realized that the wording was not *if* but *when*. Our Father is tender and patient and knows our frailty. He knows we <u>will</u> fall. There is no question of it. But He will be present to catch us and to help us regain our footing.

CHAPTER 38

# A Hug from God

Over the preceding months, Chelsea had become increasingly dear to me. She consistently demonstrated a heart of compassion, and I'd never before met anyone who was so sensitive to the moods and needs of others. She would soon prove this in a most remarkable way.

One day was particularly difficult for me. Peter went to work in the morning. He came home for an hour before heading off in a different direction to play violin for the dedication ceremony of a new church building. After his performance, he would attend a meeting with the pastors in the church planting project. Both events were to take place at the same location, about half an hour away from our apartment. The dedication started at 4:00 p.m., and the meeting at 6:30, but somehow I got my wires crossed. I thought that everything would be done by 6:30 p.m. and that Peter would be home in the evening. As dinnertime approached, I developed a craving for a burger and decided to ask Peter to get McDonald's takeout on the way home. My mouth watered in anticipation.

He telephoned just before 6:30 p.m. to tell me that the dedication was done and that they were being served a meal. We then realized our mistake. He'd thought there were leftovers in the fridge for my dinner (they'd been polished off at lunchtime), and I'd thought he was coming home. The result was that he hadn't gotten me out any pots for cooking. The pots were stored in one of our low kitchen cupboards. In my state, I couldn't bend down to get them. They might as well have been on the moon.

I cried. I was hungry and frustrated with my own helplessness. I couldn't cook myself a decent supper and was disappointed at my unfulfilled McDonald's craving. Peter offered to call someone from church to help me get the pots, but I refused. After all, I was a grown woman; I could be creative. In the end, I prepared a grilled cheese sandwich in the toaster oven, some raw peppers, and cashews: all four food groups. I knew I could do it.

Peter later told me that he didn't share my predicament with anyone, but privately prayed that God would send someone to our door with food.

About half an hour after I finished eating, the doorbell rang. There on the step stood Charles and Chelsea. They handed me a bag of food.

"Did Peter send you?"

They looked confused. "No."

Up until that time, whenever someone had brought food it was always homemade, except for once when there were grocery store goodies. However, when I looked into the bag, there was a Big Mac meal, maple custard pie, and Coke from McDonald's.

How amazing and tender our God is! He more than cares for our every need, and even for some things we don't strictly need. It was like getting a big hug from Him.

We later shared with Charles and Chelsea that they had been God's specific answer to Peter's prayer. Charles was not a Christian, so we excitedly wondered how he might react when he heard that God had used him as an answer to our prayer. How would this change his spiritual perspective?

## CHAPTER 39

# Matters of Faith

I continued to learn about my new faith, and recorded some important lessons in my journal.

February 17, 2012

What is the relationship between faith, the flesh, and pleasing God?

Hebrews 11:6 says, "And <u>without faith</u> it is impossible to <u>please Him</u>, for he who comes to God must believe that He is and that He is a rewarder of those who seek Him."

Romans 8:8 says, "Those who are <u>in the flesh</u> cannot <u>please God</u>." (emphases mine)

Is there a connection? Perhaps there's a link between being in the flesh and having a lack of faith. Both are conditions in which we can't hope to please God.

What does the Bible say 'in the flesh' means?

- Those in the flesh set their minds on the things of the flesh as opposed to the things of the Spirit. This results in death.[1]
- The flesh is hostile toward God.[2]
- The flesh doesn't subject itself to God's law and can't even do so.[3]

What about 'without faith'? What is faith?

"...the assurance of things hoped for, the conviction of things not seen..."[4]

Faith is trust; faith is submission to the plans and power of God, beyond the realm of the seen. It enables us to subject ourselves to God's law <u>because</u> we're sure of certain things we can't see. Faith allows us to experience life and peace because our minds are set on the things of the Spirit. The corollary to "without faith it is impossible to please God"[5] is 'without faith it is impossible to live a Spirit-led, Spirit-centred life', because it's not about me leading my life. It's about the <u>Spirit leading me</u>. This is only possible when I submit myself to God, knowing my assurance lies beyond the seen, in the unseen.

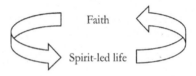

One causes the other, causes the other. No wonder the cycle has to be started with God, "the author and perfecter of our faith"[6]. He is the only One who can break into the loop; only He can start the cycle.

In Hebrews 11, one passage reads like a hall of fame for the giants of faith in Jewish history. There, I came across a phrase I'd not noticed before. First, the passage describes Abraham and his faith. He became a pilgrim to the land God had promised as an inheritance. Even after his arrival, he lived as a foreigner there. His faith was so deep that Hebrews talks about him looking for a city <u>with foundations</u>. This suggested something already constructed, not in the planning phase. God had promised; therefore, Abraham knew it was done. It was something steady and unshakeable.

"Lord, please help me to think of Your promise of healing as already accomplished," I prayed. "You are not changeable, and nothing can thwart You. Therefore, 'It is finished!'[7] You will be faithful to complete the work You have started, and because You are faithful it's already complete."

I realized that faith holds on to God and His promises against all odds. It may be shaken, but looks to the Father with trust for provision and replenishment. It isn't fazed by what the eye can or cannot see but waves the verse "we walk by faith, not by sight"[8] as a banner to give itself hope and encouragement. Faith waits upon God because of the conviction that victory <u>has already taken place</u>.

Up until this time, I'd continued to pray for healing even after God had promised it. However, I realized now that I needed to appropriate the victory and 'doneness' of God's promise. From then on, I accepted that healing had already been guaranteed. I stopped entreating, "God, please heal me" and instead acknowledged, "Thank You for healing me. Please complete it speedily."

# CHAPTER 40

# Scribbles and Scratchings

I would occasionally write poetry as my thoughts began to solidify around core ideas, and in some cases, my definitions of basic Christian concepts underwent radical redefinition.

> What is worship?
> It is a choice:
> The choice to praise
> In the midst of adversity.
>
> The choice to pursue
> A God who is silent
> Because He's worth it.
>
> The choice to believe
> That God is love
> When our comprehension of what love is
> Fails.
>
> The choice to press on,
> To keep shouting at the ceiling,
> To never give up
> Because He never gave up
> On me.
>
> What is worship?
> It is the choice to be broken,
> The choice to be healed.

The choice to be humbled
By our own weakness,
So we can revel
In Him.

Because when He finally speaks
We realize
That His voice is enough
To turn a parched soul
Into lushness and beauty, and
We are satisfied.

While in Canada, Julia, Peter, and I held weekly Bible studies together. In those times, God continually refreshed us with new insights in His Word. At one point, we discussed our relationship with Him and the fact that He is sometimes silent when we call.

"I don't understand why He wouldn't answer us every time we come to Him." Julia's eyes looked pained.

"We must be missing something," Peter said.

"The Bible compares our relationship with God to a bunch of human ones: king and servant, husband and wife, father and child—"

"How can a father not answer his child?"

"Wait a minute." My brow creased. "What if that's not the one we should be focusing on? What if there's something in the husband-and-wife relationship that could explain this?"

"Go on," Peter encouraged.

"We should look in the Song of Solomon. That's about romance. If there's something about the husband/wife connection, I'll bet it's in there."

We turned to our Bibles and started reading.

"I've found it!"

The others looked to me expectantly.

"Look in chapter 5. The woman thought her beloved would be there, but he was gone. She searched for him but couldn't find him. She called for him, but he didn't answer. She even got injured in her search. She was so earnest."

"Okay, but what does it mean?" Julia trailed off.

"Well, think about it. In a romantic relationship, it would be disheartening to always be pursuing someone but never be pursued yourself. Someone who's always passive and never initiates anything is emotionally dysfunctional; and so is someone who's content with the other person always being passive. God is anything but dysfunctional. He wants to have a healthy relationship with us. What if, in those times when God is silent, He's giving us a chance to pursue Him?"

"So when God is silent, He's really letting us show Him that we love and want Him too."

"Well that puts a whole new spin on things."

I'd often wondered about the silence of God and what it means to the Christian in his walk. Now I wondered if, like love, there was another dimension to it.

> The silence of God:
> A rest in the music,
> A break in conversation.
> Incredibly painful,
> Of unknown duration.
> But a musician would say
> A rest
> Turns
> Cacophony into a symphony.

## CHAPTER 41

# Fellowship of Suffering

Hanna and I continued our weekly Bible study, using a book called *Pilgrimage of the Heart* as our guide. I sometimes found great encouragement in its pages.

One February night in 2012, I couldn't help laughing with delight as I finished that week's chapter. In it, there was a partial summary of the key verses and thoughts on which I'd been meditating for the past several weeks, even before this study. Now I sent a note to the friend who'd recommended the book in the first place.

What amazing encouragement and confirmation of the things I've been learning, I wrote. What a sense of fellowship with people who have gone through these experiences before! I've realized over the last little while that an ordeal like this entails a degree of isolation and loneliness. It's an inseparable part of the experience and a necessary component of the trial. I've been able to connect with a few of our ministry partners who are in similar situations of suffering. Encouraging others always encourages me, so I've felt this 'fellowship of suffering' to some degree before; but it's really quite a delight to find it, unexpectedly, in the pages of a book.

Even as I considered these things, something else clicked in my brain. 'Fellowship of suffering': that was the phrase used in Philippians 3:10. I hadn't meant to repeat it just then. I'd put that phrase in quotes because it seemed oddly appropriate, but I didn't want to make it sound like I was snooty and part of some sort of exclusive club.

To my mind, the biblical 'fellowship of suffering' had always been some sort of association of people who had suffered, much like the alliance in Tolkien's *Fellowship of the Ring*. But I now realized that it truly was what it said: a form of fellowship.

The experience of suffering could be pretty terrible. If I were not a Christian, I might have gone insane with the pain and seclusion. I realized that unless someone had also gone through a similar trial, they could not hope to understand. Even Peter—who had been around the most and had been so understanding—sometimes made comments demonstrating a degree of incomprehension. Loneliness was not just physical (though that was important), but emotional too. The helplessness and unknown duration took a huge toll.

Those partners who were going through their own valleys of distress had generally been in that place for much longer than I. When e-mailing them, I always prayed that God would give me wisdom. In my lack of knowledge, I didn't want to say something that seemed good to me but might hurt them a little more. I thought that this understanding of separation, loneliness, and suffering must be the fellowship Paul talked about. It was very sweet and very precious. There was always an aspect of "I wish you weren't here with me, but at the same time I'm so grateful you are."

## CHAPTER 42

# Time Marches On

God continued to increase in me a passion to see the people of Okinawa come to know Him, and confirmed past promises of fruitfulness for His kingdom.

One day when I turned to my devotions, God led me to a special verse: "After you have suffered for a little while, the God of all grace, who called you to His eternal glory in Christ, will Himself perfect, confirm, strengthen and establish you."[1]

"This is for you," His Spirit whispered to mine.

At around that time, He also allowed me to see some of the effects of my ministry. In February, Seaside Chapel commissioned and sent off a new couple to start their own church with regular services. Peter told me that when the new pastor and his wife were speaking, they described some of the verses I'd shared with them when they'd come to visit. They'd decided to claim them as their theme for the new church. I felt incredibly honoured and encouraged that God had used some of my fumbling communications to touch them like that.

Nevertheless, a new dismay snuck up on me and struck a difficult blow.

One evening, Peter made an offhanded remark that caused me to go into an emotional spiral. It wasn't anything horrible or profound.

"Can you believe it's the end of February?" he said.

And I couldn't. By the end of February, I'd wanted to be so much further along. I'd wanted to be almost better, but I wasn't, and reality had just crashed in on me.

That day in the driving rain, I'd seen a spider's web between the spokes of our balcony railing. The rain was pummelling it, yet it remained intact.

"Please help me to be like the spider's web," I prayed. "These feelings may pummel, but You are my strength. Anchor my web in You, for Your foundations are good and sure."

As we contemplated the previous month, gratitude returned and we couldn't help thanking God for the work He was doing in spite of, or perhaps even because of, my injury.

We realized that our relationships with the Japanese people were deepening at an unexpected rate. It was almost as if the fact that we were going through adversity was acting as an accelerant to our relationships. The concept of mutual indebtedness is really integral to developing deep relationships in Japan. This was a foreign, and sometimes unwelcome, concept to our North American mindset, but we learned to really embrace it. It usually takes years and years to build up sufficient mutual indebtedness for significant relationships to blossom. Before my injury, the indebtedness would likely have been seen as very unbalanced. After all, we'd just left our country and family to come and serve in Okinawa. However, now the church was able to care for us with visits, food, and other gifts; meaningful relationships were being constructed.

Meanwhile, there were more and more instances of people being influenced by the verses and encouragements I shared with them from God's Word when they visited. It would seem that though I wasn't up and about as much as I would have liked, God was using most encounters for significant impact.

In considering this, I felt as though God had given me a glimpse of a reality different from the one I usually saw.

"You don't need to surround yourself with activity to be effective," He said. "Just surround yourself with Me."

# CHAPTER 43

# 'Potential'

Despite God's assurances of value and effectiveness, from time to time the physical experience of being restricted to bed seemed to overwhelm my spiritual reality. To my chagrin, a few people who were not direct observers of our situation seemed to succumb to this trap as well. Their comments only served to reinforce my own misconceptions about my value, until one day I started to question the labels that had been applied to me.

March 5, 2012

I've been ruminating on two phrases over the last few days. The first is 'out of commission'. I've almost used it to describe my situation over the last little while, but I realize that it's a bit of a misnomer. A child of God is never out of commission. He always has some use for us.

At one point in this journey, I read Psalm 43:5, which says, "hope in God, for I shall again praise Him." I said to myself, *Yes, when I'm better I'll praise Him again.*

Another psalm talks about declaring God's glory in the assembly[1]. Again, I thought, *I can't wait until I'm better so I can do that.*

The second phrase is something that someone else said to me, as he talked about looking forward to me being better. "You have so much to offer," he said.

I know what he meant, and the surface sentiment is lovely, but I wonder if such a statement has a faulty premise.

"You have so much to offer"—what does it mean? You have so much potential (thank you!), but maybe you're not living up to it? What if potential—if fulfilment of potential—is a subjective human construct? What if this statement does not take into account the plans God has for us—plans so much higher than human ones that we can't even begin to comprehend them? What if God's plans for us are higher than our own plans for ourselves?

What if the only potential I have, in and of myself, leads to hell? All other 'potential' is God's grace to me, giving me His gifts.

My promise doesn't lie in the things I could do. It lies in the One who makes all things possible.

My being injured is not wasted potential. I am not out of commission. I am still a commissioned officer serving under Jesus, my commander. I am still useful in God's kingdom. Don't be lulled into seeing the world through your physical eyes.

My mission field is different. My relationships with people here are different. But by saying, "You have so much potential", you invalidate my ministry now—the new, different one that God has given me.

We give lip service to putting our relationship with God above ministry. But when our expectations are taken away—when all we have left is God—are we content? Do we really believe what we've been saying?

When God chooses to give us a different ministry than we expected, is it good enough? Or do we stomp our foot like an obstinate toddler, demanding the one we wanted?

Ministry will flow out of our relationship with God. It's simple. It doesn't matter if we can run and jump and play, or if we're bedridden. The question is: will we see it? Will we allow God to work in our weakness? When all eyes are turned to people more able than me, will I still be an instrument of God's glory?

## CHAPTER 44

# Friends of Job

The preceding months had alternated between struggle and victory, despair and joy, turmoil and peace. But there was also another—darker—undercurrent present in our lives.

Some from our organization, whom we considered friends, had their own speculations about the reason I was still recovering from my injury. At first unaware of this, at one point we were copied on a string of e-mails meant for someone else. We were horrified. The person whom they depicted was like a grotesque caricature of me—barely recognizable. The implication was that I was a neurotically fearful person who didn't want to go through more pain and was suspicious of doctors. Deeply traumatized at these portrayals, we called our mentors, Joshua and Sophie. They suggested that we pray over the string of e-mails, as Hezekiah prayed over Sennacarib's letter in the Bible[1].

When the call ended, we printed out the chain of e-mails, laid the papers on the floor, and prayed for wisdom and God's intervention. Afterward, I had a mental image of Jesus standing before Pilate, silent.[2] I went to share this with Peter, only to find that God had given him the exact same picture in his mind. We were not to respond. We no longer needed to defend ourselves. God would be our defense.

That night, I had a horrible sleep. My mind kept playing everything over and over. I tried to take thoughts captive and quoted scripture to myself, to no avail. Eventually, I decided to use the time productively, and prayed for others.

Then my mind started to wander. I don't know if I was awake or asleep, but in my mind's eye, I saw a larger-than-life version of the horrible caricature in those e-mails. It started to laugh, and as it laughed, it changed into a terrifying skull. The laughing mouth opened wider and wider until it stayed fixed and became the mouth of a tomb. My field of view zoomed out, and I saw not far away Golgotha and the three crosses there.

"I died to defeat this," Jesus said to me. I knew that He meant the grotesqueness of lies and sin and death.

I slept soundly.

The next morning, I reflected on the previous night.

"You didn't just die to defeat those things," I said to Jesus. "You *became* them—for me."

I felt sick at the thought of His beauty marred by such ugliness, and cried a few tears of gratitude.

Over the next few days, Jesus continued to gently and tenderly hold our hands as we walked through the dense web of innuendo around us.

One morning before dawn, I woke up and thanked God for the freedom of knowing He was our defender.

Galatians 2:20 came to mind: "I have been crucified with Christ; and it is no longer I who live, but Christ lives in me; and the life I now live in the flesh I live by faith in the Son of God who loved me, and delivered Himself up for me."

At that moment I saw my reputation, the truth about myself, nailed to the cross along with Jesus'.

"It is no longer I who live, but Christ lives in me."

My chest started to feel lighter, as if the air I was breathing had somehow changed; as if all my life I'd been inhaling thick, greasy gravy, but now I was breathing true air—breathing as I was meant to, all along. The air seemed alive somehow. The lightness continued to spread, and my whole torso felt like it had become a giant lung, filled with this living air. There was such a sense of joy and peace and utter belovedness. All I could do was breathe. All I *wanted* to do was breathe. In and out, in and out.

I laughed to myself when I thought of that song:

> This is the air I breathe:
> Your holy presence,
> Living in me.³

I felt myself, and yet not myself. I don't know how to describe it other than to say that there was a sense of being together with God, but not as individuals. I was not the dominant personality, nor did I want to be. I was just happy to be loved, and to be breathing.

In and out, in and out.

I fell asleep.

---

Sometimes, like Job's friends, a few people who were godly on the surface would say things that sounded good, until we deeply thought about the underlying implications and held their words up against the lens of scripture. I once more picked up my pen and began to sift through truth and error.

March 11, 2012

> I've been thinking about the words 'invalid' and 'invalid'. One is a noun; the other, an adjective: prejudice built right into our language. How many times do we think of invalids as invalid? How many times do we say, "Tsk, tsk," and shake our heads at the 'wasted potential'?
>
> It would seem to me that unless someone's ministry has already been publicly proven (like Joni Eareckson Tada's), we don't often look at invalids as having huge potential to be used of God. This is really sad, because I've seen myself how easy it is to buy into others' opinions of my usefulness and to fall into the trap of dreaming

about all the things I'll do when I'm 'better'. But <u>now</u> is the time I've been given. Waiting until I'm better does not honour God.

Over the last little while, I've realized that Job suffered much more than I once thought. His tribulation did not end with the loss of his children, possessions, and health. It was augmented by the false consolations of his friends. Their words of 'wisdom', their questioning of his integrity, their prescriptions for godliness yielded another form of suffering. I've found that this sort can be much more insidious and can pierce much more deeply.

So let us not allow our words to inflict more suffering, to falsely limit an individual's true value, or to invalidate the people whom God loves and uses.

## CHAPTER 45

# The Spring

Our organization connected us with an agency in Canada called MissiMed, that deals with missionaries' health while they're overseas. One of their doctors was able to consult and give advice while I was physically unable to go and see a specialist in Japan. He emphatically confirmed that I was doing the right thing by avoiding the car vibrations that had worsened my condition. I was relieved to find someone who understood my logic, and happy to have medical feedback on my situation.

The time of our organization's annual spring conference on mainland Japan was now at hand. Given my injury, we weren't able to travel there with the other missionaries, but we did call in to participate. The first day was training for short-term missionaries.

I had been developing a friendship with the coordinator over the preceding months, and she asked me to lead a devotional that morning. The things I shared were well-received, and I enjoyed contributing.

The Internet connection at later sessions wasn't very good, and the signal cut out quite regularly. We strained to hear each word, which was draining, but the truths we gleaned from the speaker's messages were well worth the effort. I recorded them in my journal.

March 18, 2012

God has been at work, yet again. It started when He told us that we didn't have to defend ourselves. I've been gradually releasing this responsibility and leaving my defense to Him.

When I find my thoughts spooling, rehashing everything, and getting mired in negativity, I've started saying, "You don't have to defend yourself, Valerie, even to yourself."

At one point, Luke 12:11-12 came to mind: "…do not become anxious about how or what you should speak…for the Holy Spirit will teach you in that very hour what you ought to say."

God has been rooting my security more and more in Him and has also been gathering trustworthy people around me so that I feel less threatened. However, with everything that's happened, there's still that tug toward paranoia and self-protection.

The speaker at the conference we're now attending has shared some pertinent reflections:

"If we insulate ourselves from hurt, we also insulate ourselves from intimacy," he said. "Self-protection is a huge barrier to relationship."[1] (I've seen how destructive self-protection can be, particularly to people who are relationally close by. I don't want to be like that!)

"We need to focus on giving honour to God and not be fearful."[2] (I sometimes struggle with this. But fear has no place here[3], and I reject it in favour of Jesus' love.)

Somehow I need to forgive, even while people are still acting against me. I think it's significant that Jesus prayed "Father, forgive them" while He was being crucified. He didn't wait until after He was resurrected, or even until just before He died. He prayed as they were dividing His clothes, <u>while He was still suffering</u>.

Father, please enable me to forgive. Jesus, mine is not the standard by which all other suffering is measured. Yours is. Mine is not unique or even that severe in the grand scheme of things. You've gone through far worse. Please help me to live my life "by faith in the Son of God, who loved me, and delivered Himself up for me"[4]. Help me to crucify my old sinful tendencies and desires, and enter into Your truth, peace, and love.

Luke 6:27-28: "...do good to those who hate you, bless those who curse you, pray for those who mistreat you..."

# CHAPTER 46

# Compassion and Suffering

I found myself ruminating now and then on the nature of suffering, and the interactions that take place between those who experience and those who observe it. One morning as I journaled, my thoughts finally coalesced into something meaningful.

> March 19, 2012
>
> We evaluate others based on our own experience. It's human nature. We are our own frame of reference. The degree to which we've suffered becomes the standard against which we measure others. But this is not productive.
>
> If someone has endured more than we, then we venerate him. Yet a suffering person does not need this. He needs to be understood. He needs community. If someone who has not been afflicted as deeply desires to help, the best thing that person can do is to assume the humble posture of a learner, avoid meaningless prescriptions, and listen. Veneration is not particularly helpful, and can actually be harmful to the sufferer should he currently be in a phase of self-pity.
>
> If someone is enduring less than we, the tendency is to disdainfully dismiss him as shallow. Self-righteousness grows within our hearts, and the sufferer is not helped. There is no love or tenderness imparted—or at least, none of a genuine quality.
>
> But suffering is relative. It has everything to do with the maximum a given person has encountered thus far in

life. If the current trial exceeds all previous experience, then it will be felt more greatly. If it is a fraction of the past, it will be felt less.

We cannot possibly know the levels of hardship which others have encountered. There is a reason Jesus said, "Do not judge lest you be judged."¹

This is one thing I love about the cross. It becomes the standard by which we judge suffering. Its emotional, spiritual, and physical misery and shame are so much greater than everyone else's. Where, then, is veneration? Where is disdain? They are both crucified with Christ, for with Him and Him only does suffering begin and end.

Jesus' cross enables us to be truly compassionate people.

It would be rare, if not impossible, to come upon two situations where suffering is humanly judged to be equal. There are too many variables. If one person judges equality, likely the other will not. But that's not the point. Under the cross, all suffering is changed from a subjective measure to an objective one. All is put into perspective. Our estimation of ourselves diminishes. Veneration and disdain are non-issues.

The one who has endured more is freed to empathize. The one who has endured less is freed to listen and learn. The awareness of 'me' fades away, and we are empowered to be compassionate people of grace.

"For we do not have a high priest who cannot sympathize with our weaknesses…."²

## CHAPTER 47

# Glimmers of Hope

Though my recovery continued to progress, it was painstakingly slow. I passed the majority of time laid up in bed, waiting eagerly for the next opportunity to exit my prison, if even briefly. I'd spent December in pain, able to be up just long enough to take care of bathing and personal needs. By the end of January, I could be up for an hour per day, fifteen to twenty minutes at a time. In late February, it was two and a half hours per day, thirty minutes at a time. At the end of March, my capability leapt to six hours per day, in segments of one hour. I was still unable to sit or bend significantly, but was greatly encouraged as the bonds that held me to my bed loosened.

The Japanese school year ends in March, there is a holiday, and the new year starts in April. Similar to North America, many church programs parallel the school schedule, so by this time we were gearing up for the coming year.

Our previous ESL course had finished, so we began a new twelve-week one: *Highlights from the Life of Jesus*. Thrilled with the classroom discussions on God and His Word, we keenly anticipated His continued revelation to the students.

During this period we also planned to start a few new ministries in addition to our established ones. With all this focus on the future, I yearned desperately for the completion of my recovery and a return to full health and capability.

Even as I prayed for accelerated healing, I began to feel the stirrings of discontent. From past experience, I knew these had the potential to spin out of control. Dietrich Bonhoeffer once wrote, "Everything we cannot thank God for, we reproach Him for."[1] So I asked God to enable me to be grateful. In response, Jesus reminded me of my deeper desire: for Him.

Beginning in February, I started to experience a strong feeling in my spirit. If I had to put a label on it, I'd call it anticipation.

I told Peter about this. He reacted with surprise. He'd experienced the same feeling.

When we asked God what this could possibly mean, one word was imprinted on both of our minds: "June."

We eagerly wondered what God could possibly have in store for us.

In my Bible study book, I came across a line that summarized the exquisite anticipation we now experienced: "Somewhere in the darkness is the imperceptible glimmer of hope that comes to the heart of a pilgrim during trial."[2]

This reminded me of a story I'd once heard in church. Researchers were curious about the effect that state of mind can have on behaviour, so they decided to run a rather cruel experiment using rats. Their goal was to measure the influence of hope. They placed a rat in a basin of water in an entirely dark room and timed how long it would swim before giving up. The basin's walls were too high for the rodent to escape, and it struggled to stay afloat for about three minutes before finally succumbing to the cold and dark.

Following this, the researchers placed a second rat in the same tub in the same room. This time, however, they left the room's door open a crack. A sliver of light shone in, just touching the water where the rodent swam for its life. This one lasted for thirty-six hours—more than seven hundred times longer than its compatriot.

*How much more hope do we have*, I thought, *not just in a little beam of light, but in the God of the universe!*

We constantly felt God's hand of encouragement and blessing upon us. Studying Japanese, I forged ahead toward linguistic improvement. Eleanor, my language helper, continued to visit several times a week for conversation practice, and I appreciated the opportunity to hone my speaking and listening skills. Sometimes we held impromptu Bible studies if one of us had learned something special in our devotional times.

One day, I received a really high compliment. I'd just started learning informal verb forms in my Kumon studies. Up until then, I'd only known formal ones and had been using them with everybody.

Eleanor was sixty-eight years old, and age has a big impact on social status in Japan.

"I'm assuming that I should use the formal form with you," I said.

"No, no," she said, "use the informal, the form for friends."

Wow!

There were also strong signs of hope in my body's recovery process. I felt almost ready to start experimenting with the limits of my physical capabilities, and in mid-April, I wondered whether to try sitting.

*I haven't felt a twinge of pain on the toilet for a couple of weeks at least*, I thought. *Maybe it's time.*

A few hours after this, there was a sharp pain, as if God were saying, "Not yet."

*Perhaps I should try climbing the stairs again*, I wondered next. I was tempted to do this even though my body didn't quite feel good enough for it.

The next day in my devotions, I read:

> "Cease striving and know that I am God;
> I will be exalted among the nations,
> I will be exalted in the earth."
> The Lord of hosts is with us;
> The God of Jacob is our stronghold.
> (Ps. 46:10–11)

"Okay, God, I get the message," I prayed. "I won't force it. Please continue to guide me and help me to submit my desires for speedy healing to You. It's enough that You have promised."

## CHAPTER 48

# A Change in Plans

Most of Peter's former and current Bible ESL students who weren't Christians were men. This was really special in Japanese culture because women typically make up the bulk of the Christian community. After having attended Bible classes, by this point all but one had started coming to church on Sundays. Several of them reached out to Peter socially and expressed a desire to become friends outside of the classroom.

Meanwhile, I continued to invite people from the church into our home. We developed a regular rotation of about twenty visitors. Some came on a monthly basis; others came biweekly or weekly.

As my recovery continued, the doctor from MissiMed recommended that I engage in physiotherapy to aid in rehabilitation. However, we were told that in Japan, physiotherapists don't make house calls.

I contacted a Canadian chain specializing in backs and asked if they would help me remotely. The lady I talked with was hesitant to open her practice to liability problems, since she hadn't physically examined me. I prayed for favour with her, explained my situation, and told her I would be happy to sign a liability waiver.

God granted my request, and in her, I found a new champion for my cause. In the end, she contacted her head office on my behalf and connected me with the most senior physiotherapist in the entire organization. From our first phone call, despite my repeated offers of payment, he insisted on giving consultations free of charge. Once more, God had provided for me; those exercises became integral to my ongoing improvement.

On the night of April 17, we received an e-mail from a leader in our organization requesting a phone call on the following day. We found ourselves anxious at this and went to God in prayer. He gave us some Bible verses and reminded us of our hope in Him:

> No king is saved by the size of his army;
>     no warrior escapes by his great strength.
> A horse is a vain hope for deliverance;
>     despite all its great strength it cannot save.
> But the eyes of the Lord are on those who fear Him,
>     on those whose hope is in His unfailing love,
> to deliver them from death
>     and keep them alive in famine.
> We wait in hope for the Lord;
>     He is our help and our shield.
> In Him our hearts rejoice,
>     for we trust in His holy name.
> May Your unfailing love be with us, Lord,
>     even as we put our hope in You.
> (Ps. 33:16–22)

Our lives changed dramatically the next day, April 18. Our organization told us they had decided that given the delicate stage of my injury, the lack of a firm diagnosis, and the unknown timeline for recovery, the best course of action would be for us to end our ministry and return to Canada. Permanently.

We asked not to go into details, but arranged to have a follow-up call in two days. We needed some time to absorb the news.

Until then, I'd only been able to stand for an hour at a time before needing rest; but when we finished the call, I found I'd unwittingly been up for two hours.

Shortly after this, our doorbell rang. To my surprise, there was Eleanor. She'd come for our regular language practice, and it was all I could do not to burst into tears in front of her.

After that session, Peter and I ran to God in prayer. We poured out our hearts to Him for two hours. Then I felt a whisper in my spirit.

"Go downstairs and walk around the park."

"Was that You, God?" I asked. "Your voice is so soft. Did I hear you right?"

"Go downstairs and walk around the park."

I hadn't been able to do this for almost five months. I was scared of incurring a setback but obeyed anyway. We strolled around. Savouring each step, I smiled at an old man (he smiled back) and prayed for some kids who were with their parents.

Finally we came to the bottom of the stairs leading to our apartment. This was the part I'd really feared. Climbing stairs had been hard on my body in the past, but this time, I felt the same afterward as I had before going out.

When I later reflected on everything that had happened that day, there was a strong impression on my spirit: the plans God had for us were no less exciting than they'd been two days ago.

Distressed over our organization's decision, Peter and I decided to fast and pray from Wednesday until the phone call on Friday. Those two days, we cried out to God as we never had before. We soon fell into a rhythm: praying intensively to exhaustion for one or two hours, resting for one or two hours, and starting again.

We requested God's intervention on our behalf—that He would change the hearts of the decision makers, that He would give them dreams and visions, and that He would speak to their spouses as He spoke to Pilate's wife. That was on Wednesday.

On Thursday, we sent an SOS e-mail to a few of our closest friends and family. Hopeful of a change in our organization's opinions, we didn't give details but simply shared our weariness at a particularly intensive spiritual battle, and asked for special prayer for both ourselves and the decision makers in our situation.

After this, Peter and I continued in our own marathon. We fervently asked God to change either our hearts or those of the people in charge. That Thursday, our attitudes began to shift. A darkness settled over our spirits—not oppression per se—just the feeling that God was not going to do what we'd asked the day before. I think He was preparing us for what would come next.

After Friday's call, it was apparent our organization did not believe that in my injured state I had a ministry at all. It would not change its decision; an appeal would not be entertained. They had determined that our work would end on May 31. We eventually negotiated to stay in Japan until my body was physically able to handle the plane ride back to Canada without sustaining further injury.

After the call was over, I tried to contact my sister but she was driving, and it was unsafe to talk. Less than a minute later, the phone rang. It was someone from an organization named TragIssist International.

On one Sunday in 2011, while still in Canada, Peter and I were having lunch with the pastor of a partnering church when the conversation took an interesting turn. Pastor Alden indicated that he was friends with the chief operating officer of TragIssist, which focused on carrying out relief efforts in Japan and around the world.

This man had been using a special means of planning how to get emergency provisions to disaster areas. He'd been approaching this type of problem from a mathematical perspective, but this was the exact area of my engineering speciality, and I knew some of my tools could complement his methods.

A few months after agreeing to put me in touch with the chief operating officer, Pastor Alden died, and the possibility of working with TragIssist faded into the background in light of all our other preparations for Japan.

In April 2012, a week before the news from our organization, TragIssist Japan had come to mind. I'd filled out an online form volunteering my services, since there was no way to contact the chief operating officer directly.

That Friday, TragIssist responded to my inquiry. It turned out that the executive I wanted to contact was now doing relief work in Thailand. The lady I talked with took down all the information on potential benefits of my expertise and passed it on to the planning department.

We had no idea if TragIssist was where God was leading us, or if He was simply encouraging us in our time of need. Whatever the case, our spirits were buoyed by that call.

When we were later able to get in touch with Julia, she offered great encouragement and a listening ear. We spent the following day absorbing the news and phoning the rest of our family to explain everything to them. Each conversation encouraged us in a different way: yet another one of God's provisions.

Our newsletter was due out shortly after we were told of our termination. In it, we wrote:

> When we got the news, our world caved in, and we spent the next forty-eight hours fasting and praying. God was wonderfully vocal in our distress, and we've come away with several strong impressions on our spirits. I will share two here.

## On the Potter's Wheel

1. From *The Lion, The Witch and the Wardrobe*: "Aslan is on the move."[1] God is at work here. We don't understand what He's doing, but we know He is very active. Often the darkest points in our lives herald the dawn.
2. God's plans for us are no less exciting now than they were two weeks ago.

We're often bewildered by what God is doing. He could have stopped this before it even started. But the fact is that He has been incredibly active and wonderful: teaching us countless lessons and using us in many ways. We trust in His plans for us.

Thank you so much for standing firm with us. It only took one morning for three thousand people to come to Christ on the day of Pentecost. We serve a big God, and we still believe He will do big things. We encourage you to join us in our sense of expectation as we watch to see what our great God will bring about. In our anticipation, we can't help but ask: "What will He do next?"

With the news of our termination, I completely deflated. All my motivation to engage in language study, and any of the other projects I'd been tackling, evaporated.

Early in the morning of April 22, God woke me up. "Dear one, I know you are suffering," He said. "I know your pain. I will not command you to do this, but I will ask: Would you be willing to keep learning Japanese? You may not be able to use it for much longer. You may cry with every word you memorize, your heart will rip a little more open with each bit of grammar you learn, but if you're willing, this will be your act of love to the Japanese: increasing your ability to communicate with them over your last months."

My answer was yes, but I knew I would need God's strength to do it.

I continued to process this interchange during the following morning.

"God, if I do this, I have a request to make of You," I prayed. "Please supernaturally enable our minds and mouths. We don't have time to learn the language well. Please give us the gift of tongues, that we may be able to proclaim Your love to all we meet—in the language of their hearts."

After we sent out our newsletter, our friends and family responded with overwhelming support and prayer. The Japanese church in general would not know of the organization's decision for another month while Higa sensei and the church board put forward an appeal. However, in the end it would be unsuccessful.

## CHAPTER 49

# Releasing

We were in mourning, in every sense of the word. I looked around the land we loved, around the place which we'd made as a home, and was bereft. My digestive system was in an uproar. It would only tolerate the blandest of food. I took naps in the middle of the day, and wasn't sure if it was because I was exhausted from staying up late night after night to call and explain the situation to partners back in Canada, or because for a few hours the sleep afforded me a blessed escape from the powerful emotions buffeting my already-bludgeoned soul.

Two weeks ago, I would never have thought I could come to the place where I now found myself: starting to accept the very real possibility that our time in Okinawa was ending and that we might be going back to Canada.

A small voice whispered to my spirit, "I'm not finished with you yet." But we also started to feel small releases from Okinawa, as if God were saying, "I will take care of the people here. Don't worry about them."

One of our ESL students, Felix, was a professional photographer. Virtually all of Peter's non-Christian friends had just bought new cameras. A few weeks before, we'd talked with a Japanese Christian family from church about the possibility of starting a camera club; now we discovered they'd decided to move forward with the idea. The church would hold a class, with Felix as the teacher.

"I don't need you…" God said softly.

Peter had become good friends with Daniel, a man passionate for reaching the lost. Daniel was full of ideas and enthusiasm; it was rare to see such passion flowing from someone who was not himself a new Christian. At one point, Daniel worked at a seniors' centre; whenever there was a celebration or festival, he would bring Peter in to play hymns on the violin. Daniel would then share the gospel by explaining the meanings of the hymns.

Throughout their friendship, Daniel had developed many ideas for ministry. Peter had gently challenged him to get them off the drawing board and into reality. As a result, Daniel had started following his advice. He'd recently quit his job and spent the past few months deciding what to do next with his life.

Meanwhile, we'd been concerned about the future of the church in Okinawa. Many pastors were older, with no clear successor to carry on their ministries. Indeed, the average age of pastors throughout Japan is between sixty and seventy.

One day over lunch, Daniel announced to Peter that he would be returning to Bible college.

"...to take care of them," God said.

*Oh, but I so wanted to stay here, to be part of Your plans for this place*, my heart cried.

Sadness and joy and release—somehow all woven together.

In Psalm 50, God makes it clear He does not need sacrifices from His people. Instead, He commands:

> Offer to God a sacrifice of thanksgiving,
> And pay your vows to the Most High;
> Call upon Me in the day of trouble;
> I shall rescue you, and you will honor Me.
> (Ps. 50:14–15)

"Okay, God," I prayed. "You have said You do not despise the brokenhearted.[1] You will rescue me. My sacrifice, my act of worship, is to thank You for the good things You have done, are doing, and will yet do."

> But as for me, I will watch expectantly for the Lord;
> I will wait for the God of my salvation.
> My God will hear me.
> Do not rejoice over me, O my enemy.
> Though I fall I will rise;
> Though I dwell in darkness, the Lord is a light for me.
> (Mic. 7:7–8)

"These things I have spoken to you, that in Me you may have peace," He responded. "In the world you have tribulation, but take courage; I have overcome the world."[2]

Peter and I continued to have digestive problems. Often nauseated and unable to eat, we lost a lot of weight. But God was gentle with our broken hearts. From the day we learned of our termination, He began to open our eyes to a variety of possibilities for future ministry.

"I'm not finished with you yet," He said again.

## CHAPTER 50

# In the Park

The park across the street from our apartment was awash with all sorts of life: from many types of trees and foliage to bugs and fish, small animals, and people. The Japanese have a talent for creating picturesque landscapes that incorporate all of the senses. Several terra-cotta-roofed pavilions, offering shade from the sun and protection from the rain, were scattered along a meandering path. Benches and rocks to sit on, two playgrounds for the children, and a gushing waterfall easing into a large stream and pond completed the park's delights. The joyous laughter of children on holiday, or just out from school, often wafted up to our apartment. I took great pleasure in finally being able to regularly visit the park once more.

Sometimes at night we would hear what sounded like cats screaming or howling in pain. One day in late April, I walked around the park and saw two cats. They were very skittish, so I mimicked the sound of the little welcoming trill our pet cats used to make when we were growing up. They revealed themselves a little more, and I saw that someone had cut off their tails in different spots.

"Who cut off your tails?" I asked.

A prayer began to form in my mind. "God, I don't know if You'll be bringing us back here, but there's a scrappy part of me that wants to stay and fight the darkness in this place, to be here when You overcome it." With a touch of sheepish melodrama, I continued, "Please give me a sign. If we'll be coming back, just let these cats follow me as I walk."

## On the Potter's Wheel

I kept talking to the cats and softly doing the welcoming trills, and soon they were both following me. After I completed one circuit of the park, I went up to our apartment and collected the bowl of dinner that I'd been unable to eat earlier because my tummy was in turmoil.

When I arrived back downstairs, the ginger cat was no longer hiding under the car where I'd left him. The black-and-white one was nowhere to be seen. When I made the trill, the ginger cat came running. I threw him some of my dinner; he didn't really like it either.

He and I followed each other back across the stream to a pavilion. We had a good petting. He even licked my hand a little! The small black-and-white cat reappeared and allowed me to stroke him once or twice too.

We started to wend our way back, stopping at another enclosure for more petting. The ginger cat let me pick him up and place him on a picnic table so I could reach him better.

Eventually, I made my way back home. The cats accompanied me: the ginger one following a few paces behind, the black-and-white one—a kitten, really—bounding ahead and sporadically waiting for me to catch up.

They followed me right to the bottom of the stairs. It was absolutely delightful.

Peter and I later named the orange-and-white cat Ginger. He had half of his tail remaining. The black-and-white one, we christened Rhombus. He had just an inch-long stump.

A few nights later, I went for a walk in the park to try and find them again. They hadn't been around the day before, perhaps because the park had been exceptionally busy with children off of school for a holiday called Golden Week.

I found Rhombus pretty easily. While petting and feeding him bits of hot dog, I noticed a black cat sitting some distance away, watching us. I threw it a bit of food too, but it didn't come any closer.

I have nothing against black cats. My beloved childhood pet, Scamper, had been black; but at this point, I grew inexplicably uneasy. Then Rhombus' body language changed, and he started to growl. I remembered that back in my hometown, cats were used for witchcraft now and then. Remembering Jesus and the herd of swine, I knew that animals can at times be vessels for unclean spirits.

I'd been chattering away to Rhombus but now self-consciously decided to try an experiment. Turning my attention to the black cat, I said, "In the name of Jesus Christ, I command you to leave us alone."

The cat ran away, lickety-split. Then it turned around and tried to come back. I picked up Rhombus, usually very squirmy but now perfectly still, and prayed for God's protection over both of us.

With growing certainty, I kept commanding the unclean spirit in the cat to leave us alone and leave the park in the name of Jesus. Every time I said His name, the cat ran further away. Finally I declared that I was staking Jesus' flag on the park and asked the Holy Spirit to fill it. I didn't see the black cat again.

Later I found Ginger. We all had a nice petting and shared the hot dogs. When I telephoned Peter, he came down to meet Rhombus. Ginger had by that time gone off to engage in more interesting pursuits.

What a bizarre night.

## CHAPTER 51

# Surrounded

*Turn again our captivity, O Lord,*
*as the streams in the south.*
*They that sow in tears shall reap in joy.*
*He that goeth forth and weepeth, bearing precious seed,*
*Shall doubtless come again with rejoicing, bringing his*
*sheaves with him.*

—Psalm 126:4–6

Through this time, our hearts were in great flux. Sometimes they would be calm, as though God had poured oil on our troubled waters; at others, they would be full of anguish and pain. When we were utterly tired of the strong feelings buffeting our spirits and bodies, we would try to numb them by doing things that required no thought, mindlessly watching sitcom after sitcom on television.

I often felt stuck in a limbo of survival—just trying to hang on until things got better. But I didn't want to only survive. I wanted to thrive, to experience the abundant life. I asked God to help me take hold of His victory, to be triumphant even in difficult circumstances.

One morning, I tried to run away from those things that tore at my guts and chest—emotions so strong that I felt physically sick. There I was, playing a game on my phone and trying to escape from them—and by extension, from God. After all, He is truth; and as I faced Him, I knew my feelings would also come to the surface. But I knew I couldn't run forever. I needed Him too much.

He was tender and patient with me; after experiencing His rest again, I wrote in my journal.

May 2012

> Thank You for the richness of Your life—a life so alive that everything else is by comparison inanimate, frozen in time and space.
>
> Thank You for the rain pounding down outside; it brings vitality and nutrition to Your creation. Thank You for Your waters of blessing in here that soothe and refresh my spirit. You are God, and there is no other. Heaven and earth may pass away, but You remain: glorious and infinite and ALIVE.

Through this time, troubles swirled around us: the heartbreak of a lifelong dream being ripped away; the abandonment of a dear friend from Canada, who joined with our former organization in opposing our ministry in Japan; the vocal opinions of former colleagues, that I couldn't be useful on the mission field in my injured state and should go home; the ongoing stress of dealing with my injury; the loneliness of being an alien in a foreign culture where we couldn't communicate easily, and the only people who spoke our language had now rejected us; the requirement to act as though everything were normal with the people involved in our ministries while Higa sensei appealed the decision to send us home; and the uncertainty of whether we would be allowed to stay in Japan until I'd sufficiently healed, knowing that if negotiations failed I faced lifelong injury from the journey out of the country. At one point, we took a stress test to gauge where we might fall along the human continuum. Our result was three times higher than the point at which people start to have heart attacks.

Surrounded, as we were, it was easy to focus on the distresses encompassing us; it would have been simple to angrily centre our attention on those who'd caused us hurt, but God had bigger plans for us than this.

In my devotions one day, I read the last chapter of John. One section struck me.

After His resurrection, Jesus was together with His disciples near the end of His time on earth. He'd just foretold Peter's future imprisonment and death.

Peter pointed to John. "Lord, what about this man?"

"If I want him to remain until I come, what is that to you?" Jesus said. "You follow Me!"[1]

I felt as if God had spoken directly to me: "If I want to do something with others, what is that to you? They are Mine; I will deal with them. <u>You</u> follow <u>Me</u>."

This became my new mantra. Whenever I felt myself getting sucked into anxiety about the attitudes and actions of others, I repeated that phrase to myself: "You follow Me." Eventually, I found that Jesus filled my view and that there was no room for distractions. As I centred my focus on Him, in my weariness I could no longer identify myself apart from Him. Even in simple e-mails, "In Christ" was the only phrase I could pen as a sign-off. Life became much simpler.

When I was a little girl, my mother told me a story about a farmer who owned a brood of chickens. One night there was a fire in the hen house, but it wasn't discovered until it was too late to rescue the birds. The farmer and his family worked through the night to save the surrounding buildings from also being destroyed.

The following morning, sooty, sweaty, and tired, the farmer went out to survey the wreckage. At one point, in frustration he kicked at a rock lying in the midst of the scorched remains. To his surprise, a line of chicks scurried out from beneath it. The farmer knelt down to examine the rock more closely. In shock he realized it was the charred body of the mother hen. Shielding her chicks with her body, she had sacrificed herself to ensure their survival.

I always remembered this story whenever I happened upon a Bible verse that talked about God spreading His wings of protection over His people. One day, I continued this meditation in my journal.

Early Summer 2012

> Singing beneath the shadow of His wings denotes confidence in Him. We do not have to cower and quake and hide there until destruction passes us by. We are confident enough in the power and protection of our great God that we don't care if destruction knows where we are. It cannot touch us, for our refuge is in our Father: the mother hen who will indeed give up her very life for her offspring.
>
> There is a difference between 'hiding' and 'taking refuge'. One denotes fear; the other, quiet confidence.
>
> Thank You, Father, that we have nothing to fear. You alone are God, and our hearts expand in Your refuge. We do not have to shrink to avoid observation. In fact, we invite it. For as men observe us, their hearts will also be turned to praise You, and our singing becomes the adoration of a choir.

For a few weeks, the physiotherapist had been encouraging me to try sitting. I'd resisted for awhile, fearful of the repercussions. However, at this point, I decided to go ahead. After about one minute, the results were not good. A substantial amount of pain returned.

For several days following, I was in denial. *Sitting was hard on my body*, I thought. *It will take some time to bounce back.*

A week and a half later, I had to accept the reality that I'd regressed. Only then could I once more become ultra-vigilant to the requirements for healing.

God continued to draw friends around us, to encourage and strengthen us. My correspondence with pen pals was one of His chief methods, and one day I sent a note to a friend whose husband was also going through a time of physical suffering.

May 16, 2012

> I love that line in the song you shared, about how God "kindly veils our eyes"[2]. It's so true that we often wouldn't be able to face the future if we knew what it held.
>
> The other day I asked Peter if he would have been able to handle our current situation if not for his crisis of faith back at the beginning of the year. He said that he wouldn't have, and I think the answer is the same for me. Our Father has lovingly prepared us for this.
>
> But He's also confirmed to us again and again that He has something wonderful in store for us. In the nine days following the decision to send us home, He showed us nine different ministries that we could eventually start or join—both in Japan and back in Canada. He gave us no indication on which (if any) from that list might come to fruition, but we couldn't help finding some comfort in knowing we're never discarded in our Father's eyes.
>
> I can't remember where, but Paul talks about being afraid of becoming useless to God: of being put on a shelf. That's always been a fear of mine, but He's been so tenderly assuring us of the opposite that we can't help thanking Him for His comfort.

And so, we press on. We don't know what God will do next, or when we might come back to Canada, but we do know His purposes for us are higher than our plans for ourselves, and that's enough.

So here we wait, with open hands, asking for His guidance and wisdom. Because He is greater and wiser and higher and more in every way. Our life's ambition—the real ambition at the core of it all—is to be rooted in relationship with Him. We have no idea if this season in Japan is now over, but we can't help praising Him because He has made our deepest, most desperate dream come true: the dream to know and follow Him.

## CHAPTER 52

# Betrayed

It was now May 20, and while reading through some of my old journals, I came upon an entry from mid-November that talked about my fears. I felt a muted emotion and tried to ignore it, to stuff it back into whatever crevice it had seeped out from.

Instead, I initiated a conversation with Peter about the future. Somehow we ended up talking about my health and how much I'd missed the cats and walking in the park since trying to sit the previous week. This setback wasn't as bad as it could have been. My sensitivity to vibration continued to decrease; I could still bend to a good degree, get down on my knees, and do physiotherapy exercises on the floor. But I wasn't able to stand or walk as much. I couldn't help looking wistfully at that decision to sit and wishing to take it back.

Peter reminded me that for an entire month beforehand I'd considered trying to sit. It was the right decision; we needed to know how my body would react. We had no way of knowing without trying. Even the physiotherapist had thought we should do this. Nevertheless, I refused to be comforted; and Peter took me to task, confronting my desire to wallow and find someone to blame.

"What's this really about?" he asked.

"When I was reading my old journals this morning, I came to an entry with a list of all of my fears. And I realized: they've all come true. I turned them over to God, and they all came true."

"How does that make you feel?"

"Betrayed."

"By whom?"

"God."

"I'm going on a walk. You need to talk this out with Him." Peter left.

And there I was, lying in bed, avoiding this conversation for as long as possible by journaling out the history of what had happened in intricate detail. Now the history was complete, and the words I'd built up as a shield between me and God were falling away. There were very few left before I had to face my feelings head-on. The time was here.

Deep breath.

The time was now.

"God, I feel betrayed," I prayed. "Not just because my fears came true. I gave them to You because I couldn't handle living with them anymore. They were too heavy. You gave them back to me, as reality, in more manageable pieces. I can see how, in this, You've been caring for me.

"But the word that really stands out to me right now, out of all the words I've used today, is *pieces*. Pieces of dreams, shattered all around me. Pieces of fears, broken down into bite-sized chunks. When they're reassembled, they make a horrifying mosaic that, at the moment, I find completely overwhelming.

"I feel as though You've led me on a wild goose chase for more than a decade. I've used 'the best years of my life' to pursue a dream You planted in my heart—only to have You shatter it on the eve of its completion.

"I feel betrayed by You, Your people, and my body. Why did it have to go and wreck everything? Why did You have to go and wreck everything?

"You *say* that You have wonderful plans for me and my future, but how do I know those won't be ripped away as well? Am I just going to be a horrible object lesson for the rest of my life? An illustration of who-knows-what? Grotesque caricatures have been painted of me and my character. Will I eventually become them?"

I now realized that all those years ago, when He first placed that call to Japan on my heart, He'd said, "This is where I want you to go," not, "This is where I want you to *stay*." How many other heartbreaking times would I misinterpret His direction? How much more would I have to endure? How much of my life would be devoured by this?

"'For I know the plans that I have for you,' declares the Lord, 'plans for welfare and not for calamity to give you a future and a hope.'"[1]

When God brought those words to mind, I wept at His tenderness. Now I was faced with a choice: I could choose to keep wallowing and allow the enemy to make a play park of my brain, or I could choose to trust Him and all the wonderful experiences I'd had with Him.

"I can choose to trust You even when it looks like You've betrayed me," I prayed, "because even a circle can look like a straight line if it's big enough compared to the point of observation. You are bigger than the biggest circle, and I am smaller than the smallest dot. I choose You. I choose to trust Your promises because You don't change and neither do they. Because You've already proven Yourself to be true and faithful and altogether wonderful. Thank You for Your direction and guidance—to wherever that is in the future. Your ways are perfect, and I am complete—and content."

## CHAPTER 53

# Endings

*We are, not metaphorically but in very truth, a Divine work of art, something that God is making, and therefore something with which He will not be satisfied until it has a certain character. Here again we come up against what I have called the 'intolerable compliment'. Over a sketch made idly to amuse a child, an artist may not take much trouble: he may be content to let it go even though it is not exactly as he meant it to be. But over the great picture of his life—the work which he loves, though in a different fashion, as intensely as a man loves a woman or a mother a child—he will take endless trouble—and would doubtless, thereby give endless trouble to the picture if it were sentient. One can imagine a sentient picture, after being rubbed and scraped and re-commenced for the tenth time, wishing that it were only a thumb-nail sketch whose making was over in a minute. In the same way, it is natural for us to wish that God had designed for us a less glorious and less arduous destiny; but then we are wishing not for more love but for less.*[1]

—C. S. Lewis

Endings are very important in Japan, so we'd developed the habit of throwing a small party to celebrate the completion of each ESL level. With the end of Peter's class in May, another party was on the horizon.

In considering it, I wondered if my inability to sit, and the subsequent stabilization period, was God's way of directing me again. Pre-sitting, I'd been planning on walking to church as

## On the Potter's Wheel

soon as I was able. I hadn't been praying about it. What if God still didn't want me to go to church? What if He didn't yet want me to meet whoever-it-was?

This brought up another question. We'd planned to have an ESL party at our apartment. The last time we'd tried to have Grant and Felix over, I'd gotten sick. Would someone else get sick and be unable to attend this time?

In the end, scheduling conflicts prevented us from hosting the party as planned, though we did get together socially with several of our students in the following months. However, events always conspired so that Felix was never able to join us when I was present. A few months later, he moved back to his hometown on mainland Japan.

At around this time, Higa sensei finally ascertained that our former organization would not reverse its decision concerning us. Until then, it was possible something might change following his appeal. He didn't want to upset everyone until he knew the results. On our last Sunday of official ministry with the church, he announced the organization's decision to the entire congregation. It was really hard to know for more than a month that we were being sent home while most people weren't aware of this. We'd felt kind of like we were lying to them, but could see the sense in Higa sensei's reasoning. Now we were relieved the news was out in the open.

Our final week was particularly tough as we wrapped up all the 'lasts' of our ministry. The day Peter gave his last violin lessons was difficult for him because now the students would have to change teachers. He knew this would likely set back the most talented girl about a year, based on her current level.

How guilty we felt for letting down those who depended on us; how desperately we wished we could have stayed!

The first day of June dawned: the day after our ministry in Japan officially ended. Throughout the preceding four months, Peter and I had both experienced a growing sense that something amazing was going to happen in June. Now that it had arrived, I started my day with a sense of thirsty anticipation.

At lunchtime I looked in the fridge, saw some leftover taco fixings from two nights before, and decided to combine them with noodles from the previous night's meal. It would be quite a tasty combination: noodles topped with spicy ground beef, yellow peppers, fried onions, tomatoes, and cheese crumbled on top. I heated the appropriate ingredients and was in the middle of cutting up the noodles when disaster struck. Without realizing it, I'd placed the plate unsteadily on the counter. It tipped over, depositing everything on the floor. I stared at the mess and began to cry. It was a pathetic little metaphor of my life.

Bits of ground beef had been flung quite widely abroad, like shards of glass, while the peppers and noodles remained closer to the epicentre. And there I stood: staring, disappointed, and hungry. I'd been looking forward to this lunch, but now it was scattered on the floor, inedible.

"It would have been so yummy," I said.

Peter nodded. "I know."

"It seems like such a waste."

"Yes, it does."

"It's my fault. Maybe I could have been more careful. With the noodles. With my body."

"It's not your fault."

"Why did gravity—why did things beyond our control—have to come along and wreck everything?"

"Without gravity, there would be no delicious things to eat."

"We could have been really fruitful here. We would have been really fruitful."

"Yes."

# On the Potter's Wheel

"Why can't I just have noodles? All I wanted was some noodles. What's wrong with that?"

"Nothing."

"Is there something wrong with me?"

"No."

"You know, I never wanted to come to Japan before God told me to. It was one of the least interesting countries to me."

"I know."

"I don't want to be a masterpiece. I just want my noodles. I know it's an oxymoron, but why can't God just leave us alone and let us serve Him?"

Peter smiled. "You know, those noodles on the floor have done more for you than I ever could have. You've been busy putting a brave face on things, but sometimes you need to allow yourself just to feel. You don't always have to frame or interpret things."

"I need to survive this."

"Did Jesus say, 'I came to help you survive this life'?"

"If I don't survive, I won't be able to experience abundance afterward. I can feel later."

Silence.

I couldn't bend down to help Peter. "I guess you'll need to clean this up now. I'm sorry for making a mess."

"That's okay. I'm not sorry. I'll let the noodles dry out on the floor a little first. Then they'll be easier to clean up. And maybe that's part of the reason we're not going home right away."

Having now looked my grief in the face, I was ready to see more of God's reality within our situation. Insights continued to pour into my journal.

>End of ministry 2012

God, if there's one thing I've learned through this time, it's that so often reality does not lie in what we can see. True reality—the one You see—is not bound by the things that seem sensible to us. Likewise, Your wisdom seems like foolishness to those insensitive to Your Spirit.[2]

There are those who would say that it is foolishness to let me stay on the mission field while injured. But we've seen Your wisdom working powerfully through this situation for the furtherance of Your kingdom. Please let me not be blind to this.

The evil one may appear to be winning, but he also appeared to be winning on the eve of Your greatest triumph: the day You defeated sin and death for all time, the day You slapped shackles on Satan and imprisoned the imprisoner.

Right now my eyes tell me that our ministry with Seaside Chapel is ending, that our time in Japan may soon be over. Perhaps this is true—I don't know—but I do know You are not finished: not in Japan, and not with us.

# CHAPTER 54

# A New Family Member

Now that May 31 had passed, our previous organization, which still had control over our Japanese visas, told us that we were no longer allowed to engage in any sort of formal ministry. Peter got special permission to continue playing his violin on the church worship team, which was a relief. However, all of Peter's other ministries, ESL classes, and violin lessons ceased. We felt bereft and, with lots of time on our hands, adrift. Stuck between two worlds, we were unable to fly home to Canada because of my injury, but also forbidden to work with the Japanese church.

Though we might not be able to lead formally, we realized this could not prevent us from living our lives for Christ. He eventually showed us informal ministries we could start without breaking the rules. These new ministries had a much different dynamic than we'd experienced in the months before.

According to Japanese societal norms, in our previous position as missionaries, we would have been viewed as slightly more elevated and apart from those to whom we ministered. However, stripped of our position, we found ourselves operating solely on the basis of 'friend'. This implied a more level social playing field and facilitated deepening relationships.

Since my ministries over the past months had already been on an informal basis, my activities didn't change much. We still visited with many people each month. The one noticeable difference was that fewer people came by our apartment on an impromptu basis. However, we compensated by being more proactive in our social invitations.

Peter had made great connections with many of his ESL students over the previous months. After each class, he shared his stories with me, and I wrote them down.

One week, the class studied the account of the lame man who was lowered through a roof and healed by Jesus.

"How would you have felt if you were one of the people in the crowd and heard Jesus say, 'Your sins are forgiven'?"

"Jealous," one of the students, Grant, replied. "I have a lot in my life that I need to be forgiven for."

Peter asked, "Why can Jesus forgive sins?"

No one in the class could think of an answer.

"Because He's God," Peter said.

On another week, the story was of Jesus and the Samaritan woman. That week, Grant had hurt his back. After class, he approached Peter and said, in a physical context, "I need living water, and I think so does your wife."

"Yes, she does."

For some months, Grant and Felix had been coming to church on Sunday mornings. Each week Grant looked thoroughly bored with the sermons, but as we were learning, reality is often much different from what we can see.

In one of our last classes, Peter taught about the sermon on the mount and loving our enemies.

"Would you forgive someone who murdered your brother?" he asked.

Grant piped up. "At first I would be angry, but I think I'd eventually forgive."

Over the preceding months, Peter and Grant had engaged in several conversations whose content demonstrated that Grant was listening intently to Higa sensei's sermons every week. The changes in his thinking were very evident that night.

Grant later posted a message on social media: "Today's class was very good: 'Love your enemies and pray for those who persecute you.' I want to live my life like these words."

Grant first came to ESL at the invitation of Daniel, who was Peter's best friend in Japan. On the evening of June 10, after a long talk with Daniel, Grant decided to follow Jesus and be baptized.

# CHAPTER 55

# Followed by Evil

One night, I was wakened at about 5:00 a.m. by Peter gasping, "Jesus!" in his sleep.

I woke him. "What's wrong?"

"I was trapped in my dream," he said. "It was about demon possession, and I couldn't escape. Somehow, though, I knew Jesus could help me. I tried to call out His name, but the words wouldn't come. It took all of my strength, but finally I was able to say just one word: 'Jesus'."

Demon possession?

"We need to pray."

"There's a demon in the park across the street," Peter said after we were finished praying. "We need to get rid of it. It's the same spirit that's been following me for the past fifteen years."

"What do you mean?"

With that, he told me a remarkable story.

When he was twenty, Peter was praying in his parents' living room when a fiery face appeared before his eyes. It was floating, very ugly, and otherwise indescribable.

This was the scariest moment of his life up to that point. He prayed fervently, and eventually, the face disappeared.

The following year, Peter traveled to Mexico with an itinerant mission group. Billeted in a host family's home, he shared a room with his friend Abbott.

"This is strange. I feel like there's some sort of presence in this room," Abbott said. "It seems to be moving from left to right, across the room."

Then it pinned Peter down in bed. He felt as though he were suffocating, and couldn't move.

He struggled to get the word out of his mouth, and was finally able to gasp, "Jesus!"

The presence vanished.

Later, Peter went to Poland with the same mission organization. One evening, he was standing on the balcony of a monastery with a different friend, Jude.

Peter had a strange feeling. "Jude, go inside."

"Why?"

"Just do it. I'll be right behind you."

However, Peter couldn't follow; he suddenly couldn't move. He was standing halfway between the building and the edge of the balcony, and started having strange thoughts.

*I wonder what it would be like to fall. Would I get hurt? Maybe I could fly. It would be fun. I should try it.*

He recognized these thoughts weren't his, yet his body felt pushed by an unseen force toward the edge. He grabbed hold of the balcony railing to slow his momentum.

"Jesus!"

Everything went back to normal, and he went safely inside.

After Peter told me these stories, we prayed. He sensed that we should go down to the park. I'd not been able to walk up and down the steps of our apartment for a month, ever since I'd tried to sit. But I was convinced he should not go alone.

We descended to the park together, praying all the way, and I was fine. We came to a clearing in the trees.

Peter stopped. "That evil spirit is here."

We both spoke to it. When I opened my mouth to cast out the spirit, I felt a spasm in my rear. It was the only pain I experienced on our walk. It left as soon as I started claiming Jesus' power on our behalf.

We walked a little further. God guided us to an enclosure overlooking a children's playground. Peter had the sense that we should pray for the area to be spiritually cleansed. After this, we started back to our apartment. We looked at the dog idols on our building, proclaimed their eyes closed in Jesus' name, and declared that the only spirit with the right to be there was the Holy Spirit.

We came back up to our apartment and slept soundly.

The next morning, I didn't know what to make of these experiences. The night before had been truly bizarre. I wondered if some things, like the bit about the enclosure, were just flights of fancy. But then I remembered that I'd felt God prompting me in that direction. When I'd gone to tell Peter, He had told him the same thing. One thing I did know: we were in a spiritual war, and it would seem that Peter and I were under attack.

## CHAPTER 56

# Connecting

In the Japanese culture, having a guest into one's home is a rare and significant relational leap. Having people unexpectedly drop by and willing to come in is completely countercultural; yet in our case, this had been happening with a number of visitors, including a lady named Irene.

"It must be very hard for you to go through such a long recovery process," she remarked during our first visit.

"Yes," I said, "but there's also great joy in knowing God is with me and teaching me many important lessons."

She visibly started at the word 'joy'. "What did you say?"

We ended up having a wonderful discussion about how God can use even our suffering for good.

The day before my birthday, Eleanor came by with Irene. They gave me beautiful white lilies and strawberry cake. At the end of our conversation, Eleanor asked if Irene could come along for another visit. Not having seen Irene since the announcement that we were being sent home, I was happy to know she was still open to continuing our relationship.

June 16, a Saturday, dawned bright and sunny. I'd not been looking forward to it because I would be spending that birthday by myself. Peter was playing violin at a wedding in the morning. He had regular camera club with his Japanese friends in the afternoon; and in the evening, he would be attending Ando Cafe, the church plant. I knew all these activities were good and tried to reason myself into not caring that the day would be a lonely one.

*We can always celebrate tomorrow*, I told myself.

We eventually found out camera club had ended the week before, so Peter and I spent the afternoon together.

Evening came, and Peter trekked off to Ando Cafe. Twenty minutes later, he returned.

"I forgot something. Come here and see."

There, standing at the door, were fifteen of my friends and Peter's ESL students singing "Happy Birthday"!

They'd planned a surprise party for me, bringing cake, ice cream, and gifts. A friend from church, Edward, had seen on Facebook that my birthday was coming. He'd hatched the idea of a party and had been arranging everything since the week before.

It was truly wonderful. I finally was able to meet several of the ESL students for whom I'd been praying. After such excitement and joy, I couldn't fall asleep that night until several hours past bedtime. My cheeks were sore. I hadn't smiled so much since our wedding day.

In Japan, the decision to be baptized is very important. There are so many people who have accepted Christ at one point, only to fall away from Him later, that baptism is seen as a firmer commitment. It shows the person hasn't simply said yes because it's culturally impolite to say no. As such, baptism is celebrated with the same joy and vigour as North American Christians would celebrate a person making the initial decision to follow Christ.

After a few months of attending ESL classes, one of Peter's students, Helen, decided to rededicate her life to Christ and be baptized.

Before my birthday, Helen and I made several attempts to visit together, but our plans had always fallen through. However, at the party I finally got to meet her and invited her to drop by anytime.

A week later, Helen was in the neighbourhood and came over. We talked partly in English, partly in Japanese, and she stayed for over two hours. Our conversation was broad: ranging from languages we know to the Japanese educational system, to tapping maple trees for syrup, to the British Commonwealth.

It was a sweet time of fellowship. She marvelled that I was always smiling, and we shared our favourite Bible verses with each other. Later we went on to discuss the nature of truth in Christ.

It was so good to talk with her, and it seemed that she enjoyed our conversation too.

At the end of our time together, she looked at me with a hopeful expression. "Can I come and visit you again?"

"Please come back!"

The following day, I was still uplifted by this new friend and was so glad that she'd taken up my offer to visit. She'd even felt comfortable enough to come alone.

A Japanese person once said to me, "We Japanese love *magokoro* (literally, 'true heart' or 'sincerity'). We always observe others' behaviours, not their words." Peter and I ever afterward kept this thought in mind as we tried to show the Japanese God's love through our lives.

By this time, I was able to stand for an hour at a time, with an hour's bed rest between each up time. When our friends surprised me with the birthday party, Peter and I realized that hosting large-scale events from our home was no longer out of reach for us, even with my limited physical capabilities. So during my birthday party, we invited everyone back to celebrate Canada Day with us in two weeks' time.

Peter was sick during the last week of June but was completely recovered shortly before Canada Day. We cooked up a storm in preparation for the party. We expected fifteen to twenty people to come, but twenty-seven actually did! Our apartment was packed, and we couldn't believe we managed to fit so many into our 450-square-foot abode. It was fortunate that I'm always a little paranoid about running out of food and tend to cook much more than is generally needed.

I'd spent the previous week making decorations, planning games and door prizes, and selecting Canadian music for the party. We decorated our place with a variety of paraphernalia, including flags, art displays, and Canadian money. Everyone got to pick out a key chain with either a moose, bear, or beaver on it. The kids played on the Wii; the adults talked and laughed.

The food was based on a traditional Canadian summer barbecue: grilled sausages, two flavours of chicken wings, potato salad, coleslaw, broccoli salad, green salad with homemade dressing, and devilled eggs. And that was just the main course. Everyone was stuffed by the end and seemed to really enjoy themselves.

"How many hours did it take to cook everything?" someone asked.

"Two days," we responded.

Our guests were really touched. In Okinawa, spending that amount of time in preparation is very meaningful, so this was a great way of saying, "We care for you." I got my second hug from a Japanese person on that day.

Soon after, Peter found out that Daniel had plans to participate in a local festival. One of its events was a talent show, and Daniel had decided to form a church band and sing songs about

Jesus. When Peter heard of this, he also learned that Daniel had named the band "Peter and Friends".

In Okinawa, personal planning tends to be last-minute by Canadian standards; we never knew who would show up for a given event. There were several people who had to drop out of the festival because of scheduling conflicts, but one thing was certain: both Daniel and the band's namesake would be there. They practiced on Sundays after church for a few weeks. On the day of the performance, the band had eight members, including two who weren't Christians. We felt privileged to again engage our friends and sing about Jesus' love to those who didn't know Him.

## CHAPTER 57
# Offerings of Faith

Shortly after Higa sensei ascertained that our former employer would not reverse its decision, he visited us to request that we look into finding a new organization so we could continue ministering in Okinawa.

At first, we were wary of this request, wondering if there was some sort of miscommunication. Perhaps we were reading our own wishful thinking into his words. However, when he began actively brainstorming possible outfits we could work with, and introducing us to people who might help us to stay, we realized there was no misunderstanding. So we started researching and applying to organizations we might be compatible with.

As the months wore on, we continued making phone calls to our donors to explain our termination. We also fielded many questions by e-mail from people who didn't understand why our official ministry had been cut off while we were still in Japan. We didn't understand either. Both we and our partners lifted up our voices in asking God to clearly guide us in the way we should go next.

By mid-July, we only had a few phone calls left, to people we'd had difficulty contacting. One day we had a video call scheduled, so I got up from bed and prepared to talk while standing. However, there were technical issues. In the end, we called our partners' land line, and I decided to lie down while we talked.

Later, Peter challenged me on this. "Why would you get up from bed when you thought they would see you, but lie down when you knew they couldn't?"

"I didn't want to be vulnerable in front of them."
"Why does that matter?"
*Good point. Why?*
"These people love us," Peter continued. "They've given sacrificially for God's kingdom. They know you're injured. They've been praying for you. There's nothing to prove. They have only our best interests, and the interests of God's kingdom, at heart."

So why did it matter to me?

In mulling over this question in my journal, I remembered the attitudes of our former friends. I'd started buying into their distorted views again, I realized, and was treating myself as useless. I only felt valuable when uninjured, and wanted to be standing when people saw me so they would view me as valuable.

I numbly looked at these realizations on the page. Something tickled my cheek. I was crying.

"Lord God, please show me what You think of me," I prayed. "Am I valuable, even like this? I need You to tell me that this is not a waste. That I am not a waste."

Shortly after this, I had an unusually good night's sleep, the best I'd had in a long time. But I didn't sleep all the way through the night. There was a point when I woke up, aware of the presence of God.

We didn't really say much. We just enjoyed each other's company.

I remembered a line from one of Amy Carmichael's books. When she worked as a missionary at an orphanage in India, sometimes the children would approach her in an especially sweet way. Without any ulterior motive, they would simply come up to her, gaze at her, and say, "I have come just to love you." Their focus was on her and not on something they wanted. They craved her companionship simply because they loved her.[1]

That's what this was like. God and I were together, just loving each other.

As I was about to doze off again, a song came into my mind, and I sang it in my head to Him. I asked Him to finish healing me soon and, trusting His promises, thanked Him that I <u>was</u> healed. I fell asleep.

At the beginning of August, I got a boil in a sensitive place. Its location made it impossible for me to distinguish between pain from my injury and pain from the infection. I realized it would be best to stay in bed while the boil healed in order to avoid unintentionally aggravating my injury. During this time, the summer Olympics were taking place.

It was an interesting experience to watch the Olympics in a foreign country. We understood none of the television commentary, but since Japan participates in different events than Canada, we did get to watch games we'd never seen before. That year included table tennis, rhythmic synchronized gymnastics, and loads of judo, a sport we came to enjoy immensely.

Throughout the Olympics, I gradually became aware of a strong emotion exerting itself in my spirit: jealousy. I wasn't jealous of the superhuman feats of the Olympians, exhilarating as they were. No, I was jealous of the people in the stands. The people who were free of injury, who were leading normal lives, who could sit and walk to their hearts' content, and who could get up and fly on planes wherever they wanted. I felt pathetic.

With this realization came another: for the last few months, I'd lost my contentment. I'd had moments, even extended moments, of peace, but this was not the overarching theme of my life as it had been before.

Paul said, "I have learned to be content whatever the circumstances."[2] For a time I'd been able to say that too. What had changed?

I opened my journal and began to write.

> August 2012
>
> A large part of contentment is the development of habitual gratitude. I'm a strong Type A personality: very results-driven. But what about the times when results are not within my power to obtain? What about situations where the very setting of goals can be detrimental because then I will try to push my body to meet them, courting further injury? Am I willing to submit myself to God and His plans? Am I willing to trust, and even to thank, Him for the place I'm in?
>
> In my devotions, I came to the following passage:
>
> > Better is the little of the righteous
> > Than the abundance of many wicked.
> > (Psalm 37:16)
>
> What if this applies to me?
>
> Through my injury and recovery, God has been refining Peter and me—showing us delights in Him we never dreamed of. What if the *little* I have now is better than the greatest *much* I had before?
>
> Everywhere I turn, it seems that God has been bringing verses about waiting on Him, and promises of His good plans for us, to my attention. The verse I've been meditating on in recent days is Psalm 46:10 (NIV): "Be still"—my favourite translation says, 'Cease striving'—"and know that I am God."
>
> Now I meditate on two words of that verse at a time. Somehow, in the stillness, all frustration and impatience melt away. I am content.

My season of discouragement was not over; I continued the struggle to take my thoughts captive and submit them to Jesus'

authority. To my chagrin, the boil took a few weeks to completely resolve, and I found myself easily frustrated and discouraged. Those feelings poured out in my journal.

> August 20, 2012
>
> Lord, I need encouragement. I'm at my wits' end. I feel trapped here. Trapped in Japan, unable to go home to Canada. Trapped in our apartment, unable to visit the park or the doctor. I'm in a cage—my bed—with nowhere to turn but to You.
>
> You are the One who has put me here—and for what? To be fired by our organization? To be prevented from doing ministry here? To waste away and die?
>
> Peter and I both feel like we're going insane with the waiting, without being able to do anything productive. Why must we wait? What do we have to learn? What is the purpose—my purpose? Where are You? The all-powerful God tarries. Why?
>
> Must I go through this fire indefinitely? Where is the abundance You have promised?
>
> And then I have a thought. It's more of a memory, a line that Peter's fond of saying: "It's okay to cry."
>
> I feel like crying, and that's okay. My crying does not have to denote a crisis of faith. It can simply be an acknowledgement that this is hard.
>
> You are tarrying. Sometimes You give healing, and at others (like now) You retract it a little. Through it all, it's okay to cry. Faith is not dependent on a smile. My tears can also be an offering of faith.

Over the next few days, God answered my requests for encouragement and contentment, once more using His creation. In the park across the street was a pond, and a frog moved in. His croaking was so loud! We could hear him outside, even when our doors and windows were all closed. Hearing him made me smile every time: here was a frog happy to be a frog, and doing froggy things. It helped me to remember that I, too, could be happy doing the things I could do. Sometimes I thought that the act of taking joy in my *little*—the few things I could do now, with my injury—was a way of worshipping our God, the giver of *much* abundance.

With all the chaos and commotion of the preceding year, we continually struggled to make sense of our situation. At times, God would give us insights into parts of His larger story. More importantly, though, the ongoing theme of this period was that He was ever present—teaching, guiding, and refining us.

I woke up one morning grieving at the prospect of leaving Japan, and possibly the mission field, forever.

In a conversation the day before, Peter and I realized that if my injury had happened a year earlier or a year later, or if we had started our mission work at a different time, this probably wouldn't have happened. We realized that many factors in this situation had been carefully timed.

By whom? By God? He was the only One I knew who could orchestrate with such precision. Did He intend for this to happen all along, or did He just allow it?

Peter and I kept coming back to the story of Jonah. Was it God's will that he run away? No, God asked him to go to Nineveh. But Jonah did run. He got swallowed by a fish, and when he was spit out, he must have looked (and smelt!) like death itself. Did this lend power to his proclamations of coming doom? Probably. Did this help the Ninevites turn from their wicked ways in repentance? Possibly.

So the question was: Did God choose Jonah because He knew he would run? Did God choose us because He knew what our reactions would be?

I couldn't help thinking of one of my favourite childhood books, *Jonah and the Worm*, which was told from the worm's perspective. The worm was called to embark on an arduous journey to go and eat the vine in Nineveh that eventually sheltered Jonah. Along the way, he exhibited far more faith than the prophet did. When he ate the vine, his part was done.

Had we now eaten our vine?

"Is this dream, which You placed in my heart since I was seven, now done?" I prayed. "It seemed to me that You were saying You have more for us, but right now I'm so sad. I can't see past this feeling. I can't help fearing that perhaps I just read my own wishful thinking into this situation."

When I opened my Bible for devotional time with God, He came to meet with me. The last portion of reading that morning was based in Acts 27. Paul was on his way to Rome and got shipwrecked because those in charge wouldn't listen to his warnings. But he still eventually got to Rome.

*We may be shipwrecked at the moment*, I thought, *but this doesn't change our final destination.*

We'd thought our destination was Japan. We might have been wrong. However our Captain, Jesus, had known our end point all along. He would guide us on the route we should take.

## CHAPTER 58
# Obon

That year in Okinawa, the weekend bordering August and September was *Obon*. A three-day Buddhist holiday that revolves around worshipping the spirits of people's departed ancestors, *Obon* takes place throughout Japan. Okinawa's version depends on the lunar calendar; it occurs about a month later than in the rest of the country.

The festival begins at sunset and involves a variety of preparations, including *Eisa* dancing, meant to summon and welcome the spirits who are said to come and visit for the duration of the celebration. On the first evening, Okinawan people will often burn candles to guide the spirits toward their homes, standing out in front to welcome their ancestors as the sun sets and darkness shrouds the islands.[1]

Dazed at the obvious physical mirroring of a grim spiritual reality, we decided to use that weekend to concentrate on praying for the people around us, and asked some of our North American prayer partners to join us in this venture. We all prayed for the Japanese Christians; and for our friends who were still seeking spiritual truth, that their eyes would be opened to see the true Light of the world in the midst of such darkness.

We reminded ourselves that the victory is already won—not a victory over people, but one over sin, death, and the spiritual forces seeking to enslave and destroy those loved by God.

*Eisa* dancing is a practice unique to Okinawa. Each day and night as the *Eisa* dancers traversed the town's streets in colourful robes, sashes, and head kerchiefs, their drumming and chanting was loud and incessant. We couldn't escape it, even with all our doors and windows tightly shut.

Our spirits were greatly disquieted whenever the dancers were nearby. In fact, we soon noticed a pattern. We'd been fighting with each other every day since *Obon* started, and our fights always seemed to ignite a few minutes before we began to hear the *Eisa* dancers coming through. Spiritual warfare was running high.

We needed a strategy, and decided to run to God in prayer as soon as there were disturbances in our spirits. Each day when the drumming started, we turned on our Christian worship music, prayed, and praised God with all our hearts as the procession passed by once more.

Sometimes we would look out our window, watching and praying for the dancers themselves. That was when we noticed another pattern. They would go up and down all the other streets in our area once, drumming and chanting throughout, but paid special attention to the park across from our house. They circled the park not once, but twice.

I'd long felt a deep conviction that somehow the park was of strategic, spiritual importance. I'd found a witch doctor's charms there once, and now the *Eisa* dancers were also paying special attention to it.

When they left our area after the first of many such campaigns around the city, I felt a prompting in my spirit.

"Go around the park together and pray," God said.

I was nervous about doing this because at that point I'd not walked the four flights of stairs to the park in more than two months. But we obeyed. Circling the park, we earnestly asked God to deliver the people around us from the spiritual oppression that hovered so densely above. I felt no ill effects following our return home.

## CHAPTER 59

# Surviving or Thriving?

I once read a paragraph describing the mentality prisoners adopt during their incarceration.

> How do you survive for years in prison? You don't think about years, or months, or weeks. You think about today—how to get through it, how to survive it. You wake up tomorrow, another day is behind you. The days add up; the weeks run together; the months become years. You realize how tough you are, you can function and survive because you have no choice.[1]

How closely it described my own experience during my injury. Yet, unlike a prison sentence, there was no known end date. There was no countdown to the time when I would be free from the shackles of injury.

As this incarceration stretched on without any resolution in sight, the hope the Bible talks about—that unceasing state of expectation—was almost a form of torture. In that state, my hope attacked my faith because it remained unfulfilled. Eventually, I assumed a more 'sustainable' balance between the two, where my hope was instead a vague expectation of future healing.

One day, after listening to a sermon on the Internet, I was challenged to take a hard look at my attitudes. Had my prayers become too anaemic? It was true that to some extent I'd stopped praying for healing. Part of this was because God had already promised to heal me. But I'd also become resigned to my fate, and to the fact that God alone would determine what He would do and when.

This approach was less painful because I didn't have to keep hearing Him tell me to wait a little longer. But was it truly biblical? Perhaps not. Perhaps one of the reasons He'd kept me waiting was because He was waiting for me to ask.

"Okay, God, I'll ask," I prayed. "But if the answer is 'no' or 'not yet', please be gentle with me. My heart is pretty battered right now."

On the following day, my prayers of renewed hope continued.

*It's easy to be dependent on God when I can't do anything for myself*, I thought. *But when more things are possible, will I still pray for His guidance in every action, in every decision? Is this the reason I'm still in bed: to learn true dependence?*

I found myself strangely excited by the thought.

God spoke up. "I want you to be connected with Me, praying and following My guidance every moment of every day."

Every moment?

The size of His request was overwhelming. How could I possibly pray to Him at every moment? Why was God asking this of me when He didn't require it of so many other Christians?

Considering this, I couldn't help being eager: a future with such intimacy and dependence on Him would have to be pretty amazing. That was my future!

"Okay, God," I said. "Please help me to remember to pray in everything. Please help me to hear Your voice, to distinguish it properly from all my own desires.

"When I asked You to teach me to pray all those years ago, I was just thinking of those times we set aside for intense prayer. But You had a much bigger plan, didn't You?"

I smiled at the thought. Then another wiggled to the surface.

*What about right now?*

"God, should I be on my side or my back?"

"Back."

"That was fast. I'm so comfortable on my side. Maybe that was just an echo in my mind of my own question, so—"

"BACK." The instruction was almost a shout in my mind. I couldn't miss it.

"Okay, God, I'm turning over. Thank You for starting out so clearly. I know this is of You."

When I later told Peter of God's instruction to pray for guidance in every decision, he wasn't sure what to make of it. Such direction seemed odd, to say the least, but he decided to hold his peace and see what happened.

*After all*, he reasoned, *the test of whether God was actually speaking to a prophet in the Bible was whether or not the prophet's prediction happened. The results were the test of truth. I'll wait and see if this makes a difference in Val's recovery. The results will be the test.*

He only told me of these thoughts months later.

In the meantime, I struggled with a heart of disobedience and had a hard time remembering to pray about every little thing. Sometimes it would have been more convenient to forget to obey.

At times, when He told me no in response to a much-desired request, I regretted praying. Occasionally I tried to argue with Him, and one day caught myself being flippant in my disobedient attitude. Sure, I obeyed His commands outwardly, but often my heart wasn't in it. Much of the time, I lusted after that former control over my life and decision-making.

Again and again I had to repent, asking Him to forgive and cleanse me of these things. I didn't want the saying 'familiarity breeds contempt' to be true of my relationship with Him.

Soon I noticed the language of my prayers beginning to change. I asked less for God's help, where I might be mistaken for the primary mover, and He for a source of supplementary resources; and instead asked Him to enable me, recognizing that He was the primary mover, and I was merely a sidekick.

God gradually enabled my heart, as well as my actions, to be obedient to His direction. However, another problem emerged. My relationship with Him started to shrink down to just that one dimension: God as guide in my decision making.

Missing the intimacy of our former relationship, I developed another strategy. At the start of each day, I began asking Him to help me live in companionship with Him and to remember my identity as His child, not just as His follower. Soon the delight between us began to return.

Though God was the source of my hope, sometimes I apprehensively tried to limit what He could do with me, according to my will. In Bible study one day, there was an exhortation to ask God to teach me to pray.

I resisted.

Why?

Fearful that His answer would mean more long months of injury, I wanted to add the proviso "But only if it means I'll still heal quickly." Over the previous months, I'd become increasingly aware that we cannot put restrictions on God. My solution: avoid praying that prayer altogether!

After two days, I finally gathered up enough courage to be honest with God. "When all pretenses are stripped away, a stark question remains: Will I trust You with my future, with my recovery? Or will I avoid praying prayers for godliness, for fear of what the answer might mean?

"Lord, open my heart to trust You again. Please release me from fear into Your freedom."

As time went on, I became increasingly convinced that I should be grateful for each step of the journey. One day, I came across a special Bible passage: "For everything God created is good, and nothing is to be rejected if it is received with thanksgiving, because it is consecrated by the word of God and prayer."²

My back was created by God, <u>and it was good</u>. I'd never before considered it a gift.

"Lord, thank You for creating my back, just the way it is," I prayed. "Thank You for the lessons You've taught me because of it."

# CHAPTER 60

# Changes

Less than two weeks after I began praying for God's guidance in everything, the nature of my recovery began to change.

One evening, I was up from bed and asked God to guide me in what to do next.

"Read," He said.

Over the past few days, I'd been going through *The Necessity of Prayer*. That night, my daily chapter was on praying with perseverance. Partway through the reading I experienced some strong pain twinges and, on checking with God, felt that He was telling me to go back to bed.

I read a little further. Challenged to ask for God's healing right then, I prayed. It wasn't very long, but it was earnest.

At the end, something strange happened. For lack of a better description, there began to be a throbbing in my head—a linguistic pulse of the word "Yes." The word came to the forefront, grew in intensity, and then started to recede, only to increase in strength once more.

"Should I get up from bed again?" I'd only been resting for ten minutes.

"Yes."

I ended up standing for a total of two hours, with only that ten-minute break in between.

What ecstasy over this remarkable leap in healing!

## On the Potter's Wheel

In the past, I'd discovered that climbing the four flights of stairs to our apartment was a risky endeavour. If I climbed too quickly or continued for too long without taking a break, my recovery could be negatively impacted for the next several days, or even weeks.

It was possible that I could get stuck: unable to get back up to our apartment, but also unable to keep standing because I needed to lie down again. In my physiotherapy exercises, which required stair climbing, I took the pragmatic middle-road: gradually developing my abilities by climbing and re-climbing the half-flights closest to our apartment. In that way, I could strengthen my muscles, while at the same time remaining near to home in case there was trouble.

By the end of September, I still hadn't traversed all four flights or gone to the park in about a month.

One day as I ended prayer in my devotions, God said, "Go."

"Go where?"

"To the park."

Trepidation rose in my chest. "Please show me clearly. Is this really Your command and not just my own desire?"

"Yes."

"Are You sure? Is this really You?"

"Yes."

I realized that at any other time He'd affirmed His guidance so clearly, I'd simply obeyed. Was I asking for more verification because I was fearful?

"Okay, God," I said. "I believe this is You. You're telling me to go to the park. Please help me not to be anxious."

I randomly opened my electronic Bible, and the verse there before my eyes was Psalm 46:2 (KJV): "Therefore we will not fear, though the earth be removed, and though the mountains be carried into the midst of the sea."

I laughed to myself, and went down the stairs with Peter.

Together we walked around the park, on the short path. We prayed for a man riding a bike. Another man was taking the shutters off of his windows; we prayed that Jesus' light would shine clearly into his heart and life. We admired some pretty flowers.

On returning to the stairs of our building, I felt God telling me not to climb them yet.

"Where should we go?"

"Walk back to the street and go straight."

We went in that direction for a few blocks.

"Now stop and turn around."

We returned home. As we approached, four people descended: our downstairs neighbour, whom we'd not seen in months, and three of his guests.

We bowed to everyone. "*Konnichiwa!*" (Oops, that means 'good afternoon', and it was still morning!)

We would have missed them if we'd gone up right away.

I made it back up the stairs with no twinges of pain.

## CHAPTER 61

# Typhoons

Between August and October, we experienced a few major typhoons in Okinawa. These weather patterns were new to us, and we approached them with a great deal of curiosity. A typhoon is basically the same as a hurricane, the main difference lying in its location. Hurricanes originate in the Atlantic or east Pacific Oceans,[1] whereas typhoons originate in the west Pacific. There is a popular myth that typhoons spin in the opposite direction to hurricanes, but in actuality, they only have reverse spin if they're south of the equator.[2]

Our first exposure to Japanese attitudes on typhoons came when Peter asked our ESL students what they did to prepare for them. Everyone started smiling. Staying home from work on a typhoon day is typically greeted with the same anticipation as Canadians feel for a snow day.

Okinawa is remarkably well-prepared for large storms. The rest of Japan's buildings are constructed to flex with numerous earthquakes. However, because Okinawa doesn't experience many substantial quakes, its buildings are made primarily of rigid, reinforced concrete. Every structure, including the trees, is fortified to better handle typhoons.

Because everything is so well-built, unless a typhoon was a category four or higher, we soon discovered that there was no real cause for concern. Sometimes power or water would be knocked out, so we always had spare bottles of water, canned food, battery power, and our crank-operated radio on hand.

With all the natural disasters Japan faces, emergency-preparedness handbooks and kits are everywhere.

The Japanese generally refer to typhoons by their number rather than by name. Each year, the numbering system is reset. The Okinawan islands are small, so often storms will blow right by with little effect. However, in that year there were three that had significant impact.

According to our radio, typhoon number 15 (a category four, named *Bolaven* for the non-Japanese) was the biggest to hit Okinawa in thirteen years. At times, the wind sounded rather alarming. The roar, which is so dramatically depicted in disaster movies, was surprisingly accurate. Even so, we saw virtually no damage, apart from a few downed tree branches.

A baptism had been scheduled for the weekend when number 15 blew through, but both the baptism and church service were postponed.

The following Sunday, an announcement was made at the end of the morning. "We're going to be having a baptism service today, but we don't know when—oh, Daniel has the tide schedule. Low tide is at 4:00 p.m. Okay, the baptisms are at 4:00 p.m. Be at the church at 3:30 and we'll head over to the ocean."

Okinawan culture is typically far more spontaneous than that in the rest of Japan. We found ourselves enjoying the off-kilter feeling of never knowing what would happen from one moment to the next. When Peter showed up promptly at 3:30 p.m. for the baptisms, Higa sensei told him that he wanted his help. The ocean's tides were a little much for a seventy-year-old man to handle by himself. So Peter ran home to get his swim trunks and had the privilege of helping to baptize his ESL students, Helen and Grant.

Typhoon number 16 (*Sanba*) started out as a category five, but was downgraded to a category four by the time it hit us, and later to a category three. Our Japanese friends told us that at its strongest, number 16 was one of the biggest typhoons in

## On the Potter's Wheel

recorded history for our area. At one point, its winds reached about 290 km/h.

The last major typhoon that year was number 17 (*Jelawat*). Whereas the eyes of most storms (numbers 15 and 16 included) crossed over our island at a single point, number 17 travelled up the entire length of the island, knocking out power and water for many people. It was fast-moving and did more damage to our area than any typhoon in the previous sixty-two years. It was also my favourite.

Though we were inconvenienced by the power outages, number 17 was so fast-moving that it disrupted our lives much less than its predecessors. Between the fluctuating barometric pressure before and after a typhoon, and the roar of the winds for a couple of days, we could generally expect four to five days (per typhoon) of almost complete sleep deprivation. However, since number 17 travelled so quickly, our sleep was disturbed very little, apart from the time when the winds were at their loudest.

At the end of September, in the wee hours of the morning, I couldn't sleep. Typhoon number 17 was coming in, and the wind was very loud. So I rolled over and checked e-mails on my phone. There was one from a potential mission organization that had decided not to process our application until we could prove my health was no longer in question—back in Canada.

As I lay in bed, listening to the typhoon buffeting our building and feeling the floor of our apartment shake, I felt as if there were a little typhoon tearing through my heart and destroying everything in its path too.

Somehow, I couldn't help feeling that this storm was exquisitely timed. In a strange way, it gave vent to my feelings perfectly.

"Thank You for this typhoon, God," I prayed.

We knew that if we went back to Canada without first finding a new organization, our chances of returning to the mission field would be almost nonexistent. Assuming we could find an organization whose operating strategies matched our own, there would still be a lengthy application process, and we would have to go through the initial stages of fundraising all over again. There would likely be many questions and concerns about my ability to actively engage in ministry, which would mean even slower progress. In realistic terms, it would take five years or more to come back to Japan, and we weren't sure that we had the stamina to go through such a marathon—again.

There were times when the grief swamped me like a tidal wave. At one point while Peter was out, it hit me particularly badly. The emotion was so intense that I couldn't even cry. All I could do was groan and gasp for air.

After the worst of it passed, I opened my journal and wrote a prayer to God. "You are still worth it. When I waxed poetic all those months ago about what You're worth, perhaps some of my musings were only in theory. But now, even as I grieve, even as I suffer, my soul gives an emphatic nod, a triumphant shout, a joyful declaration: 'You are worth it!'"

His Spirit tenderly whispered back. "You were worth it too."

Over the following days, we entered into another period of mourning. We were keenly aware that only one organization remained on our list of possibilities. The rest either didn't operate in Okinawa, had an incompatible missions vision with ours, or refused us because of my injury. Our outlook was realistically bleak.

CHAPTER 62

# Thanksgiving

In Japanese architecture there is often a sunken vestibule, called a *genkan*, which means that a person must step up to enter the rest of the building. People are often uncomfortable with going to a place they don't know, and this serves as a barrier to them exploring church. In expressing this concept, the Japanese metaphorically say that the step into the church building is too high.

When we first started teaching ESL classes, Peter's friend Daniel invited four of his friends to attend: Felix, Grant, Neil, and John. Felix and Grant came regularly; but for Neil and John, the class' language level was too high, and they stopped attending. However, the metaphorical step into the church had been lowered. Since becoming familiar with the building, they all began to attend the Sunday church services. Though Neil and John were no longer part of our English classes, Peter eventually became friends with them too.

Eight months later, changes were afoot in the life of Felix. By this point, his wife and child were attending church regularly with him on Sunday mornings. However, in September, he and his family moved back to Tokyo in search of stable employment. On their last Sunday, Felix's wife brought along her new Bible, followed along with the sermon, and seemed to be much more engaged than in times past. Before they left, Felix told Peter that his family intended to find a church in Tokyo so they could keep learning about Jesus.

Shortly afterward, Neil telephoned Daniel. "I want to talk with you," he said.

*Oh well, it's been a good run,* Daniel thought. *I bet Neil would like to tell me that he no longer wants to come to church. Well, at least he got to hear the good news about Jesus.*

When Daniel went to visit, Neil told him he wanted to become a Christian and be baptized!

With this change, I remarked to Peter that we might encounter a problem. "Felix's family is moving back to Tokyo, and some of the others have come to Christ. Now we're in danger of running out of friends who aren't Christians!"

"Given the reason, it's a good problem to have!"

I agreed.

A few weeks later, we transitioned into Thanksgiving mode and planned to hold another party for our friends. The Canada Day party had consisted mostly of cold salads. The idea of cooking a hot meal for about twenty people was daunting, particularly when we considered our facilities: a toaster oven, a small microwave, a kettle, a two-burner stove (no oven), and two square feet of counter space. We knew the key to success would lie in the planning. Peter's parents, accomplished church caterers in their own right, graciously gave us tips on precooking and reheating our planned turkey, ham shank, vegetables, and desserts.

We were able to obtain the North American ingredients necessary for an authentic Canadian Thanksgiving meal, including cranberry sauce and canned pumpkin. Many of our friends had never before tasted pumpkin pie. I looked forward to introducing them to one of my favourite desserts with great anticipation.

We held the party on the afternoon of October 14 and invited our guests to bring vegetables to supplement the menu. Nineteen people came, including five whom we'd not previously known. They weren't Christians, but members of Charles' family. We all had fun sampling each others' cooking, chatting, and playing games, including a Thanksgiving version of a classic children's game. Our variation was 'pin the feathers on the turkey'. To our surprise, the adults joined in colouring their feather drawings beforehand, sitting on the floor along with the kids. This was yet another testament to the group culture so prevalent in the Japanese mentality.

As we later reflected on that party, we took joy in knowing Jesus had heard our conversation about running out of friends who weren't Christians, and had blessed us with several new contacts in that category.

# CHAPTER 63

# Unstuck

One of my pen pals was a lady whose husband was experiencing long-term health problems. We could relate quite well to each others' situations, including the all-too-familiar sensation of slogging through the muds of time.

I think one feeling must be pretty common among people who are going through some sort of health problem: the feeling of time, and indeed of life, passing us by. Sometimes it can be difficult to see others going about their lives while we end up feeling stuck. But God kept bringing me back to those three little words Jesus had replied to the apostle Peter when he was inquiring about John's future: "You follow Me."[1] It was good to be reminded that this was not about comparing ourselves to anyone else, for there could be no comparison. God had set us on a different path, and our sole responsibility was to abide in, and follow, Him.

Eventually, God began to open up further ministry opportunities for me. One, particularly beloved, came in the form of my friend Isabella. Many years before, while I was still in university, she had moved to Canada for a year to study English. During her stay, she became a dear friend, and eventually a Christian. When she went back to her family in Asia, we developed a habit of telephoning each other once or twice a year. With a start, I realized that through all my time in Japan I'd not spoken with her. So I decided to contact her as quickly as possible. We arranged to connect over Skype.

When I saw her, I was shocked. She was very thin, painfully so, and as we talked I realized she was depressed. On grasping the extent of her depression, I recognized the need to connect with her more frequently. She expressed a deep spiritual hunger, so we started studying the Bible together, weekly.

Those Bible study times were an immense blessing to both of us. She told me that she found tremendous comfort and hope for the future in the Word of God, and I found a great deal of fulfilment as I was finally able to be the person I was made to be, using the gift of teaching God had given me.

I delighted to watch her learn and grow, and it was a privilege to be involved in the memorization of her first Bible verse. During the week following, she had a difficult time at work, so she quoted the verse to herself.

"That verse had nothing to do with my situation at the time," she later told me, "but when I quoted it, I was amazed. There was real power there. The Word of God has power!"

## CHAPTER 64

# Faith Without Risk

> *Was not Abraham our father justified by works, when he offered up Isaac his son on the altar? You see that faith was working with his works, and as a result of the works, faith was perfected; and the Scripture was fulfilled which says, "And Abraham believed God, and it was reckoned to him as righteousness," and he was called the friend of God. You see that a man is justified by works, and not by faith alone.*
>
> —James 2:21–24

Together with Isabella, I delighted in God's power through His Word, and the lessons of His Holy Spirit. One day I meditated in my journal on the concept of faith without works, and particularly on James 2:21–24. This was the story of how Abraham was justified: "by works".

November 7, 2012

> As I think about this passage, I realize that faith without works is toothless and anaemic. It has none of the vigour of vibrant faith, and eventually requires life-support. If not addressed, it leads to death.
>
> In considering this vignette of Abraham, I see that a synonym for 'faith without works' is 'faith without risk'. Are we so addicted to our life of comfort that we're unwilling to risk our hopes, our dreams, our very selves—on God? I wonder if this is actually a symptom of doubt. (Perhaps our view of God is unfounded. Perhaps our God

is not as strong and powerful as we say He is. Perhaps we don't want to find out we're wrong.)

So our solution is to sit timidly in a corner and not risk anything. We end our prayers with, "Thy will be done", couching our doubt in 'holy' terminology. Are we really so feeble that we can't handle a relationship with our Heavenly Father where He might say no?

Faith versus works: theology versus practice. What we say versus what we do. The world has a term for people whose words do not match their deeds: hypocrite—and rightly so.

We do not exist solely in the spiritual realm. Our bodies are an integral part of our existence, and our spiritual reality is often played out in the physical sphere. That's why we are to present our <u>bodies</u> as living sacrifices—because in so doing our spirits are also purified. Faith without works is dead because the spirit cannot exist without the body in this life. In the next, faith will become sight, and deeds will no longer be required.

In the meantime, if we are unwilling to risk, and unwilling to put ourselves on the line, then ours is an unhealthy, passive relationship with our Father. We want Him to do all of the work and take on all of the risk in our relationship. He, after all, put Himself on the line by sending Jesus to die for us.

Our works and answered prayers serve to increase our faith, and our faith in turn increases the amount we are willing to risk. So faith and works feed each other, growing bigger and bigger. Without this cycle, the plant of faith has no food, and is left to shrivel and die. Not only this, but our view of God begins to shrink, and we begin to place him on the shelf of our own convenience.

An unwillingness to risk robs us of the joy of seeing God at work, answering our prayers and blasting our pitiful dreams and expectations out of the water to something beyond good. What joy to realize the greatness of God, the Creator of the universe, who cannot be contained by the imagination of any man!

And what sorrow to see those unwilling to risk, walking around as faint shadows of who they could be, were they to step out in faith and allow their God to amaze and delight them.

## CHAPTER 65

# The Pendulum of Grief

Some days we would be happy, taking joy in our relationship with God and with each other. Other days, the grief of leaving the land and people we loved was overwhelming. Some nights, sorrow would insistently command an audience, banishing all rest from its presence. Such was the case at one point in November, as the newborn day blinked its way into existence. Everything poured out in my journal.

November 12, 2012

My God, my God, why hast Thou forsaken me?[1] Why hast Thou rejected me? My eyes stream with rivers of tears. My heart is broken, my insides quiver. My organs melt, my spirit is so bruised it chokes in its own bloody vomit. I am nothing, a worm, worthless and cast out. I have no intelligence, no success, no godliness to recommend me to You. I have nothing but failure and defeat and agony.

Where are You, Father? Oh Jesus, how I need You! I'm a fighter, but how can I fight when my skin has been stripped off, when all that's left is bone and a bit of sinew? How can I raise my fists for another round when there's so much blood and pain?

My soul screams. Do You hear?

There it is again.

I can't stop.

Run to me, Father. Envelop me in Your arms. Stroke my hair, hug me fiercely, and tell me that everything's going to be ok. That You're here. That You love me. Oh Jesus, I need You, how I need You…

When friends and family asked about our welfare, the answer would vary with our grief. This was the case when one of my pen pal friends happened to e-mail later that day.

"How are you doing" is a pretty loaded question at the moment, I responded. The last couple of days have been particularly hard for us, as we've both been deeply suffering over the things that have happened. At some times, it hits us harder than others, and it would be easier to crawl into a hole and not interact with the people we love here, because it causes us pain. But though this has been difficult, we also hope and pray that God will continue to use us in the lives of our friends for His good purposes.

On the following day, the pendulum swung back to a measure of peace. Jesus continued to enfold us in His presence and love.

## CHAPTER 66

# The Terror of the Telephone

Living in Japan, we were often amazed at how much we could understand and communicate to others, simply by using facial expressions and actions. These tools were incredibly powerful, both to our own understanding and to being understood by others. That was what made the telephone so daunting: the visual aids that helped us so greatly were absent.

Over the past few months, as my language abilities improved, the telephone became marginally less intimidating. I successfully navigated several Japanese-language calls from various people—some friends, some strangers.

Tuesday nights were our date night. As a special treat, we sometimes got takeout: sushi or McDonald's. One night in late November, I decided to stretch myself and try ordering pizza delivery from a place called Pizza-La, for dinner.

"If our dinner doesn't show up tonight, then we may have to cook something ourselves," I joked.

First came the preparation. We had a Pizza-La menu, which I scoured for details. Knowing that the key to a successful conversation would be in the groundwork, I made a list of options to select: *M-saizu* for medium size, *hando-tosu* for the crust selection, and *Maragurita* for the flavour (tomato, onion, and basil). In my dictionary, I looked up the word for 'delivery'. Hmm, maybe the Japanese word for 'try' would be useful. I looked that up too. I added up the cost of the items in the order. If the total that Pizza-La told me was the same as my calculation, I would know I'd ordered the right things. I pulled up my own name in our address book. In the stress of the moment, I didn't want to forget a key component of our location.

The conversation went something like this:

Pizza-La: [a bunch of things I didn't understand] Pizza-La [a bunch of other things I didn't understand].
Me: (in Japanese) I'm sorry, I'm Canadian and my Japanese isn't very good. This is my first time calling to make an order for pizza.
Pizza-La: If you wait, I can find someone who speaks English to help you.
Me: Thank you, but I would like to try using Japanese. Is this okay?
Pizza-La: Yes. Please go on.
Me: I would like to have delivery.
Pizza-La: Delivery. I understand.
Me: First, *Maragurita* pizza, *M-saizo*—
Pizza-La: *Maragurita*, yes. *M-saizu*, yes.
Me: Oh, sorry, *M-saizu. Hando-tosu.*

And so we went on: I would state my selection for an option, and he would confirm it. Eventually we came to the end of the order.

Pizza-La: [a few things I didn't understand] number [more I didn't understand]
Me: Do you want my phone number?
Pizza-La: Yes.

I told him our number, proud I could now read the digits off without thinking about what the Japanese words were.

Pizza-La: [I didn't understand anything.]

## On the Potter's Wheel

I knew the request for my address should be coming up. The word I knew for address wasn't in his previous sentence. However, deciding to assume he'd asked for our location, I rattled it off. It seemed to be what he was expecting.

He repeated my order to me, and I proudly understood everything he said.

Pizza-La:   [something I didn't understand] minute.

Hmm, it sounds like he's talking about how long it might be until the pizza arrives.

Me:   I'm sorry, can you please say that again?

He repeated himself. Yes, I was right. The pizza would arrive in thirty to forty minutes. Then he told me the cost of my order. I didn't quite hear the last two numbers, but the first two matched my calculation. We were in the ballpark! I thanked him and hung up the phone.

Twenty minutes later, the delivery boy dropped off our order—and everything was exactly as I'd intended. I've never before felt so victorious in ordering a pizza. And let me tell you: after such an accomplishment, that meal tasted pretty wonderful!

# CHAPTER 67

# An Unusual Encounter

A quartet of black-and-white kittens lived in the park across the street from our apartment. Their tails had been hacked off, and the leftover stumps indicated a messy chopping job that was clearly not genetic. They were skittish, but we slowly made friends with them and adopted the practice of going for evening visits in the park.

One night in early December, after feeding Ginger and the kittens some hot dogs, we turned to go home.

God had other plans. He told us to cut through the park and stand on a street corner by the local drug store.

We obeyed.

"What do You want us to do now?"

"Wait here."

A minute passed.

"Should we go somewhere else now?"

"No, just wait."

Five minutes passed. I felt kind of stupid just standing there as traffic whizzed by.

"Okay, you can go now," He finally said.

Just then a Japanese woman ran up to us.

"I want to pray for your happiness," she said. "You're Christians, right?"

Alarm bells started going off in my head. How did she know we were Christians? But I also felt a great love for her.

"Should we let her pray for us?" I asked God.

"No."

"What if we also pray for her?"

"Yes."

I prayed for her, partly in Japanese, partly in English. Peter went next.

Then she told me to close my eyes. I did, and silently asked God for protection, but after a few words God shouted into my mind, "NONONONONO!"

My eyes shot open, and I knew He wanted me to rebuke the unclean spirits she was addressing. I felt an almost-physical oppressive presence, but it started to lighten as I prayed to God and quietly whispered rebukes to evil spirits (with my eyes open).

She started by closing her eyes. "Thank you, thank you, thank you," she intoned. Then she raised her hands, parallel to us, palms outward, and spoke for awhile. After this, she brought her hands inwards, put them together in a praying posture, and reverently said thank you three more times.

Turning to Peter, she repeated this pattern.

"Should we invite her to our place?" I asked God.

"Yes."

We exchanged phone numbers and gave her our address. She would come for tea the next day at around 5:00 p.m. Her name was Charna.

After the exchange, God wouldn't allow Peter and me to return to our apartment for quite some time, and we got the sense that we needed to cleanse ourselves before entering our home. My body felt abnormally achy; Peter felt dizzy. We prayed together outside for about half an hour.

"I wonder if she's a *Yuta*," Peter said. We'd heard of matriarchal shamans in the Okinawan religion, but hadn't met one before now.

In our experience, her behaviour was atypical of a Japanese person. A single woman running up to a couple of complete strangers to pray for them? Agreeing to come to their home? Knowing that we were Christians, though we'd never met?

"Yeah, I've been wondering the same thing. Maybe she's the *Yuta* who's been active in the park and whose charm I found last year."

Just over a year ago, I'd asked for *Yutas* to come to know Jesus. Was she the first?

"Lord, I have no wisdom or experience in this type of situation, and neither does Peter," I prayed. "Please guide us. We don't know what to do."

On the day of our appointment, we spent the whole morning praying, and soliciting the prayers of others. Just as we were going through the armour of God that afternoon, the phone rang. It was Charna.

"I cannot come today. I am busy."

"I understand." I paused to ask God for guidance. "If you like, you can come for tea tomorrow or on Thursday."

"Yes, that sounds nice. I will telephone you when I am able to come."

She didn't come on Wednesday or Thursday.

The following morning we received an e-mail from one of our Canadian friends. We'd left a phone message for her, explaining the situation and requesting her intercession.

"I have no peace from God on the possibility of having Charna into your home," she wrote. "I strongly feel that though she might be allowed to stand on your threshold, she should not enter."

When we told our friends and family about the cancellation, several of them echoed the sentiment that this was God's way of protecting us.

"I wonder why God wanted us to meet Charna, if we wouldn't be able to spend time with her again," I later mused to Peter.

"Maybe He just wanted her to know there are now Christians here."

"Or maybe it was to show her that Christians aren't afraid of her spirits."

"We have no idea what she prayed. What if God wanted to show her that He can protect those who trust in Him?"

We never did end up having a visit or talking with Charna again.

Why? Perhaps we'll find out one day.

## CHAPTER 68

# Strong in Me

I'm no stranger to depression. Both my mum and sister have struggled terribly with it for many years. In that period of self-loathing and brokenness, before Jesus healed my emotional wounds, I also experienced it to some degree. I've seen the tearful hopelessness of never-ending struggle and battle fatigue in the eyes of those I love; the devastation that can follow in the wake of a well-meaning Christian who blithely suggests that depression is a 'spiritual problem', solvable with the correct scriptural regimen; and my sister's spiral toward the fateful nadir that culminated in her suicide attempt. Though depression is not a part of my general psyche, I know it. I know what it looks like. I know what it can do.

As we approached Christmas 2012, I was not feeling depressed. There was no downward spiral, no monotonous drone of hopelessness. Yes, my lifelong dreams had been ripped away; but God showed me over and over again that He had something more planned, and injected me with hope for the future. As unknown as that future was, an inexplicable sense of love and security accompanied me.

Sometimes I was overwhelmed with the pain of our situation; but this was grief, not depression. Along with those seasons of grief, there were also times of peace and happiness.

A week after we met Charna, Peter was out at a Christmas function and I was alone at home, reading.

At one point, I stopped. Numbness encased my heart, as though I were staring at something so massive, so incomprehensible, that my mind couldn't absorb it.

## On the Potter's Wheel

A tidal wave crashed over me, and I was suddenly submerged in despair. Struggling to stay emotionally afloat, I found myself sucked downward, unable to breathe.

Ah! The pain! It sliced through my chest, almost a physical sensation.

I clenched my teeth, ground them a little. A puff of air escaped my throat, almost a sigh.

*How can I go on? I don't want to go on.* That thought swirled around me.

I went out to our balcony and stared over the edge to the ground four storeys below, transfixed.

It was nighttime. The lights in the park across the street shone in the darkness. I barely noticed them.

Looking down at the pavement again, I stroked the balcony ledge. The rough concrete prickled along my fingertips.

A sharp breath in.

My limbs felt heavy.

I couldn't do it.

I came back inside, drained, despising my own cowardice.

"God, right now everything seems futile," I prayed in my journal. "I feel completely bereft, empty of hope, void of joy. My soul is bruised, beaten, bleeding, close to death. I cannot feel anything because the nerves of my heart have taken in the maximum they can handle. The beating has gone on for so long, has been so severe that there's nothing left to feel. Not even love. I wish I could say that I love You right now, but I can't. I don't want to lie to You. You deserve love, but such an emotion no longer exists for me. I'm sorry."

I went to sleep.

On the following morning, as suddenly as it had come, the despair was gone. I felt guilty over my earlier struggle but shoved the feeling aside, not wanting to examine why. Something was amiss, and I was afraid of what I might find within myself.

The next day I continued to avoid my feelings, and God.

The day after, I began to think about that night of despondency and what it had meant. My faith had been so weak. I came to God and asked for His help in figuring out what had happened.

He slowly poured His understanding into my mind. He reminded me that Japan is known for its high suicide rates. There is an evil spirit of suicide who is partially responsible. That night, it had visited me.

"The forces of evil are stronger than me," I responded in my journal. "That has never been in dispute. But the God who created everything is stronger still. And it is to Him that I have entrusted myself.

"Before this happened, I thought my faith was strong. It had been proven in fire and could weather anything. But I had it slightly wrong, didn't I, God? I was one small step away from self-sufficiency. My name means 'strong'. But I am not strong in You, Jesus. You are strong in me."

Later that day, my devotions were based on Revelation 1. John's reaction when he saw Jesus struck me. The One with whom he'd been best friends in life was fearsome and awe-inspiring.

"You are a great God, fearful and majestic," I prayed. "But—in the midst of all the trembling and awe in heaven—will I get to hug You?"

A cascade of His love suddenly enveloped me. "Yes."

His love continued to pour into my spirit, as if I were an empty vessel. Well, not quite empty. I'd been full of pain. But as His love poured into me, it displaced some of that hurt.

The closest analogy I can think of is when I was in a car accident and got shards of glass in my arm. The doctor at the hospital had to dig them out, which was painful. But it was a good kind of pain because he was removing what shouldn't have been there.

In the same way, my soul's pain was being removed and making room for more of God's Spirit. This process stung a little. But it was good pain. I felt safe and valuable and cherished.

CHAPTER 69

# According to Plan?

Chelsea, Karin, and Helen had repeatedly indicated an interest in learning how to cook in a North American style, so I decided Christmas baking would be a good place to start. On one Saturday evening in November, I invited them over. Their children enjoyed licking out the batter bowls after our goodies were in the oven, and we planned to bake together again in early December.

Meanwhile, as we neared the year's end, Peter and I arranged a party for Christmas Eve. However, we didn't want to invite only those who knew or had heard about Jesus. We also wanted to invite our neighbours and introduce them to local Christians. Our neighbours' low comfort level with us and lack of familiarity with people from the church were the main potential barriers.

So I came up with a plan, inserting stages of familiarity into our invitation. Peter bought small, decorative boxes to house my Christmas sweets from the baking session; and when we handed them out to our neighbours, I also invited the ladies to join us next time. We hoped they would become comfortable with us through that time, and receptive to the idea of their families attending our Christmas party.

The night before the next baking session, God told me to sit. I got nervous. Wondering if I was hearing Him properly, I asked for more confirmation. Still, He persisted.

I was scared. The last time I'd tried to sit was in May, and then there had been a regression.

"Where should I sit?" I asked.

"On the open toilet seat, with your pants up."

Probably more filled with fear than with faith, I did what I was told. Two minutes was the commanded time.

When I sat down, I asked, "Is this what You want?"

His answer throbbed in my mind. The word "yes" started small, gradually built until almost a shout, and then slowly receded only to intensify again.

"Yes (this is what I want)."

"Yes (this is Me telling you to do this)."

"Yes (you heard properly)."

"Yes (I am with you)."

"Yes (you'll be fine)."

"Yes (you'll be okay tomorrow for your baking party)."

When it was over, I got up and continued on with the evening. The next day, I experienced no ill effects.

When the time to bake arrived, several men showed up along with their wives. Peter had gone shopping for my Christmas gift, but I called him back so our male friends would feel comfortable. They had fun chatting together and eating samples of the ladies' cooking. Eleven people came, including several kids. We made chocolate truffles and sugar cookies.

One of the ladies had made cookies before, but only the kind that are rolled up in a ball and dropped onto an oven tray. When I pulled out a rolling pin, their eyes grew ever so round. The kids had a lot of fun, and we adults enjoyed watching them. They eventually abandoned the use of cookie cutters in favour of making their own original shapes.

Afterward, Peter and I planned to give this batch of treats to our neighbours too. As was our custom, we prayed for God's guidance before each action.

"Okay, God, You know that tonight we're planning to invite our neighbours to the Christmas party. Who should we go to first? Our neighbours across the hall?"

"No."

"To the other family on our floor?"

"No."

"What about the neighbour who lives directly below us?"

"Yes, go there."

To our knowledge, this neighbour was a single man. When Peter and I gave him the treats and invitation, his reaction was strange to our Western thinking. I wondered if we'd somehow offended him. Perhaps we'd been too pushy by Japanese standards. Given his reaction, I knew he wouldn't be coming.

When we asked God who we should approach next, He wouldn't allow us to give out any more invitations. Though disappointed that none of our neighbours would attend the party, we eventually shrugged it off and obeyed.

Christmas Eve finally arrived. We'd been sick for the week beforehand but managed to recover a few days prior to it. I spent that time cooking. Many traditional Christmas foods and desserts weren't readily available in Okinawa, so I made virtually everything from scratch. God graciously gave me the energy for each day.

On the morning of the party, we got a call from Higa sensei.

"Peter, can you play violin for one of our church members? We will be going to see him this evening, before carol singing."

"Carol singing starts at 7:00 p.m.?" Peter queried.

"Yes. Can you play?"

"Yes, I think so."

The call ended.

I wigged out. "Our party was supposed to finish at 7:00 p.m., and now you're going to be leaving before it's even over!"

"Don't worry," Peter said calmly. Too calmly. "Okinawans have a way of working everything out. Timing won't be a prob—"

"Now I'll have to hold down the fort all by myself because you can't say no!"

I had organized this great event, but now it was in ruins, like all my other plans of late. I'd planned to be a lifetime missionary with our former organization, then I'd been injured and undergone a long recovery, they'd cut us loose, and now the party plans were in shambles too. What was the point of even making plans?

Eventually I calmed down, resigned to the coming disaster. God was going to do whatever He was going to do. Though I didn't see much point in making plans, I knew it was futile to fight Him anymore.

Four o'clock rolled around, and the doorbell rang for the first time. It was our downstairs neighbour, Richard, and his wife Rose. She was pregnant, due in April. I got them settled, had them sign our guestbook, and gave them apple cider. No one else showed up for almost half an hour, which was a little awkward. I did my best to converse with them in Japanese, and they seemed to understand me.

Finally, Helen also arrived. She was able to talk with them while I finished my preparations. Daniel had invited some people whom he'd recently met at a community English class, and four of them came. Two were Christians, two were not. Most people started arriving at 5:00 p.m. (an hour late), at which point I served dinner.

We had a main course of chicken, ham, rice pilaf, honey carrots, cranberry sauce, bread, stuffing, gravy, and potluck contributions (pizza, rice balls, and salad); after which we played a game with ¥100 gifts, equivalent to presents from the dollar store.

Everyone took a randomly-assigned number and then either chose a gift from the central pile or stole someone else's. We'd been worried the Japanese would be too polite to steal, but after we went first, there was quite a lot of exchanging between moms for some hand soap. At the end, the kids pulled chicken wishbones for a few leftover gifts.

Then we had dessert: chocolate truffles, candy canes, shortbread, maple cookies, pumpkin pie with whipped cream, and sugar cookies with an icing-and-sprinkles decorating station. At this point, Higa sensei arrived. He and Tsuneko sensei were able to meet the new people, enjoy dessert, and join in the group photo.

After this, our neighbours and the English students made their exit. The rest went with Higa sensei to sing at the church member's house. It was some distance away—requiring a car ride—so I stayed at home. Peter later told me that the fellow was rather old and infirm and not able to get to church, but was a new Christian. Greatly encouraged that they would go to him, he gave Peter two scarves as Christmas presents.

A few minutes after everyone left, Patrick showed up. He'd just finished work. I gave him dinner and dessert, though not in that order. We chatted a bit and then he left, choosing not to go carolling.

When everyone else returned from the church member's house, we walked to some local stores and sang Christmas carols outside. It was 18°C, but our friends were all cold. After the first place, Higa sensei was ready to stop, but everyone else wanted to go on. So we sang another two songs down the street outside of a convenience store.

Peter was playing violin, so he saw more than I did; I was concentrating on my song sheet and just trying to get the Japanese words right. The classroom by the convenience store opened up its windows and people poked their heads out to hear; several in cars rolled down their windows; some passersby stopped to listen, while others cast glances over their shoulders as they strolled on; and one man riding a bike started to

## On the Potter's Wheel

veer into traffic before stopping to have a cigarette and enjoy the music.

After Higa sensei and Tsuneko sensei left, the younger generation came back to our place to warm up. We served hot cocoa and homemade apple cider, and watched the cartoon version of *The Grinch Who Stole Christmas*. Peter explained to Daniel what rhymes are.

It was a school night, so our friends and their families left for home. Peter and I cleaned up everything in less than an hour. Then we hit the sack, souls full and hearts grateful.

At one point in the night, I woke up.

"Wasn't that a good night?" God said.

"Yes, Lord."

"Your plans don't work out because they're too small. I want to bless you, Valerie. I have better plans."

I bowed my head.

"Trust Me, Valerie."

I repented. "Yes, Lord, I will."

CHAPTER 70

# The Little Giant

When we left Canada, Peter's grandfather was ninety-five years old. We'd signed up as missionaries for a three-year term and knew that in all probability we were saying goodbye to him for the last time.

He was so proud of us, and our family said he was always telling his Japanese friends that we had gone off to share the good news about Jesus in Japan.

As my language abilities improved, I began to write him letters in Japanese. At first, they were simplistic, written in the Japanese phonetic alphabet, but as my language studies progressed, I was able to use more and more of the Chinese characters (*kanji*) employed by adults. Grandpa was always gracious in his enjoyment of my abysmal Japanese and would respond with correspondence of his own, also in his native tongue.

It had been many decades since he had lived in Japan, so some of the characters he employed were not in general use anymore, and I couldn't even find them in my dictionary. Still, I would painstakingly translate his letters into English; type out what I wanted to say in Japanese, leaning heavily on my dictionary; teach myself how to write the characters required; and meticulously write out responses by hand. After this, I would need to rest from letter writing for a few weeks because the process had been so mentally draining!

One of my proudest moments was when Grandpa received my last letter. On reading it, he exclaimed to his daughters, "Did she type this? It's so neat. I can't believe she wrote this!"

## On the Potter's Wheel

I would write him two more letters, but one would arrive after he passed away in early 2013. The other would never be mailed because he died the day after I finished it. Its envelope still remains tucked into the cover of my journal.

In the days before Christmas 2012, Peter's grandfather was admitted to the hospital. At first the doctors thought he was having heart problems, but the following week, they found that his difficulties most likely resulted from cancer. Dark spots were visible on the scans of his liver and lungs, but with his advanced age and weakened condition, the doctors thought it unwise to engage in a biopsy.

We rang in the New Year rather soberly. Peter's grandfather had been given three months to live. His daughters began to consider moving him to a home as they could no longer care for him properly. Peter and I discussed the possibility of his return to Canada for a brief visit to say goodbye.

In the first week of January, we heard that Grandpa had become fearful of going to sleep because he didn't want to die then. Pastor Ito, who had led Grandpa to Christ seven years before, came to visit and reassured him of his eternal security. After that visit, Grandpa was much less fearful.

One morning later that week, Grandpa was sitting in the chair of his hospital room, eating breakfast.

The nurse came in just as he finished. "Mr. Hashimoto, we're going to move you to a different floor for a few days while we sort out your future accommodation. Someone will come in for you after breakfast, okay?"

"Okay," he said. Then he took a deep breath, and died.

"I've never seen anything like it," the nurse later told his daughters.

We were grateful that God had granted Grandpa's desire: he hadn't died in his sleep.

Because of immigration issues, Peter wasn't able to make it back to Canada for the funeral. So we participated in the ways we could. Peter sent a recording of himself playing two of the funeral hymns on his violin, and I wrote down a few recollections to be read during the service:

> Most of our memories of Grandpa involve him sitting contentedly, eating some sort of snack, and listening to his family around him. He was always a quiet man, and it wasn't until Peter was in his late teens that he realized how funny Grandpa was. He was good with his hands, and very talented at many things. He loved gardening, and we were always amazed at the size of the vegetables he nurtured. He was artistic, and loved practicing calligraphy.
>
> He really liked the Blue Jays and the Leafs, and always wanted to watch their games on TV, so we would scout out the sports schedules whenever he came over to visit. Several years ago, Peter remembers that Grandpa said he didn't think he would see the Leafs win the Stanley Cup again, and he was right!
>
> He was really proud of his Japanese heritage. When he found out we would be going to Japan as missionaries, he was so excited. He sat us down beside himself to look at the Japanese newspaper and practice reading the characters. He was so enthusiastic, and we got tired out before he did! After we'd been in Japan for awhile, and our language had improved a bit, we had the amazing opportunity to correspond with him in Japanese. We will miss you, Grandpa. We're so glad we will see you again.

It was difficult for us to be so far away, and unable to love and interact with our family in the ways that came most naturally to us. The delay between death and funeral, where the reality of his passing was lacking, was elongated for us. A thoughtful cousin videotaped the ceremony, so eventually we did experience a measure of closure. But at the same time we knew part of our mourning would be deferred until we stepped back onto Canadian soil.

Grandpa had recorded many of the events of his life before he died, and entrusted them to Pastor Ito, who read selections aloud during the funeral ceremony. Short in stature, Grandpa was large in perseverance and care for his family.

Pastor Ito's summary was incredibly meaningful to us. "As I look at his life," he said, "I can't help thinking that here was a little giant."

# CHAPTER 71
# Where You Are

As matters beyond our control swirled around us, Peter and I sometimes felt as though we were merely observers of our own situation. However, the events that had transpired and continued to play out seemed to be more intertwined than we'd imagined. We could see God at work not only in many dimensions of our own lives, but also in the lives of people around us. I mulled over these ideas in my journal.

> January 2012
>
> God's methods appear messier than we would like. Sometimes it would be more comfortable to have everything visibly neat and tidy. But I believe part of the reason things appear messy is that they're actually far neater and more connected than we realize.
>
> To a one-dimensional being, a square would appear to be an unfinished line. However when we step into two dimensions we see that the square is a complete shape in itself. Because we don't exist in the same reality as God, we don't fully realize all that He is doing.
>
> However, this verse is true: "God causes all things to work together for good to those who love [Him], to those who are called according to His purpose"[1]. We can't always see this because we haven't stepped into His plane of existence. We are still being, and eventually will be, conformed to the image of His Son, according to our predestined eternity.

## On the Potter's Wheel

As God continued to guide me toward healing, I couldn't help feeling a little self-conscious at times and avoided telling people outside of our immediate families the details of God's direction. His approach seemed odd to say the least. But then I remembered the Israelites. God led them, too, with His pillars of cloud and of fire. In their case, He was fine-tuning the leadership of a nation. In mine, He was leading an individual, and I couldn't help delighting in the intimacy and love of the journey.

I rejoiced in the affirmation of the Bible, where there were several conversations with God similar to mine; and the confirmation of my own experience. Peter and I were amazed at the results God was giving. I could now stand and periodically walk for all my waking hours (fifteen to sixteen hours per day, every day). This was longer than I'd ever been able to stand, even before my injury. My sister, a nurse, remarked that even an uninjured person would struggle to do some of the things that now came easily to me.

At one point, God had another lesson in store. Over the past months, I'd been asking for His guidance in every action and decision. When He gave direction, I simply obeyed.

"What should I do now?" I asked one day.

"What do you want to do?" He countered.

And He allowed me to make a decision on my own.

On another day, He told me not to eat a treat I'd been craving.

In the past, I would have regretfully put it away, but this time was different. "Actually, I really want to eat this. You know I'll obey whatever You tell me to do. But I'd like to ask Your permission again."

To my surprise, He responded, "Okay, you can eat your treat."

It was then that I realized something new. Our relationship was no longer solely one of command and obedience; God was now allowing room for conversation.

# CHAPTER 72

# Appointments

When we started feeding the kittens in the park, it seemed that each of them had been imprinted by a different fear, perhaps associated with their recent tail trauma. One would panic whenever there was anything over his head, whether an umbrella or an outstretched arm. Another was terrified at the sight of a human hand.

As the months wore on, they began to trust us. The day when we were first allowed to stroke them was one of true delight. Soon they rather liked being touched and would come to us even when we had no food, just for a petting.

Peter's favourite, Blackie, adopted him as her protector. A little black cat with white paws, chest, and belly, she would follow Peter anywhere—even into situations where she was afraid of her surroundings. She loved to be petted but was fearful of hands. Her solution was to approach Peter and then quickly turn her back to him. This became her way of asking for a petting; she could enjoy the pleasure of being stroked without having to suffer the fear of seeing his hand.

My favourite, Buddy, was a white cat with black blotches. He had the widest feline eyes I'd ever seen, and approached life with a great deal of curiosity and wonder. He loved to climb trees and would head-butt my legs whenever he thought I was paying him insufficient attention.

The remaining two kittens, females we named Trap and Quad, were explorers by nature and would only attend feedings that fit into their travel plans.

As we continued to interact with them, we found that God seemed to be healing us through the kittens, and the kittens through us. Our hearts began to unwind from their tightly-coiled pain, and the kittens learned how to play again as we brought them cat toys.

When we told stories of our evening outings to a Canadian friend, he remarked that this would likely be a powerful testimony to the people in our neighbourhood. Perhaps those outings were just what he suggested: a visual parable of the healing Christ can bring.

During this time, we began experiencing a high number of 'appointments' that seemed to have been set up by God. These largely stemmed from my practice of praying before each action and decision. God used those prayers to direct us in reaching out to people around us.

The first instance was during an evening walk in the park, a few weeks before Christmas.

"Should I go to the park tonight?" I asked.

His love flooded into my soul. "Yes," He said.

It felt different. Another sensation was also included in His yes, as if He were anticipating something with delight.

*Maybe I'll get to see and pet the cats tonight*, I thought.

But He had different plans.

"Should I go now?"

"Not yet."

A little later, "Now?"

"Not yet."

I eventually gave up hope of going, thinking I'd misunderstood His instruction.

Peter kept encouraging me to ask again.

Eventually the waiting ended. "Yes."

Peter and I started out on our usual walk, but God soon brought me up short with a small pain in my rear.

"Am I doing something wrong?" I asked. "Where do You want us to go?"

"Turn around."

We obeyed and walked along the way He directed, praying for His leading at almost every step. Eventually, He had us circle a small playground at one edge of the park. On our first circuit, we noticed a group of high school girls there.

"Go into the park," God said as we were starting our second circuit. "Now, go and talk with the girls."

At this point, I was scared. Our Japanese wasn't very good, and packs of teenage girls could be so daunting. How would they react? Would they run from us, screaming?

"I think God is telling us to go and talk with those girls," I said, "but I don't know what to say."

Peter paused. "Well, let's try just walking by and saying 'good evening' in Japanese."

When we went by and delivered our line, one of the girls said something I didn't quite catch.

"I'm sorry, can you please repeat that? My Japanese isn't very good. We're from Canada."

When they heard that we were from Canada, a couple of them squealed, and all ten gathered around us.

"Where in Canada?"

"Do they have snow there now?"

"Your skin is so white! And your nose is so pointy!" (Directed to me, not Peter!)

"How long have you been here?"

"Why did you come to Okinawa?"

We ended up talking with them for more than forty-five minutes. They were all seventeen. We had a chance to tell them about Canada, and that we'd come to Okinawa as missionaries because we love Jesus.

# On the Potter's Wheel

Almost bursting with excitement, that night I wrote in my journal, "Thank you God, for this amazing encounter. It was so much better than cats!"

The next day during language practice, I told Eleanor about what had happened. She was also excited. From her reaction, I gathered that the openness we encountered was really unusual in Japan.

We later saw a few of the girls in the park again, and hoped that if we were able to stay in Okinawa they would be interested in joining our ESL classes.

Reflecting on this encounter and the one with the suspected witch doctor, I gained some new insights on the human perception and experience of reality. I recorded them in my journal.

*Early 2013*

I read Matthew 16:24-25 in my devotions today.

> Then Jesus said to His disciples, "If anyone wishes to come after Me, let him deny himself, and take up his cross, and follow Me. For whoever wishes to save his life shall lose it; but whoever loses his life for My sake shall find it."

Followers of Jesus must deny themselves and be willing to suffer. Our physical lives, and the value we place on them, are inversely proportional to our spiritual lives. Which reality will we embrace?

It's interesting to note the Matthew 16 passage implies that we can only choose to live well in one reality—or perhaps it's possible to live half-lives in both. If we wish to live fully, though, we have to jettison caring about the other reality. Over the last few weeks, I've been learning to cast off what others think of me as God has me wandering around. I used to worry about looking stupid. Now I've started caring more about obeying Him than about human appearances. If we're always cognizant of how short the time is, then we're willing to risk more in the physical realm.[1]

One evening in the new year, I felt like going for a walk—not to do anything in particular, just to amble with Peter. We wandered around the aisles of a local grocery store. While there, we picked up some dry cat food. It would probably be better for the cats than the hot dogs we'd been feeding them.

When we went out the next night for our regular kitty time, they all seemed to like the new food.

Partway through the feeding, four boys came up to us.

"Hello," they said.

We introduced ourselves.

"Are you from the Mormon Temple?" Many Japanese people are leery of Mormons.

"No." We showed them the address of Seaside Chapel.

They wanted to know all about Canada, so we told them a few things. They asked about Canadian weather, Christmas, and cultural customs.

I gave them some dry food, and they enjoyed feeding the cats too.

We talked with them for about half an hour. This was no small feat because they knew even less English than the high school girls whom we'd met earlier. We eventually parted ways, but it was a great first encounter.

I looked at my watch as we left and was surprised at the length of our conversation; usually junior high boys don't have such long attention spans.

"Maybe it's not a coincidence that God wants us to feed the cats in a well-lit area on the busiest part of the path," Peter commented on the walk home. "Maybe this way people will see us regularly, and eventually we might be able to connect with them."

## On the Potter's Wheel

In mid-January, university students from Campus Crusade for Christ (CCC) Korea came to Japan for a short-term mission trip. Over a hundred people, divided into teams, came at the same time. All but one of the teams were stationed in Okinawa. Seaside Chapel was assigned eleven people. Many didn't speak Japanese, but all spoke some English.

They carried out a series of outreach events, with Peter and the rest of the church helping out. The crowning event was "Korea Night", a special evening showcasing their culture. Approximately a hundred people attended, one-third of whom had never before come to Seaside Chapel. The mission team cooked everyone a Korean dinner and subsequently put on a presentation consisting of dance; mimes telling the gospel story; and a Tai Kwon Do demonstration, which was a big hit since Okinawa is the birthplace of karate.

I was still unable to walk to church or travel in a car, so the team planned to visit me at our apartment. The day beforehand, I needed supplies for our guests. However, when I prepared to go to the grocery store, I felt a check in my spirit.

"Not yet," God said.

I went through most of the afternoon asking, "Can I go now?"

Always the answer was the same.

Finally, when I'd resigned myself to not shopping until the following morning, and was about to wash my face from the day's humidity, the instruction came: "Go now."

"Really, God? Can I wash my face first?"

"No. Now."

I went. It was my habit to say good afternoon to anyone on the street who made eye contact. I didn't get very far before an older lady smiled at me.

"Good afternoon!"

To my surprise, she stopped. "Where are you from?"

We ended up having a conversation entirely in Japanese (she spoke no English), and I understood 90 percent of what she said.

"Why have you come to Okinawa?"

"My husband and I are missionaries. We're working with a church in this area."

"Which church?"

"Here's the address." I pulled out my business card. Showing people the church's address often served two purposes: it let them know we weren't Mormon (most people knew where the Mormon temple was, and avoided it); it also helped them to become familiar with the church's location, should they want to visit later.

She peered at the card. "I'm sorry, I've forgotten my glasses. I can't make out what this says."

"Oh, sorry. We're working with a church called Seaside Chapel, which—"

"Seaside Chapel? I know that church. It's right over there, isn't it?"

"Yes, that's right."

We must have talked for fifteen to twenty minutes.

"I have enjoyed our chat. I will stop to talk again the next time I see you in our neighbourhood," she said.

With that, we continued along our different paths.

After this encounter, I began to carry a notepad and pen in my pocket whenever I went out. Who knew if I might need to exchange contact information with someone after another 'appointment'?

The Campus Crusade team came over the next day. We served them banana split sundaes. After they devoured all the ice cream in our house, we made note to never underestimate the stomach capacity of university boys!

Peter set up our TV to play a slideshow of the past two weeks of ministry, and videos of their performances during Korea Night. It was a great time of prayer and fellowship.

At the end, they all gathered around in a semicircle and sang me a song. Then they prayed for me, Peter and I prayed for them, they sang us another song, and we took pictures. What refreshment to my soul. I felt incredibly loved, and thanked God for His amazing message of tenderness to me that morning.

On the day of their departure, the mission team went to say goodbye to some of the school children to whom they'd ministered. They arrived in the school yard at 8:10 a.m. and realized they were late. School had started ten minutes before. Some of the children saw them from their classrooms and crowded around the windows to wave goodbye.

The principal saw what was happening. He came out to greet everyone and invited them into the building to say a proper farewell. Eleanor, my Japanese language tutor, is a retired school teacher. She was with the team at the time and later told me that she knows this man.

"I'm sorry we could not have you into the school this year," the principal said as the team departed. "If the mission team comes back next year, I'll make sure that we have a special school assembly so you can make a presentation to the students then."

We were once more reminded that though we may be delayed, God's timing is never late.

CHAPTER 73

# Compassion

Reading through the Bible, I made a startling discovery in the book of Ezekiel. In chapters 25–26, God gave prophecies of judgement and destruction against five different nations.
*Why were they being penalized?* I wondered.
It turned out that three of the five were being judged not for their actions, but for their attitudes. They'd rejoiced in the downfall of God's chosen people, Israel; they had exulted in Israel's destruction. They'd said, "Aha!...now that she lies in ruins I will prosper."[1]
I took this as a solemn warning to never exult in the judgement and punishment of God's people, regardless of the deeds that might have brought them to such a fate.
Nevertheless, in the early days of January I started to notice a disturbing trend in my thinking and emotions: the feeling that I wouldn't be altogether sad or sorry if God punished the people who had hurt me. I remembered that earlier lesson from the book of Ezekiel and asked Jesus to help me have a godly attitude in these things.
A couple of days later, I came to Psalm 51 in my devotions. I didn't get very far in praying for God's cleansing before He stopped me. As quickly as thoughts and prayers came into my mind, they dissipated—like watching a video of the ripples on a pond after rocks had been thrown in, on double- or triple-speed. The ripples of my thoughts became smaller and smaller.
"Be still," God said.

It was a weird experience. In the past, when He'd asked me to be still before Him, I'd felt filled with His love, united with Him. But this time was different. I was still, and my thoughts were largely empty. There was a sense that He was with me and that I was safe, but there was also an impression of separateness, as if He were across the room.

In the stillness, the pain from my emotional wounds evaporated.

My thoughts flitted around, quickly snatched away and quieted. "I'm not very good at thinking about nothing. Can I think about Jesus?"

"Yes."

I thought about Jesus with the children, Jesus on the cross, Jesus living His life. I didn't know what He looked like. I imagined Him with a beard, without; fat, thin. "I would have loved You any way You looked."

I thought back to Psalm 51. "Please give me a clean heart."

"You are clean," He said

A pause. "Lord, I don't just want to be empty of sin. I want to be full of You."

Immediately, I felt joined with Him, as if a pitcher of His love and Spirit had been poured into my soul. We were together again; there was no separateness.

But then I noticed something. The emotional pain was back. Just a little, deep in my belly.

"Why is the pain back?" I asked. "When we were separate, it was gone. But when You filled me, it came back."

I had a thought. "Is this <u>Your</u> pain, Jesus? Your pain over what they've done?"

"Yes."

"Is this the way to have compassion on them, to have a godly attitude toward them? To feel Your pain?"

"Yes."

The process of forgiveness can be a long one. In my experience, the deeper the wound, the longer the time required for its healing. After having felt powerless for so long, my psyche developed a creative way to once more feel control: through criticism. It was like a dangerous animal, ready to lash out at anyone, regardless of his or her relationship to me. When this beast began to spew its venom at people I loved and respected, I realized that the imprisoned creature was me. I was neither happy nor free.

Thankfully, this state of misery only lasted for a week or two. Working through the pain in my heart, I realized it would be easy to develop a haughty spirit and look down on those who had hurt me as being somehow inferior to myself. I came across a few quotations that helped me reexamine my own heart from a variety of new angles, and my journal once more became a conduit for meditation.

February 19, 2013

> Martin Luther King Jr. once said, "I have begun to realize how hard it is for a lot of people to think about living without someone to look down upon, really look down upon. It is not that they will feel cheated out of someone to hate, it is that they will be compelled to look more closely at themselves, at what they don't like in themselves. ...[S]omeday all of us will see that when we start going after a race or religion, a type, a region, a section of the Lord's humanity—then we're cutting into His heart, and we're bleeding badly ourselves."[2]
> 
> I think that looking down on others can be an addiction. It perversely feeds our sense of pride. We become the Pharisee scorning the Publican[3]. By having someone to spurn, by having someone lower on the totem pole, we think we somehow commend ourselves to

God. We are more lovable, more 'worthy' of his attention. But Jesus said, at the end of the parable, that it was the Publican who went on his way, forgiven.

Reading this story again, I realize the Pharisee never asked for forgiveness. In his self-righteousness, he only thanked God that there was someone to look down on. <u>God granted the desires of both men</u>. The prayer of the Publican (for forgiveness) was granted. The Pharisee was thankful for someone to look down upon, and his wish was also satisfied. There will always be someone new whom we can creatively diminish.

The Pharisee wasn't really concerned about his relationship with God at all. He was only interested in his status among men. But to the Publican, whose sole request centred around God, Jesus assures us that He will open up the storehouses of heaven.

# CHAPTER 74
# New Doors

As time passed, we noticed progress not only in my healing and our language skills, but also in the relationships forming between us and the people of our community. I walked all over our neighbourhood, developing a standard route to ensure regular visits, and chatted with shopkeepers and people on the street, introducing them to the church and telling them a little about Jesus. He was my answer to the inevitable question of why we'd come to Japan.

If we were able to find a new organization and stay in Okinawa, we hoped the time we were using to build relationships in the community would later bear fruit. We also developed many ideas, based on our observations, of possible venues and methods that we might use to connect with people. If we weren't able to stay, we still prayed that somehow this work would be useful down the road for those who would remain.

Much of that February was rainy and gray. I couldn't walk around the community as I wanted to, and after several consecutive days of this, I was antsy. I mentioned my impatience to Isabella one day in our Bible study. She prayed for good weather for me.

The following day was supposed to be grey again, according to the forecast. It was actually bright, warm, and sunny. I knew that God had answered our prayers.

In the afternoon, Peter and I went for a long stroll around our neighbourhood. We ended up walking for an hour and a half! It was so wonderful.

At the end, when I realized how long we'd been out, I thought of church. Peter had told me that at my pace, it would probably take me half an hour to get there. He'd also mentioned that there would be a special speaker at church the next day.

I thought, *Why not?*

I didn't really expect the answer to be yes, but decided to ask God anyway: "So, can I go to church tomorrow?"

A wave of deep sadness washed over me.

"No," He said.

Something seemed out of place. Why such deep sadness? I hadn't been expecting a yes. I'd been content to wait on God's timing.

"Wait a minute," I said. "Is this sadness Yours, God?"

"Yes," He said. "I want you to go to church, to rejoice in being with My people, but now is not the time. Please wait a little longer."

Shortly after this, new activity sprouted at our apartment. Daniel wanted to begin a discussion group for the new Christians in our circle of friends. We jumped on board and offered our apartment as a quiet place to meet. Since we weren't allowed to head official ministries, we encouraged Daniel to take the lead on initiating the group.

He decided to market it as an opportunity to discuss the Sunday sermons after church, on alternating weeks. Since Peter's and my understanding of Japanese was rudimentary, he encouraged our friends to come out, explain the sermons to us, and share what they'd learned. We found that this freed the other participants to be more open. They, too, were allowed to ask questions if they didn't understand a concept.

Daniel, Grant, Neil, and Otto came to our first discussion. Grant and Neil were two of the newly Christian men; Otto was a shy boy of seventeen who had come to our Canada Day party and had also participated in the "Peter and Friends" band of the previous summer. That week we discussed the church as the body of Christ, and its maturation over time; everyone had interesting insights to share.

"I used to think that *gospel* was just a type of music," Neil said. "Now I know it's much more."

"I never knew that the church is like a person," Grant added. "It grows just like a human, starting as a child."

To our delight, even Otto was bold enough to ask some questions.

Peter and I were excited at this new leadership training for Daniel as he approached a life of ministry, and we all enjoyed the opportunity to dig deeper into Higa sensei's excellent sermons.

Meanwhile, our evening visits to the park continued. God still gave us opportunities to regularly connect with people in our neighbourhood.

One evening, I went out alone to feed the kittens in the park. A man in his fifties walked by, looking interested.

I motioned toward the kittens. "They're cute, aren't they?"

"Yes, they are!"

We began to talk. It turned out that his grandparents did the opposite of Peter's grandfather: they were born in Japan, lived in the Seattle area for awhile, and then returned to Japan. He still had cousins in that area of the United States, and was very interested in visiting North America sometime.

"Where are you from? British Columbia? Alberta?"

"We're from Ontario. Do you know it?"

"Yes, I know Ontario. How long have you been here?"

"About a year and a half."

## On the Potter's Wheel

"Only one year? Your Japanese is very good."

"Thank you!"

By this time we were talking half in English, half in Japanese, since it was obvious he wanted to practice his English.

"Do you come to this park often?"

"Yes."

"Well then," he said, "if I see you again, I will talk with you some more."

His name was Mori.

# CHAPTER 75

# The News

I'm easily addicted to my smartphone, so one of my personal rules is to never check e-mails in the middle of the night. However, I'm not always good at following it.

One morning, in violation of my usual practice, I checked my messages before being completely awake. There was one from Global Outreach Mission (GOM).

We'd started applying to join them five months before. Earlier that week, the man who'd conducted our initial interview had told us they would be meeting to discuss our application. This was the same pattern as that of the last organization we'd applied to, which had disqualified us because of my injury.

*Well, this is it*, I thought. *This is the meeting when they'll decide that going further is too risky.* Sighing to myself, I tucked away my hopes of remaining in Okinawa.

Now GOM was e-mailing to tell us its decision.

My heart winced as I opened up the message.

At first, the words didn't make sense to me. I read them again.

GOM was welcoming us as missionaries!

Peter was sick with a bad case of bronchitis at the time, so there wasn't much we could do to tell our partners until his voice returned. But even in this, we were blessed to have a little time to celebrate and let things sink in before our lives got really busy.

I couldn't help randomly laughing throughout the day with the joy of it.

## On the Potter's Wheel

Then I remembered my prayer, and God's answer, almost a year ago—the time when I'd asked Him to have the park cats follow me if we were to stay, and they did.

"I'm sorry for doubting," I said to Him. "I thought I was being overly melodramatic and possibly superimposing my own desires onto You as a form of self-comfort. But it did mean something, didn't it, Father?

"Was it a sin to doubt?"

"No."

"Was it my own inexperience?"

"Yes."

"Thank You for teaching me to hear and recognize Your voice. This life is so much richer with You."

Later that day, I wrote a psalm of thanksgiving.

> Oh Lord, thou hast taken heed of us.
> Thou hast looked upon Thy servants
> And hast redeemed them from the pit.
> Thou hast vindicated Thy servants
> And poured upon them Thine abundance.
>
> Let all the earth sing Thy praises,
> Let the mountains boom
> And the earth tremble with Thy majesty.
> Thou art God, Thou and no other.
>
> Man sets himself up as ruler,
> And Thou dost laugh at him.
> His kingdom crumbles at its height
> As Thy glory is proclaimed throughout the earth.
>
> Sing with me, you peoples;
> Shout for joy, and wonder at His glory.

Kneel before thy Maker
And declare His mighty works.

Jump, and shout, and exult in His mercy
For He binds up the brokenhearted,
And the proud He does not esteem.
But a humble heart will not go unnoticed,
And a willing servant He will not reproach.

Up until this time, without realizing it, I'd become tense every time Peter got sick. I didn't want to get sick as well and have to cancel our various engagements with those we loved. Aware that our remaining time in Japan was likely very short, I always wanted to maximize the time with our Okinawan family. However, after receiving the good news from GOM, I felt my whole body relax. Only then did I realize how tense I'd been.

When this happened, I knew Peter's illness would soon overtake me too. The following day, it happened. We both lost our voices and couldn't tell our families the good news for several weeks. There was something maddening and wonderful about having the secret to ourselves for awhile.

After getting better, we kicked into gear with GOM. There were several important immigration details to iron out before we could announce the good news to our partners. I was impatient to tell everyone, but Peter was much more practical.

"We've all waited this long," he said. "Just a couple more weeks and then we can rejoice with all our friends and family in what God has done." Without his pragmatism, I would surely have let something slip, but Peter was marvellous in his tender logic and methodical outlook.

Finally, the day came when we could send out our newsletter, and announce our joy to those who had loved, prayed for, and encouraged us over the months of hardship and uncertainty.

April 12, 2013

> As many of you know, coming to Japan as missionaries was a decades-old dream for us, and we finally arrived here in September 2011. When I was injured shortly after this, life became very different from what either of us had envisioned. However, we began to notice amazing things happening in our lives, and the lives of the people around us. God was teaching us many spiritual lessons; giving me a completely different ministry than I'd ever expected; and causing both Peter's and my ministries to thrive and bear fruit.
>
> Just under a year ago, we shared with you some heartbreaking news. Our organization had decided to terminate our ministry with them. This news caught us by surprise, and we spent several months emotionally winded. We didn't understand why this was happening. Was God removing our call to Japan? We'd been almost certain that it was a life-long call. Through this time, there was a recurring theme in God's messages to us: "I'm not done with you yet." We didn't know what form God's future plans would take, but we knew the Person whom we trusted, and that He would guide us.
>
> Then Higa sensei (our pastor here) approached us and asked us if we could find a way to stay.
>
> When we prayed about this, we got the sense that God was saying, "Test Me." We should look for another organization. If we were to stay, we would be able to continue on in Japan without returning to Canada. We knew the odds of finding a new organization without going back to Canada were practically nonexistent. But one of the memory verses that we'd taught our ESL class

was: "Nothing is impossible with God."[1] Were we willing to put this into practice?

We made a list of about ten different organizations, potential new partners in missions. We started through the list. Some, we were able to cross off quickly. With a few, we went through part of the application process. One organization would require us to come back to Canada; others told us that though they were interested in us, they didn't operate in Okinawa and would require us to move to a different part of Japan. However, we didn't feel that we should so easily abandon the foundation God had built for us here, so we sadly crossed them off.

Through this time, we tried to honour the restrictions placed on us (no 'official' ministry was to take place), while at the same time also honouring God and our partners. We found quite a lot of success in engaging in informal activities, and to our delight our ministry continued to grow and be fruitful.

We were down to the last agency when a friend suggested another: Global Outreach Mission. We did some research, and were encouraged. They are a worldwide organization of over 500 missionaries in more than 50 countries, whose aim is to reach out with the good news about Jesus to people on every level, using a wide range of programs. After an intensive application process, they've decided to welcome us as career missionaries.

We would like to say here that if God's long-term plan was to place us in Okinawa, but not with our previous organization, we've realized that this was the path we had to take. Before being assigned here, we didn't even know Okinawa existed; and in our communications with the various mission agencies in Japan, we've found that none of them operate in Okinawa. So, if we had initially come to Japan with any other agency, we would not have ended up in this particular area. But our God is not limited by organizational boundaries, physical restrictions, or even our own knowledge.

## On the Potter's Wheel

We're extremely excited at His guidance, and the way that He has made it possible for us to continue working with the people of Okinawa, whom we deeply love.

We've often compared our journey to an adventure with God. In fact, that's the title of our website: *Peter & Valerie's Japanese Adventure*. In May 2012, when we rented the movie *We Bought A Zoo*, we meditated on the fact that the best adventure stories include a dark period of adversity. The dark period somehow makes later joy much more profound. Against all odds, God has once more given us exceedingly more than we ever could have asked or even imagined[2]. Just as we did a year ago, we can't help looking to the future with anticipation, and asking the question: what will He do next?

# Afterword

At one point, in mulling over the radical nature of God's request that I pray to Him in every decision, I exclaimed that this was something extraordinary and that He was calling me to a type of intimacy with Him that He doesn't ask of most people.

However, as I meditate on this statement, I realize that perhaps it's not quite right. The more I get to know Him and interact with other Christians, the more I realize that our God—the God of the universe—desires delightful, unrestricted intimacy with all His people. Yet we, as His children and heirs, often content ourselves with something less than His magnificent abundance. We may experience moments of it, but tell ourselves that prolonged closeness is reserved only for a select few, and instead satisfy ourselves with less. But the truth is that we serve a limitless God whose ability to commune with us is restricted only by our own willingness to obey and follow Him.

Why do we like to hear missionaries' stories in church on Sunday? Is it because they are full of faith? Because they experience God in a way we don't think is possible for us? That is simply not the case. Our Father is not Father to only a select few, with the rest of us belonging to a lower spiritual caste. He loves us all equally. We are all heirs of His abundance and have been sealed with the promise of the Holy Spirit. So let us throw off these lies that only serve to defeat us, and enter into the joy and bounty He has procured for us with the precious blood of our King Jesus!

# Glossary

**chirashi zushi** – a rice-and-fish mixture
**Eisa dancing** – a practice unique to Okinawa. Dancers drum and chant, wearing colourful robes, sashes, and head kerchiefs.
**futon** – a two-inch thick mat that is unfolded directly onto the floor and can be hidden away in a closet during the daytime
**genkan** – an entranceway into a building. Entrances into peoples' homes are often sunken and considered part of the outdoors. This is the area where people leave their shoes.
**goya champuru** – a stir-fry, using tofu, spam, and the bitter melon that many scientists credit for Okinawan longevity
**hikikomori** – people suffering from hikikomori voluntarily shut themselves into their homes and bedrooms for years on end. They become recluses from society.
**hiragana** – a Japanese phonetic alphabet consisting of over 100 characters and permutations of characters, used for native Japanese words
**kanji** – a set of Chinese characters used within the Japanese writing system. In Japan, school kids are expected to learn about 2,000 of these characters in order to be considered literate.
**katakana** – a Japanese phonetic alphabet consisting of over 100 characters and permutations of characters, used for foreign words imported into the Japanese language
**kekkon no yubiwa** – wedding ring
**konnichiwa** – "Good afternoon!"
**magokoro** – literally: true heart, sincerity

**mono no aware** – an awareness of the transience of things and a bittersweet sadness at their passing

**nemawashi** – a Japanese word picture of soil getting cleared away from the roots of a tree in order to more easily uproot and transplant it. In English, the closest equivalent would be 'to clear the way'.

**ofuro** – a Japanese public bath. Men and women bathe separately, in the nude.

**Obon** – a three-day Buddhist holiday that revolves around worshipping the spirits of people's departed ancestors. This festival takes place throughout Japan. Okinawa's version depends on the lunar calendar; it occurs about a month later than in the rest of the country.

**Okinawan soba** – an Okinawan pork-and-noodle soup

**otousan** – father

**Ryuukyuuan kingdom** – the Ryuukyuuan kingdom used to be a separate entity from the rest of Japan, with its own king, culture, language, and food. It was annexed by Japan in the nineteenth century, and was then called the Okinawan prefecture.

**sanshin** – a traditional Okinawan three-stringed instrument

**sensei** – honoured teacher. This title is bestowed upon teachers and pastors, and is applied similarly to the way that English speakers would use the titles 'doctor', or 'pastor'.

**shisa dog** – typically, these are small stone lion-dog statues that are attached to buildings as guardians to ward off evil spirits

**tatami** – straw matting used as a floor covering in Japanese houses

**Yuta** – an Okinawan female shaman

# Notes

**Front Matter**

1. Names that remain unchanged are Mr. Milne, Peter, Julia, Higa sensei, Tsuneko sensei, Seaside Chapel, and Global Outreach Mission (GOM).

**Dedication Page**

1. James 1:22

## 1  Early Snapshots

1. Joel 2:25, KJV

## 2  Peter

1. Redman, "Blessed Be Your Name."
2. See Ephesians 5:18, 1 John 4:18, 1 John 4:8.

## 4  Married Life and Ministry

1. Jeremiah 29:13.

## 6  Partnership Development

1. Philippians 3:13b–14.
2. Reid, *Confucius Lives Next Door*, chapter 5 (page 16–17 of 17 in e-book).
3. Reid, *Confucius Lives Next Door*, chapter 4 (page 27 of 31 in e-book).
4. 2 Corinthians 5:7.

## 7  Speed Bumps

1. 2 Corinthians 12:9a.

2. 2 Corinthians 12:9b, YLT.
3. Philippians 4:13.

**8 Living Now**

1. Tolle, *The Meeting House Videocast*: Living in the Spirit Now.
2. Lam, Typical Adrenal Fatigue Syndrome Progression.

**10 Working Again**

1. Missionary Training International, "PILAT."

**12 Attack**

1. Ephesians 6:12.

**13 Running the Race**

1. 2 Corinthians 5:7.

**14 Waiting on God**

1. John 10:10b, ESV.
2. My paraphrase of John 3:30.

**15 March 11**

1. University of Toronto, Fukushima Engineering Lecture, 2011.
2. Some of these references can be found in: Philippians 4:7, 2 Timothy 1:12, 1 John 5:18, Romans 8:35–39, 2 Timothy 4:18, Revelation 2:11, John 17:12, and 2 Thessalonians 3:3. This is not an exhaustive list.
3. Tacitus, Annals, Book XV, 50.
4. Keller, *The Open Door*.

**16 Attitudes of the Heart**

1. Matthew 9:29.
2. Philippians 3:8, 14.

**17 Preparing to Leave**

1. Philippians 3:7–8.
2. Carmichael, *Rose from Brier*, 22.

3. Julia Clark, e-mail message to author, 2011.
4. 2 Corinthians 10:5.

## 18 Arriving

1. Wikipedia, "Ryukyuan Religion."
2. Ibid.

## 20 Moving In

1. Lewis, *The Unseen Face of Japan*, p. 45
2. See 1 Corinthians 10:19–20.

## 21 Whatever Is Pure

1. Philippians 4:8.
2. 1 John 1:9.
3. Philippians 3:13–14.
4. Galatians 2:20.

## 23 Have Thine Own Way

1. Psalm 69:32b–33.
2. 2 Corinthians 12:9.

## 24 Prayer Walks

1. Jeremiah 1:8, KJV.

## 25 Following and Feebleness

1. My paraphrase of 2 Samuel 24:24.
2. My summary, Exodus 14:11–12.
3. See Exodus 14:21–22.
4. See Exodus 15:24.
5. See Exodus 17:2.
6. See Numbers 20:2, 4.
7. See Exodus 15:25.
8. See Exodus 17:6.
9. See Numbers 20:11.
10. See Exodus 16:3.
11. See Numbers 11:4–6.

12. See Exodus 16:13–18.
13. See Numbers 11:31–32.
14. My paraphrase, Exodus 32:1.
15. See Exodus 32:33–35.
16. See Numbers 14:2–3.
17. See Numbers 14:26–35.

## 26  Setback

1. Coutu, "How Resilience Works," HBR.

## 27  Charred

1. Manion, Ada Bible Church Videocast: The Land Between.

## 28  Chomping at the Bit

1. Bull, *God Holds the Key*.
2. Morris, *The Meeting House Videocast*: Deep and Wide.
3. Matthew 6:32–33.
4. Mark 9:24.

## 29  Not Every Question

1. Carmichael, *Rose from Brier*.
2. 2 Corinthians 12:9.

## 31  Meltdown

1. Carmichael, *Rose from Brier*, 131.
2. See Genesis 26:24 and Genesis 28:13–14.

## 33  Acceptance

1. Carmichael, *Rose from Brier*, 30.
2. Job 13:15, kjv.
3. Carmichael, *Rose from Brier*, 36–37.
4. 2 Corinthians 5:7.

## 34  ESL Classes

1. Matthew 9:6.
2. See Mark 10:17–27.

## 36 Love My Chains

1. Carmichael, *Rose from Brier*, 53.
2. Carmichael, *Rose from Brier*, 53.
3. Madame Guyon, as quoted in *Rose from Brier*.
4. Author Unknown, "The Grocery Store Horse."
5. Ibid.
6. See Ephesians 3:20, NIV.
7. See Hebrews 13:5, NIV.
8. See John 14:6.

## 37 Strength for the Moment

1. Carmichael, *Rose from Brier*, 55.
2. Carmichael, *Rose from Brier*.
3. Carmichael, *Rose from Brier*, 68.
4. Rudyard Kipling, as quoted in Carmichael, *Rose from Brier*, 14.
5. See Acts 17:28.
6. Psalm 84:5.

## 39 Matters of Faith

1. See Romans 8:5–6.
2. See Romans 8:7.
3. See Romans 8:7.
4. Hebrews 11:1.
5. Hebrews 11:6.
6. Hebrews 12:2.
7. John 19:30.
8. 2 Corinthians 5:7.

## 41 Fellowship of Suffering

1. 1 Peter 5:10.

## 43 'Potential'

1. See Psalm 22:22.

## 44 Friends of Job
1. See 2 Kings 19:14.
2. See Matthew 27:13–14.
3. Barnett, Breathe.

## 45 The Spring
1. Bennett, Former Organization's Spring Conference 2012.
2. Bennett, Former Organization's Spring Conference 2012.
3. See 1 John 4:18 and 1 John 4:8.
4. Galatians 2:20.

## 46 Compassion and Suffering
1. Matthew 7:1.
2. Hebrews 4:15.

## 47 Glimmers of Hope
1. Metaxas, Bonhoeffer, chapter 26 (page 4 of 9 in e-book).
2. Martin, *Pilgrimage of the Heart*, 93.

## 48 A Change in Plans
1. Lewis, *The Lion, The Witch and the Wardrobe*, chapter 10 (page 3 of 5 in e-book).

## 49 Releasing
1. Psalm 34:18.
2. John 16:33.

## 51 Surrounded
1. See John 21:21–22.
2. Brainard, He Knows.

## 52 Betrayed
1. Jeremiah 29:11.

## 53 Endings
1. Lewis, *The Problem of Pain*, "Divine Goodness" chapter (page 4 of 11 in e-book).

2. See 1 Corinthians 1:25a.

## 57 Offerings of Faith

1. Carmichael, *Lotus Buds*.
2. Philippians 4:11, NIV.

## 58 Obon

1. Kadena Air Base, "Okinawan ancestors rejoin families during Obon."

## 59 Surviving or Thriving?

1. Grisham, *The Racketeer*, chapter 2 (pages 55–6 of 1032 in e-book).
2. 1 Timothy 4:4–5, NIV.

## 61 Typhoons

1. National Oceanic and Atmospheric Administration, "What is the difference between a hurricane, a cyclone, and a typhoon?"
2. National Oceanic and Atmospheric Administration, "Why do tropical cyclones' winds rotate counter-clockwise (clockwise) in the Northern (Southern) Hemisphere?"

## 63 Unstuck

1. John 21:22.

## 65 The Pendulum of Grief

1. Psalm 22:1.

## 71 Where You Are

1. Romans 8:28.

## 72 Appointments

1. See Ephesians 5:15–17 and Colossians 4:5.

## 73 Compassion

1. Ezekiel 26:2, NIV.

2. As quoted in *Soul Survivor* by Philip Yancy. (Originally from: Cole, Simone Weil: *A Modern Pilgrimage*)
3. See Luke 18:9–14.

## 75 The News

1. Luke 1:37, NLT.
2. See Ephesians 3:20.

# Bibliography

"Okinawan ancestors rejoin families during Obon." Kadena Air Base. Accessed 2011. http://www.kadena.af.mil/news/story.asp?id=123267647.

"Ryukyuan Religion." *Wikipedia.* Accessed 2011. www.wikipedia.org/wiki/Ryukyuan_religion.

"What is the difference between a hurricane, a cyclone, and a typhoon?" National Oceanic and Atmospheric Administration. Accessed 2012. oceanservice.noaa.gov/facts/cyclone.html.

Atlantic Oceanographic and Meteorological Laboratory, Hurricane Research Division. "Why do tropical cyclones' winds rotate counter-clockwise (clockwise) in the Northern (Southern) Hemisphere?" National Oceanic and Atmospheric Administration. Accessed 2012. www.aoml.noaa.gov/hrd/tcfaq/D3.html.

Barnett, Marie. "Breathe." Copyright: © 1995 Mercy/Vineyard Publishing (ASCAP) admin. in North America by Music Services o/b/o Vineyard Music USA. All Rights Reserved. Used By Permission.

Bennett, David. Former Organization's Spring Conference 2012. Lecture, Karuizawa, Japan, March 18, 2012.

Brainard, Mary G. *He Knows.* 1869. Public Domain.

Bull, Geoffrey. *God Holds the Key.* Hodder & Stoughton, 1963.

Carmichael, Amy. *Rose from Brier.* Fort Washington: CLC Publications, 2010. (Rose from Brier by Amy Carmichael, © 1933 by The Dohnavur Fellowship. Used by permission of CLC Publications. May not be further reproduced. All rights reserved.).

Carmichael, Amy. *Lotus Buds*. The Project Gutenberg e-book, 2009.

Chan, Francis, and Danae Yankoski. *Crazy Love : Overwhelmed by a Relentless God*. Colorado Springs, CO: David C. Cook, 2013.

Coutu, Diane. "How Resilience Works." *Harvard Business Review*, May 2002.

Grisham, John. *The Racketeer*. Toronto: Random House, 2012.

Keller, Helen. *The Open Door*. Garden City: Doubleday, 1957.

Lam, Dr. Michael. "Typical Adrenal Fatigue Syndrome Progression." *Dr. Lam. Body. Mind. Nutrition*. 2010. https://www.drlam.com/images/arcr_andrenal_fatigue_progression.png

Lewis, C. S. *The Lion, The Witch and The Wardrobe*. New York: HarperCollins, 1994.

Lewis, C. S. *The Problem of Pain*. New York, NY: HarperOne, 2001.

Lewis, David C. *The Unseen Face of Japan*. Tunbridge Wells: Monarch, 1993.

Manion, Jeff. *Ada Bible Church Videocast: The Land Between*. Videocast. Ada Bible Church. M4V. Accessed 2011. https://www.adabible.org/watch/land/

Martin, Catherine. *Pilgrimage of the Heart: Satisfy Your Longing for Adventure with God*. Colorado Springs, Colo: NavPress, 2003.

Metaxas, Eric. *Bonhoeffer: Pastor, Martyr, Prophet, Spy*. Nashville: Thomas Nelson, 2010.

Missionary Training International, "PILAT." Training course, Palmer Lake, CO, November 15-26, 2010.

Morris, Paul. *The Meeting House Videocast: Deep and Wide*. Videocast. *The Meeting House*: Deeper series. M4V.

Accessed December 10, 2011. http://media.themeetinghouse.com/vpodcast/2011-08-21-771-video.m4v

Redman, Matt and Beth, *Blessed Be Your Name*. Copyright © 2002 Thankyou Music (PRS) (adm. worldwide at CapitolCMGPublishing.com excluding Europe which is adm. by Integritymusic.com). All rights reserved. Used by permission.

Reid, T.R. *Confucius Lives Next Door: What Living in the East Teaches Us About Living in the West*. New York: Random House, 1999.

Tacitus. *Annals*. Book XV, 50.

Tolle, Eckhart. *The Meeting House Videocast: Living in the Spirit Now*. Videocast. *The Meeting House*: Duped? – Questioning the Logic of Pop Spirituality Series. M4V. Accessed September 14, 2010. http://media.themeetinghouse.tv/vpodcast/Sermon_May_03_2009.m4v.

University of Toronto, The Fukushima Disaster. Engineering Lecture, Toronto, ON, 2011.

Yancy, Philip. *Soul Survivor: How My Faith Survived the Church*. New York: Galilee/Doubleday, 2003.

# About the Author

Valerie Limmer is a missionary in Japan, with Global Outreach Mission. She enjoys drawing and learning new languages, so she's picked up a new hobby: Japanese brush calligraphy. She and her husband, Peter, are originally from the Greater Toronto Area in Canada.

To read more about Valerie and Peter's ministry in Okinawa, or to sign up for their missionary newsletter, please visit <u>peter-andvalerie.com</u>.